Copyright © 2024 by Oliver Webb

All rights reserved.

No portion of this book may be reproduced in any form without written permission from the publisher or author, except as permitted by U.S. copyright law.

ISBN: 9798867400361

This story is inspired by true events and all major events happened.

Acknowledgement

On the journey of creating this travel journal, I initially had not anticipated the need to write about my experiences. However, with each adventure, amazing stories unfolded, compelling me to share and record these experiences in writing, ensuring they remain indelible memories as I age. Heartfelt gratitude goes to my incredible family, always just a phone call away during my travels. A special acknowledgement to my family, Granny and Nigel (a family friend), for their invaluable contributions to editing the book. Their keen eyes and commitment to refining grammar and spelling have enriched the stories told.

I extend sincere thanks to Usama Zaheen for the outstanding design of the cover—a visual representation that perfectly captures the essence of this journey and moving place to place.

Each of you has played an integral role in bringing this project to reality and for that, I am truly grateful.

Follow my journey:
www.BeyondTheBorders.me

Contents

About me 1
Greece 6
Italy 16
Hungary 20
Portugal 22
Italy 26
Egypt 30
Budapest again… 50
Bulgaria 52
Nice 62
Greece again… 64
Zakynthos 66
Netherlands 68
Germany 72
Prague 75
Poland 77
Krakow 81
Romania 84
Turkey 92
Bratislava 95
Zagreb 97
Bosnia and Herzegovina 98
Serbia 102
Macedonia 106

Albania 111
Kosovo 121
Denmark 130
England 132
Morocco 133
Spain 150
London 153
Malta 155
UAE 157
Thailand 159

About me

"When will you return to normality?" is a question I frequently hear from friends and family, but you know what? This is my normality! So, what does normality mean to me? It's all about the freedom to go wherever I please and keeping my commitments minimal. However, for most people around the world, normality revolves around the typical routine of studying, working and eventually retiring – and quite honestly, that doesn't sound like much fun to me at all.

I often encounter people expressing their wishes to have done something similar when they were younger. I've taken that sentiment to heart and ensured I'm not leaving any room for regrets. Unlike many of my friends who chose the traditional path of full-time work or immediate university studies, I decided to take a different route – one that allowed me to truly live.

Why would I want to spend the prime years of my life confined to an office, with a significant chunk of my hard-earned money going to the government in taxes, when I could be in any country I choose, doing whatever I want? It just doesn't make sense to me. Unfortunately, these days, governments have set the retirement age so outrageously high that, by the time (assuming I even make it) I reach that age, I might not have the same opportunities to travel and explore the world as I do now.

The conventional path just doesn't align with my aspirations and desires. I've chosen a different way and I intend to make the most of my life. After all, who says there's only one right way to live? I'm carving my own path, seizing every chance to travel, learn and experience the world and I wouldn't have it any other way.

This perspective I've developed through my travels doesn't fit the conventional system and I've come to realise this over time. Simply following the crowd because it's the norm has never sat well with me. Critical thinking seems to be diminishing in society – everyone is believing and doing everything they're told and that is disconcerting. I firmly believe there's no one-size-fits-all approach to life and sometimes taking detours from the well-trodden path may just be the best option for personal growth and fulfilment.

Of course, this mindset comes with its own set of challenges. One significant drawback is the absence of a stable community whilst travelling. As humans, having a sense of belonging and trustworthy individuals with whom we can form profound connections is vital. The nomadic lifestyle I've chosen means consistently encountering new people, establishing temporary bonds and then moving on, which can be mentally exhausting at times. It's a far cry from the feeling of having close-knit relationships with lifelong friends and family back in my hometown.

However, there's an undeniable allure to this way of living – the sense of freedom, the endless possibilities and the richness of experiences. I've come to embrace both the advantages and disadvantages, recognising that no path is flawless, but this unique journey is mine to explore and I'm willing to embrace it wholeheartedly.

When the topic of religion arises, many consider it an outdated concept. However, for a significant number of people, embracing religion provides profound meaning and purpose to their lives. It offers them a set of beliefs to follow, something they can devote themselves to. In the absence of such spiritual fulfilment, governments have stepped in to fill that void, giving people a sense of purpose and direction. This only works if individuals genuinely believe in and adhere to the government's principles and regulations. It's akin to a collective belief system, much like a religion, complete with its own set of rules.

One can view each country as a metaphorical prison, each with its unique rules (laws), limitations on stay (visas) and requirements for extended residency (such as needing to benefit the country or 'investing' in the country). Take, for example, the post-Brexit scenario in Europe – if I were to decide to work there, I'd have to present an extremely compelling case to prove that I am more suitable for the job than a European citizen. It's disheartening to realise that true freedom is but an illusion, something we might not even notice or worry about if we choose to follow the traditional path.

In a way, we are all part of a collective agreement, akin to a societal contract, where we abide by certain norms, rules and systems, which only hold value because we collectively believe in them. It's a complex web of interactions, expectations and beliefs that govern our lives and shape the world we live in.

Now that you have a glimpse of my mentality and perspective on the world's current state, it's crucial to shed light on these ideas to understand my thoughts. So, without further delay, let's delve into the people and events that have played a significant role in shaping who I am today.

I was born in the charming small town of Emsworth, nestled in the beautiful South of England. Growing up, I belonged to a middle-class family and had a close-knit bond with my relatives. Travelling was not a common concept in my family; there was no desire to venture far from home, as everything we needed seemed to be right there. Our family holidays were mainly England based.

Throughout my school years, my grades were commendable and I was known for my diligent work ethic. However, as I observed the people around me, I couldn't help but notice that they had more stories to tell, more adventures under their belts. While I considered myself interesting in my own right, I felt a lack of captivating experiences to share.

Then came the pandemic, which acted as the final catalyst for change. The confinement and limitations imposed by COVID-19 only intensified my desire to explore beyond the borders of Emsworth. I realised that life offered so much more and I yearned to venture out, seek adventures and collect stories of my own.

This newfound longing for exploration marked the beginning of my journey, the catalyst that drove me to set out on a path of discovery, breaking free from the boundaries that confined me for far too long and with that, the chapter of my life filled with wanderlust, self-discovery and unforgettable experiences began.

I firmly believe that taking time for oneself and embracing the world beyond familiar boundaries is essential for personal growth and understanding. This journey has become more than just a trip; it's a way of life that has enriched my spirit and broadened my perspective on the world.

Months passed and I found myself continually let down by people who expressed interest in travelling with me and always seemed to find excuses to back out. At that point, I realised that my only viable option was to embark on this journey solo.

One question I often receive is how I manage to afford the costs of travelling? The truth is, travelling doesn't have to be an exorbitant expense, especially if you do it on a budget. I've found that staying in hostels and preparing my own meals significantly cuts down the expenses. From a young age, I've been resourceful in making money – I worked as a DJ covering over a hundred events and ventured into online product sales. Additionally, my supermarket job contributed to my travel funds. I live by the mantra "work hard, play hard."

It's important to understand that you don't necessarily need substantial savings to explore the world. I've come across numerous individuals who have accomplished fantastic journeys through "workaways," where they receive payment or accommodation in exchange for the work they do. Another option is volunteering at hostels, which can grant you free accommodation and even other perks, such as free meals, laundry services, or access to activities. These opportunities offer a path to complete financial freedom while experiencing the joys of travel.

So, whether it's working on the go, finding creative solutions to finance your adventures, or embracing opportunities for exchange work, there are plenty of ways to make your travel dreams a reality without being hindered by financial constraints.

The COVID-19 pandemic acted as a catalyst for my newfound interest in travelling. Being confined to one location and feeling like a slave to the demands of capitalism during the lockdown made me realise how much I wanted to break free from this routine and explore the world. The isolation I felt while stuck in my room fuelled a strong desire to venture out and experience life beyond the confines of my familiar surroundings. When the restrictions finally lifted, I was filled with a sense of urgency and a burning desire to see the world.

As a young and somewhat unconfident individual, the prospect of solo travel posed a mental challenge for me. I knew it wouldn't be easy and I needed a gentle entry into the world of travel. That's when I decided on a turtle volunteering experience, a clever way to ease myself into the journey while knowing there would be people waiting for me on the other side. It was a comforting thought to have that support and it gave me the push I needed to take that first step.

Let me tell you, travelling has been the most transformative experience of my life. It has shaped me as a person in ways I could never have imagined. The encounters, the adventures, the challenges and the moments of self-discovery have all played a role in moulding me into a more confident, open-minded and resilient individual.

I can confidently say that embarking on this journey was one of the best decisions I've ever made. It has broadened my horizons, shattered my limitations and given me a taste of freedom that I will forever cherish. Travelling has become an integral part of who I am and I'm grateful for the opportunities it continues to offer me.

I embarked on this book with a simple yet powerful purpose – to create a record of all the incredible stories and fascinating encounters I experienced during my journey, ensuring they wouldn't fade away with time. Beyond the tales, I also wanted to capture the mental struggles I faced and the triumphs over those internal battles. This book reflects my raw and authentic experiences, baring the emotions and challenges that came with my travels.

I genuinely hope that as you read through these pages, you'll find enjoyment and maybe even some inspiration to embark on your own adventures. Travelling is often perceived as a massive holiday and while that's true to some extent, it encompasses so much more. Amidst the fun and leisure, you'll find moments that are amazing, scary and exhilarating – a rollercoaster of emotions that leave an indelible mark on the soul.

So, as you read this book and immerse yourself in my stories, I encourage you to ponder your own desires and aspirations. Dare to step out of the ordinary, seek the extraordinary and discover the magic that lies beyond the confines of the known.

Greece

After the COVID-19 pandemic, my mental health took a hit. I felt like I had sacrificed a whole year of my life and I had very few stories or experiences to show for it. I wanted to change that. I yearned to look back on my life with a collection of captivating stories to share with my future grandchildren, without any regrets.

As September approached, I knew it would be a challenging time mentally. Many of my friends were heading off to university and I found myself torn between pursuing a path I wasn't passionate about or staying home with no exciting prospects. Determined to break free from this uncertainty, I made a bold decision – a month in Greece, specifically on the island of Kefalonia, as a volunteer helping with turtle conservation work.

I was overwhelmed by a sense of nervousness as I prepared for this adventure. It was the first time I'd be away from home for an entire month and I'd be doing everything solo, from catching the flight to navigating the journey. With my suitcase and a large bag in tow, my dad kindly drove me to Luton airport. As I bid him farewell with a big hug, I felt a mix of excitement and anxiety.

Entering the airport, my nerves heightened as I recalled a rough flight experience I had before, putting me in a somewhat negative headspace. To add to my worries, I began questioning if I had forgotten anything important due to the necessary COVID-19 documentation and tests.

To reach the small Greek island of Kefalonia in the most budget-friendly way, I researched and found that the cheapest option was to fly into Zakynthos (also known as Zante), spend a night there and then catch a ferry over to Kefalonia, where I would be picked up. Although Zakynthos is known as a party island, the area I stayed in was a tranquil town, far from the bustling nightlife.

As I embarked on this adventure, I was both excited and apprehensive, but deep down, I knew it was the right decision for my personal growth and the opportunity to create the cherished memories I had been longing for. This journey marked my first solo trip and with a month-long stay ahead, it made perfect sense to travel with a suitcase (though I would adapt my packing approach in future trips). Looking back, I'm proud to say that I packed wisely, avoiding the pitfall of overpacking. I made the decision to take my drone, which allowed me to capture stunning photos and videos throughout my adventure.

The flight itself was smooth and uneventful, leaving me content and relieved upon finally landing. Stepping out of the airport was a moment I'll cherish forever. The crisp smell of fresh air, the warm touch of the Greek sun on my face and the awe-inspiring scenery, so different from England, overwhelmed my senses. It was an experience vastly different from the bustling and modern Luton airport I had departed from. Here, the airport was smaller and more intimate, akin to the size of a train station, with just one landing strip.

The first thing I did was call my parents to let them know I had safely arrived and share my excitement about the incredible journey ahead. The taxi rank had fixed prices, offering transparency and assurance that I wouldn't be overcharged. I hopped into a taxi and to my surprise, the driver spoke excellent English, making communication easy. As it was a small island, I was not sure if many of the local people spoke English.

My Airbnb was conveniently located in the heart of the small town, allowing me to explore the local surroundings easily. The atmosphere was calm and inviting, filled with friendly locals. With the sun shining and the sea nearby, stress seemed to vanish entirely. The location I was staying was the calm area of Zante where the locals and families go on holiday.

Seeing Greece for the first time was a sight to behold and it was a refreshing change from my familiar surroundings in England. Greece's uniqueness was evident and it had so much to offer. The crystal blue waters beckoned, making me want to plunge in and experience the surreal beauty firsthand. Given the challenging year we had all endured due to the pandemic, I felt incredibly fortunate to be here, embracing this new adventure.

As I strolled around the area, I couldn't help but capture the mesmerising sights through my camera lens. Greece's charm extended to its furry inhabitants as well – stray cats roamed freely, with adorable kittens playfully hiding under cars and bikes. The locals were kind enough to leave food out for them, showing the warm-hearted nature of the community.

I vividly remember ordering a traditional Greek gyro and being astounded by its affordable price compared to England. It was my first time trying one and I must admit, I had no clue how to eat it. Looking back, using a knife and fork must have looked very strange and I couldn't help but wonder what the locals thought of my tourist and shocking like behaviour.

A gyro is a delicious wrap filled with mouthwatering meat, crispy fries and delectable tzatziki sauce. As I relished every bite, I couldn't resist sharing my joy on social media, posting photos that made my family and friends green with envy. It truly felt like I was on a dreamy holiday and my exciting journey had officially begun! Surprisingly, my friends were taken aback by my decision to embark on a solo trip, especially since I had been quite a different person back in school.

However, I was proud of myself for stepping out of my comfort zone and reaching this point in my adventure. Words seem to not mean much until it really happens. Finding my place of stay proved a bit challenging since there were not many street names and signs, but after a few messages exchanged, I managed to locate it. The Airbnb host was friendly and gave me a tour of the apartment. Though the accommodation was budget-friendly and basic, it served its purpose. I spent the night there and woke up refreshed and in good spirits the next morning.

An early wake-up call was needed to catch a taxi that would take me to the opposite side of the island, where I needed to catch a boat to Kefalonia. It was crucial that I caught this boat on time; missing it meant waiting for the late boat and skipping the vital orientation for the turtle project. My first real hiccup of the journey occurred when the taxi didn't show up as scheduled. I promptly reached out to the Airbnb owner, who had arranged the taxi and he assured me that it was on its way. However, the taxi ended up being over an hour late before finally arriving. The stakes were high – missing the boat not only meant losing money on the ferry ticket but also risking being late for the project orientation which would not be a good first impression. During the drive, the taxi driver repeatedly stopped to take in the breathtaking island views. Despite the stunning scenery, I urged him to keep moving, emphasizing the importance of timeliness. As per Google Maps directions, we were cutting it close, but I prefer to arrive ahead of schedule rather than just in time. This marked my first experience with the unique pace of Google Maps in the Balkans, where predicted arrival times often prove inaccurate.

Remarkably, we made it with just 15 minutes to spare. The drive itself was picturesque, showcasing stunning vistas along mostly smooth roads, save for a few bumpy and unpaved stretches. This adventure offered me a glimpse into the beauty of the Greek island. The ferry ride across the tranquil waters was a warm and beautiful experience. I basked in the sun's gentle touch and felt the soothing breeze against my skin as I sat atop the boat. Soon, I met Nicolas on Kefalonia, the leader, who warmly welcomed me and drove me to the project site. There were two designated sites, Lixouri and Argostolion. Due to the season winding down, I had the fortunate opportunity to experience both locations. The first two weeks were spent in Lixouri, followed by another two weeks in Argostolion.

Upon my arrival, Nicolas and I delved into a conversation about the turtles and the project. He told me plenty of interesting facts and how the project is working to create a future for the turtles which are currently being affected by climate change. Subsequently, we reached the volunteer house, where I encountered my new roommate and fast friend, Will. The atmosphere was serene and calm, as the previous group had just bid farewell after a final spirited night out. This initial interaction left a positive impression, highlighting the strong bonds that can form among individuals spending weeks together.

The volunteer house boasted multiple rooms and two kitchens – one on each floor. The balcony served as a communal gathering spot for conversations and meetings. Upon entering the house, equipment for conservation work was neatly stored and had to be returned daily after our tasks were done. Adjacent to the equipment storage area, a kitchen stood, complete with a fridge displaying a timetable outlining daily tasks assigned to us. For instance, cleaning duties required the attention of 2-3 people and this schedule also detailed data entry for turtle nests, beach patrols, harbour patrols and days off. Each of these responsibilities will be discussed in more detail later.

The first night, everyone was getting to know each other. It was awkward at first as I seemed to be the only one initiating conversations at the table. This was due to many people being jet-lagged and a little tired. After a good night's sleep, the next morning, I was on beach patrol with a small group. We had to make our way down to the beach to check the nests. This involved taking a bike ride, which could be a short or long journey to reach the beach early in the morning before any tourists arrived. A team leader accompanied us and showed us the route on the bike, explaining what we needed to do. The ride wasn't leisurely, especially at first when we had to navigate hills to get to the beach. The other volunteers assured us that it would get easier as our strength improved.

We set out at about 5 am, cycling as the sunrise painted the sky with magical hues. The beach, known as Xi Beach, boasted distinctive red sand and blue water. It was a long walk along the beach, where we checked nests to look for turtle tracks. Many tracks were present from other animals, such as birds and bugs, requiring us to differentiate and identify the turtle tracks. We took photos and sent them to the leaders if we were unsure whether they were turtle tracks. We also sent GPS locations to the team leaders back at the house. Negotiating tricky areas, avoiding slippery rocks and safeguarding my phone and equipment made the task even more demanding. Some areas required us to go into the water to pass rocks.

This data we collected helped estimate the number of hatched turtles. We understood the importance of accuracy, so it was crucial that we logged everything correctly. This involved investigating whether some hatchlings could be led astray by light pollution from bars and cafes, taken by predators all potentially leading to dire consequences. Amid the unfolding beauty of the beach, we were on a mission to protect the fragile journey of these hatchlings. Our search was not limited to tracks; we scoured for stranded baby turtles trapped in footprints or crevices. Every discovery felt like a triumph, a step towards ensuring their survival against the odds.

It took several days to spot a baby turtle as there were not too many nests left and a lot of them had hatched days or weeks before. Consequently, the fence around the nests was removed since no eggs remained. One evening, everyone was invited to an inventory count of the eggs. This event had a good chance of seeing a baby turtle, as they should be very close to hatching. Luckily, we did see one. The turtle was incredibly small and cute, flapping its little flippers like a determined wind-up toy from our childhoods. It seemed like it was on a mission to conquer the sea. Since it was the first time for most of us to see such a sight, we all eagerly lined up for our "turtle selfie" moment. To ensure the turtle's natural development, we couldn't place it directly in the water. Instead, we had to create a path for the turtle by digging a trench and placing it at the top. This process was essential because it allowed the mature turtle to orient itself and find its way back to the beach, where it could lay eggs in the future. The baby turtles follow the light to reach the sea. It was an incredible sight, with everyone wearing smiles and capturing numerous photos and videos. The experience was immensely rewarding, creating a genuine sense of making a positive impact.

The next day, it was my turn for harbour patrol. The task involved a short walk down past the town, followed by a leisurely stroll up and down the harbour for about an hour. The mission: to spot any large turtles. Unfortunately, due to being in the off-season, my luck was out and no turtle sightings graced my shifts. Should a fortunate sighting occur, the protocol was clear – note the time, pinpoint the location on a dedicated sheet of paper and jot down the specifics of the encounter.

While my harbour escapades didn't yield any grand turtle sightings, I did encounter other intriguing marine denizens. Playful jellyfish and swarms of small fish, often found seeking refuge under the looming shadows of the massive ships, captivated my attention.

As the sun began its retreat our work was not complete as a beach clean was underway. A busy day it was. This is where a group of us would set off to a beach and clean up any trash. With trusty bicycles at our disposal, we pedalled our way to the sandy stretches. An hour spent scouring the shoreline uncovered a harsh reality. Among the discoveries, cigarette butts reigned supreme in terms of frequency. Plastics, fashioned in myriad shapes and sizes littered the sands. Astonishingly, even sizable objects like discarded bathtubs occasionally made a dramatic appearance, which were not possible to remove.

An intriguing piece of knowledge I acquired was related to an event from a few years ago when a ship carrying plastic beads met its watery demise. The result of this unfortunate incident has left Kefalonia's pristine beaches adorned with an abundance of these tiny beads, creating a conspicuous display that catches the eye. Notably, I observed a curious sight – industrious ants collaborating to transport and remove these foreign particles from their nests, showcasing a remarkable example of nature's ingenuity.

Due to the low season and a high number of volunteers, we had a lot of free time as we typically worked for around 2-4 hours a day. During our spare moments we often did day-to-day activities like heading to the beach. It was a laugh, like a whole bunch of mates going out day after day.

My preferred spot was XI Beach, a haven teeming with entertainment options, as it offered an array of water-based activities available for hire. One day, I thought I'd have a go on a jet ski. It was great fun and they are way more relaxed with the rules compared to the UK. I even managed to hit speeds of up to 55 mph! The bloke running the rental place took a shine to us since we were regulars and let me have a bit of extra time. It was a memorable experience, one that'll stick with me.

A few of my mates decided to give this spinning ride a go – you know, the kind that's hooked up to a boat and sends you whirling through the water. Seemed like the perfect opportunity to launch my trusty drone and capture the entire exhilarating experience from above chasing them from behind. Let me tell you, it was no small feat trying to match the speed of that zippy boat, but I managed to pull it off and the result was nothing short of a spectacular success.

After that, we decided to hire a stand-up bodyboard. We wanted to see how many of us could fit on it and then we started shoving each other off and playing a game of trying to stay on it for as long as possible. These moments are some of my best memories from the trip, like the kind of games I wish I'd played more of when I was younger. Only downside was that I ended up getting sunburn that day, probably from going in and out of the water and my suncream coming off.

One of those days, we decided to rent a car and embark on a full island adventure. Our journey took us northward, about 1 to 2 hours, to a charming village that had played host to some of the inspiration for the film "Mamma Mia." The place was an absolute picture of prettiness – nestled by the water's edge, filled with blossoms and adorned with those quaint, old houses that seem to carry tales of their own. While there, I indulged in a scrumptious yogurt, a DIY affair where you could load up on everything from chocolate to fruits and various tantalizing toppings. It was the best yogurt I had ever eaten.

Following our village exploration, we geared up for a drive-up Mt. Ainos, the island's tallest mountain - renowned for its rich biodiversity and soaring over 1500 meters. The road was not smooth, though; it twisted and turned, challenged by slopes and curves. It was Emma, my trusty friend, who piloted our rented vehicle with remarkable finesse. The views that greeted us were breathtaking, until a certain point when we ascended right into the clouds, obscuring everything around. Suddenly as the mist enveloped us, a gap opened, treating us to a surreal sight of everything below appearing minuscule, like the view from an airplane window. It was an uncanny experience.

Eager to capture this unique moment, I sent my drone airborne. Yet, the clouds played tricks on my tech – they almost caused it to lose its way, confusing its descent for a landing. Thankfully, I managed to regain control and bring it back safely. Our brush with danger didn't end there, though; as we prepared to leave, we encountered a rather sizable bump that posed a challenge for our rental car. In fact, it had already scraped the car's underside. We tried various methods, including using rocks as makeshift ramps, but all efforts were in vain. Just when we thought we were stuck, a local guardian angel appeared. With a simple suggestion to angle the car and drive up, he ingeniously saved the day – a true island hero!

In Greece, dogs enjoy certain rights that protect them from abuse, contributing to their generally good treatment. While many dogs are strays, they tend to be friendly and approachable. One particularly cherished memory involves a dog that became our unofficial companion – we affectionately named him 'Bean.' Our introduction to Bean took place at the volunteer house, where he had been a resident for a few weeks, socializing with other volunteers. He'd often lounge on the shared balcony, occasionally engaging in playful interactions with us.

Each morning, as we embarked on our daily activities, Bean would enthusiastically chase after the cyclists heading to the distant beach for the beach patrol, though he could not keep up. Once he grew tired, he'd make his way to the beach accessible by foot, joining the walking group. He was a very clever dog and know exactly where to find us on the island. Bean's intelligence shone through, even though he had a few close calls when darting onto the road.

Interestingly, Bean wasn't a typical stray; he had an owner he'd return to in the evenings. This likely explained his cleanliness and well-fed appearance. I often wonder how he's doing now and hope he's thriving. Another memorable dog we encountered was a spontaneous visitor we named 'Toast' due to his similar colour. During a team meeting, Bean unexpectedly decided it was the perfect time to mount Toast, prompting me to exclaim loudly, 'Beans on toast!' It was an unexpectedly hilarious moment that added a dose of laughter.

Travelling to a distant land like Kefalonia was a completely new experience for me. It felt like stepping into a whole different world and I must admit, some things really caught me off guard. Take the stray dogs, for instance. It's a bit heart-wrenching to see them wandering around, hungry and alone. But in this place, it's kind of the norm – a tough reality to accept.

Our morning bike rides turned into a hilarious escapade with these furry locals. Whenever we pedalled past houses, these enthusiastic dogs would join in, as if challenging us to a race. Imagine a bunch of us on bikes and a pack of dogs eagerly running alongside, tongues out and tails wagging. There was even this one time when we had a full-on dog squad keeping up with us – a comical sight that left us all in stitches. It wasn't just the dogs ruling the scene. Kefalonia seemed to have a cat population that could give them a run for their money. These feline characters added another layer of charm to the island.

Staying sober when travelling is quite a challenge, especially when you're eager to socialise and unwinding over a drink seems like the perfect way to connect. Let's be honest, in most European destinations I've explored, the drinks are not only social glue but also affordable. So, you don't have to break the bank for a good time. We found ourselves a cosy bar, where these intriguing chocolate shots took centre stage. Oh, those shots were a real treat! A few of us would often go in the evening to this bar.

Cooking became a little adventure too, thanks to the convenience of nearby shops. I'd whip up meals for myself, sometimes joining the gang for an outing to a local eatery. But let me tell you, there was this Gyros joint just a stone's throw away that has set the bar high for all future Gyros I'll ever have. I made it a ritual to devour at least one of those heavenly wraps daily.

After a fortnight, those of us who were in for the long haul – the full month – were relocated to a sprawling house in Argostolion. This colossal house was thoughtfully divided into dormitories. It was nestled closest to the major nesting beaches; this was the epicentre of our conservation efforts. Yet, every coin has two sides. The downside? It was quite a trek away from any semblance of urban life – no shops, no bars, nothing. Our leisure hours were mainly split between the house itself and the picturesque nearby beaches that beckoned us. Each room boasted its own miniature kitchenette and restroom facilities, guaranteeing that essentials were never in short supply. The dynamic shifted too, as we were introduced to a fresh wave of fellow volunteers, infusing the place with a new buzz of energy.

The shift to the Argostolion base opened a whole new world of experiences, thanks to its connection with Nico, our enthusiastic leader. I was eager to dive into the fresh tasks he had in store for us. One of the most exciting routines was the morning harbour patrol. It involved a quick drive of around half an hour to reach the bustling dock. Our team, made up of four of us, was strategically positioned across different sections of the harbour where we'd rotate shifts every two hours, keeping a watchful eye on the surroundings.

During those shifts the majestic turtles, these graceful giants of the sea, would glide alongside our paths, almost like they were performing just for us. It was like a carefully orchestrated underwater ballet. Our role was more than just observing; it was about documenting their presence accurately. We had to note down their ID numbers etched onto their shells, identify their genders and check if they had any unique tags, often small metal markers attached to their flippers.

Our duty went beyond simply noting their appearances, we also had to capture their activities in detail. For instance, when we spotted a turtle munching on underwater plants, it was a positive sign. This natural foraging behaviour was a good lesson in their self-sustainability. We meticulously recorded what they were munching on, how long they indulged. Sadly, some fishermen threw food into the water, unwittingly attracting the turtles with fatty fish. Unfortunately, this fishy temptation isn't the best for their health, but it was a tough situation since maintaining a good relationship with the fishermen was vital. We were working on educating them about the potential effects of their actions.

Sometimes, the allure of the fish led to tussles among the turtles. These peaceful creatures turned feisty, nipping and snapping at each other in a competition for the fishermen's offerings. Our task was to log the duration and the feisty participants in these underwater brawls. Circular movements in the water told another story – a tale of potential romance. When the turtles engaged in these swirling motions, it was like they were dancing, a flirtatious aquatic courtship. Of course, these moments weren't left unrecorded either.

After the harbour patrol shift, a short 20-minute break gave us a chance to stock up on food or other essentials from the nearby shops. It was a brief interlude that fit perfectly into our dynamic routine.

Another intriguing task on the roster was the drone shift, which required us to venture to the more remote beaches, less accessible on foot. Armed with a high-end drone equipped with path-setting capabilities, we would unfold the iPad's map, charting a course above the water's expanse in search of telltale signs of turtle activity. This advanced drone, with its impressive range, would cruise along the designated path for around 20 minutes before needing a battery change. The data collected during these flights would be analysed later, back at the base.

Now, let me share with you my absolute favourite task, one that I eagerly volunteered for time and again – the enthralling tagging event. This was a grand operation, demanding a formidable team, drones for surveillance, ample supplies and even kayaks. The objective? To tag the turtles for tracking and conservation purposes.

Sometimes, new untagged turtles would grace the harbour, or distressed turtles in need of care would surface, necessitating our swift intervention. These situations required us to temporarily lift the turtles from their aquatic realm for about 10-20 minutes, giving us ample time to complete the crucial tagging process. The process began with voices alerting everyone to the discovery of a turtle. Then, with a flurry of activity, we would converge on the scene, scanning the water's surface for any sign of movement with our eyes and drones from above. It was here that Nico, our fearless leader and I would spring into action. We had our own personal drones that would gracefully take to the skies, following the turtle's every twist and turn communicating with each other and the people on the ground its position. The climax of this was when Nico, summoning his courage, leaped onto the turtle, capturing it with practised precision. This moment was exhilarating, for these magnificent creatures possessed jaws that could deliver a formidable bite, capable of severing a finger with ease. Nico's careful handling was a masterclass in turtle taming.

For me, it was an adrenaline-fueled spectacle, flying my drone with unwavering focus, tracking the turtle's aquatic ballet. Managing the drone's battery life was a strategic challenge, necessitating judicious flying to conserve power. If a fellow volunteer operated another drone, co-ordinated communication and altitude adjustments were crucial to avoid mid-air collisions – a feat that added an extra layer of exhilaration to an already thrilling experience.

Though some days yielded no sightings, one unforgettable occasion brought double delight as we successfully tagged two turtles. I was lucky enough to be part of the team responsible for holding down a massive turtle. It was an awe-inspiring display of strength as I leaned into my full body weight to keep the creature steady, forging an unforgettable connection with these powerful marine beings.

The project proved to be a truly fantastic endeavour, filled with rewarding tasks that left me with a profound sense of accomplishment. The experience itself was nothing short of amazing, igniting a burning desire within me to further explore the diverse corners of our world beyond the captivating shores of Kefalonia.

As my time on the island ended, I embarked on my journey back, catching a flight to Manchester. From there, an unconventional choice awaited me – a bus ride that whisked me away to my hometown. Surprisingly, this cost-effective detour proved to be more economical than opting for a direct flight to London.

Italy

After wrapping up my unforgettable time in Kefalonia, I found myself at a crossroads, eager to keep the travel momentum going. Solo exploration didn't quite tickle my fancy this time and as luck would have it, some of the cool folks I'd met on the island felt the same itch for adventure. So, I reached out to a couple of mates who I met on the trip. Lily, a fellow adventurer from Kefalonia and her friend Maisie jumped on board.

My travel style involved spontaneity and affordability; I combed through options until we settled on the intriguing allure of Venice. Our launchpad was Stansted Airport, which meant I had to camp out there overnight since our flight was set to take off bright and early. I claimed a spot leaning against a wall, aiming to catch a bit of sleep. However, sleep was playing hard to get amidst the chorus of beeps and clatters from the airport's nighttime orchestra. To fend off the impending zombie state, I surrendered to the caffeine gods and grabbed a cup of coffee – my trusty co-pilot to stay awake until my fellow wanderers arrived.

With the break of dawn, Lily and Maisie made their entrance, a few hours ahead of take off. The sight of familiar faces was like a jolt of energy, rejuvenating my tired bones and boosting my spirits. Their presence signified that the adventure was about to kick into high gear and even the thought of napping on the plane felt like a luxury at that point.

With Venice, Italy in our sights, we embarked on planning a joint escapade. Our collective goal was to capture that solo-travel vibe while relishing the chance to connect with fellow explorers. To facilitate this, we unanimously decided to stay in a hostel – a hotspot for forging new friendships and sharing tales from distant corners of the world. Now, our chosen hostel wasn't right in the heart of Venice; it was a train ride away. This savvy move not only saved us a pretty penny (or cent in this case) but also gave us a taste of the local commute.

Another trick up my travel sleeve to keep those flight costs at bay was a minimalist packing approach. Armed with a spacious Amazon-bought bag, I meticulously curated my essentials. Toiletries were picked up from a local shop in Italy, a strategic move that ensured precious bag space was reserved for my carefully selected wardrobe. I even managed to bring my drone aboard, which I was excited to use again.

Our selected hostel turned out to be quite popular and I'd made sure to check out its reviews beforehand to ensure a smooth start to my hostel experience. It had a few floors to it, a lively bar, a reception desk that never slept and even private rooms. We bunked in a shared dormitory, fitting around 10 of us and the best part was the curtains that provided a dash of personal space amidst our communal living arrangement.

The first impression was solid as we stepped in – the place had a quirky touch, with lobster cages and treasure chests where we could securely stash our stuff before we headed out to grab a bite. Eager to savour some true Italian flavours, I embarked on a mission to locate a well-rated pizza restaurant nearby. With Lily and Maisie, we managed to uncover a real gem, serving up pizza that tantalised my taste buds just right. Interestingly, my travel buddies went for pasta dishes that turned out to be an absolute revelation. Content and slightly fatigued from our day's explorations, we retraced our steps back to the comfort of the hostel. The lure of a quick power nap was hard to resist. That evening, I joined my fellow travellers for a relaxed time at the hostel bar. Engaging in casual chit-chat with fellow solo explorers provided me with a glimpse into the world of lone travel, a different kind of adventure altogether. It was fascinating to hear stories and insights from those who dared to navigate the globe on their own. This, I thought, was just what I was looking for in this trip – a chance to connect with other wanderers, exchange experiences and perhaps make a friend or two along the way.

Prior to embarking on the trip, I had cleverly marked down various spots of interest on Google Maps, effectively plotting a roadmap for our explorations. It was a nifty way to keep tabs on the places we intended to visit and, as a bonus, it allowed us to tick them off once we'd set foot there, creating a neat little log of our adventures. Armed with a determination to make the most of every minute, we set off each day early and hopped on a train bound for Venice. The anticipation was palpable as we traversed the waters and entered the realm of this enchanting city.

The Italian train system turned out to be quite the blessing – not only for its affordability and convenience but also for its double-decker design, a feature not commonly found in my native UK. The ticket vending machines were remarkably user-friendly, even offering an English language option. Yet, the frequent reminder about pickpockets, something along the lines of "Please be warned of pickpockets on the trains and platforms and keep all your belongings close by," did start to sound like a broken record after a while, albeit it brought a chuckle every time.

Given the off-season and the lingering effects of the pandemic, Venice greeted us with an unusual hush – a perfect setting for unhurried exploration. Stepping out of the train felt like entering a parallel universe, one where boats replaced cars and canals intertwined like liquid roads. The water and boats, accompanied by the serenity of the visiting tourists, painted a picturesque scene that seemed straight out of a dream. As we ventured on, we made our way over the famed "Spider Man" bridge, which features prominently in movies.

Under a brilliant blue sky, with the temperature just right, we traversed the cityscape until we found ourselves on the opposite side of Venice. It was there, in a tranquil corner, that I seized the chance to send my drone up capturing Venice from a whole new perspective without drawing too much attention. Our return journey was accompanied by the joyful companionship of ice cream and as we strolled back, we were serenaded by the talented street performers who dotted the streets.

Back at the hostel, we raised our glasses to a day well spent, only to find ourselves in an unexpected yet delightful encounter – a familiar face from our stroll, the very same busker whose music had resonated with us earlier! It turned out he was a fellow guest at our hostel, a coincidental connection that added another layer of charm to our experience. He told us tales of his busking escapades, using the proceeds to fund his travels and it was a reminder of the various paths people take to explore the world.

During it all, I crossed paths with a young traveller from the UK, a chap in his mid-twenties who was courageously navigating the journey solo. His story struck a chord, for he had worked a year in a school to save up for his pursuits. Our conversation about solo travel ignited a spark within me, his unwavering encouragement urging me to take the plunge. "Just do it," he enthused, "it'll be one of the best decisions you'll ever make." It was a conversation that stayed with me, a conversation that became a beacon of inspiration when I needed that final push for solo travel. I always look back on this conversation, if it didn't happen, I might not have gone solo travelling.

Over the next few days, our time in Venice was a whirlwind of exploration. One standout spot was a unique bookstore. This quaint establishment is known for its unusual trait—regular flooding due to high water levels. When the water rises, the books float within the various objects used for storage, such as boats. It's a remarkable sight and the entire setting creates an ambiance unlike any other bookstore I've visited. Often referred to as the "most beautiful bookshop in the world," the charm of this place is truly extraordinary. During our stay, we were fortunate that the flooding didn't occur, though experiencing that aspect of life in Venice would have been fascinating—how people adapt and continue their routines amidst the water.

As we explored the city, we noticed makeshift pathways and walkways that could be rapidly set up, such as scaffolding along the paths. Venice's ability to quickly adapt to its unique environment was quite impressive and interesting to me.

One evening, our hostel hosted a lively party. A humorous incident stands out from that night—a girl and another young lad decided to climb onto a table and showcase their dance moves (before being eventually escorted off the table). It was a comical moment that provided a lot of amusement to everyone present.

To diversify our time in Venice, we decided to make the most of Italy's excellent train system by embarking on a day trip to Verona, situated to the west of Venice. Verona, a small city, is renowned as the setting for Shakespeare's famous "Romeo and Juliet." Taking a train journey of just over an hour, I once again utilised the map to pinpoint the places we wanted to explore, ensuring we had a rough plan for the day. While the touristy and expensive Romeo and Juliet attractions weren't quite our focus, Verona did offer a grand arena and a town ripe for exploration.

Starting our journey with a park near the station, we meandered our way towards the city's roman amphitheatre. The arena's sheer scale was awe-inspiring; nestled around it was traditional Italian architecture. For a nominal fee, we entered the arena, navigating from the bottom floor to the very top of the stands, treated to breathtaking views of the surrounding area.

The following day, the girls were nursing hangovers and chose a more relaxed day. Seizing this as an opportunity to explore solo, I set my sights on one of Venice's islands, known as the 'glass island.' To get there, I hopped onto a boat bus from Venice, following a well-organised schedule. The island was a haven of glass sculptures, a mesmerising sight to behold as I strolled around. Photography was prohibited, perhaps to entice visitors to witness the sculptures in person. The range was remarkable, from large sculptures resembling oversized plant pots to minuscule ones that could perch on your fingertip. These glass creations are crafted by skilled artisans in Venice and are sold across the world. My personal favourites were the blue glass sculptures adorned with fish—so intricately detailed and reflective that they were difficult to tear my gaze away. I purchased a small sculpture, fitting for my hand luggage.

This side of the island was tranquil and less crowded, offering moments where I had the canals to myself and could enjoy the serenity. Returning to Venice proved a tad challenging, but I eventually hopped onto a random boat taxi, hoped for the best and luckily took me close to the station and my hostel.

On that evening, I indulged in a pasta delivery that turned out to be one of the most exceptional pasta dishes I've ever had. Overall, this initial trip was a resounding success. Meeting incredibly friendly people fuelled my enthusiasm for solo travel.

Hungary

A week later, I had a trip to Budapest all set with another friend I had met in Greece - Nora. However, due to Covid-related regulations, she couldn't make it. Now I was faced with a choice: cancel the trip or go ahead solo since everything was already booked. I decided to change my accommodation plans and opted for a well-rated party hostel. My knowledge about Budapest was limited, so I embarked on this journey with a mix of excitement and nerves, not entirely sure what to expect.

Arriving around 5 PM, I made my way to the hostel. The receptionist was incredibly friendly and I noticed another guy in his early twenties who had just arrived as well. He wasted no time in inviting me and a few others for a drink, which was a great relief. Within the first few minutes of arriving, I was already extended an invitation to socialise – a promising start. A small group of us, around three people, including one who worked at the hostel, headed out for a drink. He happened to be from the UK and had been volunteering at the hostel for several years. His stories were quite wild, painting a picture of a vibrant and fun hostel that aimed to unite travellers. While I hadn't come specifically for a party, it seemed like this hostel would provide a lively experience.

Settled into a 6-bed dorm, I found everyone to be friendly and easy-going. I had planned out a variety of things to do in Budapest on Google Maps and there were numerous options to explore. One of my initial stops was a cheesecake shop named 'Say Cheese.' Let me tell you, their Oreo cheesecake was an absolute delight and easily one of the best I've ever tasted. All that goodness for just £3! The exchange rate was favourable and Budapest seemed to offer a relatively affordable cost of living.

During my stay at the Budapest hostel, I struck up conversations with fellow travellers. It turned out that I ended up chatting with a girl who revealed that she was the same person who had danced on the table at the party in Venice! The sheer odds of us crossing paths again in a completely different city left me awestruck. It's incredible how travel can lead to these serendipitous connections, reminding us of the vastness of the world and the unexpected ways in which our paths can intertwine.

During my days in Budapest, I spent most of my time exploring the city's nooks and crannies. Every now and then, I'd spot fellow travellers from the hostel and sometimes we'd team up to discover the city together. There was a sense of companionship that never lets you feel alone; the hostel's vibrant atmosphere ensured that you were surrounded by so many like-minded individuals. Yet, evenings were undoubtedly the highlight. It was when everyone congregated for lively drinking games, followed by pub crawls and clubbing. The club scene was an absolute blast – dancing and partying with familiar faces made it even more enjoyable. Establishing connections with people during that week felt so natural and there were quite a few fellow Brits, which made for some shared laughter and experiences.

One standout memory was my visit to Budapest's famous thermal baths. Stepping into a public bath for the first time was an interesting experience. The warm water was soothing, but I quickly realised it could be a bit overwhelming and even make you lightheaded if you stayed in too long. It's incredible how much energy your body expends in such environments. Budapest, in all its beauty, left a strong impression on me. The fact that it was also close to Christmas added an extra layer of magic – the city's Christmas lights and the Christmas market were a delight to explore.

This trip marked one of my first solo adventures and I couldn't have asked for a better experience. The interactions with people who would likely never cross my path again, yet left such a significant impact on my journey, felt surreal. It's the unexpected moments that fuel my enthusiasm for solo travel; the anticipation of what's waiting around the next corner is invigorating.

Returning to the UK was amusing because whenever colleagues would ask about my week, I'd casually respond with, "Oh, I just popped over to another country." However, this trip also prompted a decision – it was time to re-evaluate my work situation. I had been flying back to the UK just to work between my trips, which seemed quite impractical. So, I quit my job. This was happening.

Portugal

The grey winter weather of the UK often left me yearning for sunnier shores. With Christmas on the horizon, I didn't want to venture too far. Initially, I had my sights set on the sun-soaked island of Lanzarote. However, my plans hit a snag as the island lacked hostels and it wasn't a particularly frequented spot for solo travellers. Despite having booked the flights, I eventually decided that heading to the south of Portugal was a wiser move. The allure of nice hostels and the promise of fellow wanderers made it a more appealing choice. Portugal seemed like a country where I could blend in seamlessly. My strategy was simple – stay open to the flow of things and let my journey unfold naturally.

Given my intention to return to the UK for Christmas, I had a window of about 2 to 3 weeks to explore. My first port of call was Faro, a destination I'd heard wasn't bursting with attractions. Consequently, I planned my time there meticulously, recognising the limited scope of things to do. Despite this, the hostel proved to be a social hub, where I connected with some intriguing individuals. Most fellow travellers were tracing similar routes, either forwards or in reverse, which made for some great exchanges and valuable recommendations. One interesting attraction of Faro was Capela dos Ossos (Faro), a minuscule chapel lovingly decorated with the bones and skulls of over 1000 human skeletons. I also went on some very nice walks along the beach and spent some days with fellow travellers from around the world indulging in the food and nature there.

While in Faro, I did encounter a couple of hiccups along the way. One instance that stands out was when the boat trip I had planned to take to explore another nearby island was cancelled due to unfavourable weather. This unexpected turn of events left me with an entire day to navigate and piece together alternative plans. Still, I couldn't help but be taken aback by how eerily quiet Faro was – a city almost suspended in a ghostly calm. The pubs, typically vibrant with life, seemed subdued. Faro posed some challenges for a solo traveller; without the hostel, it would've been a rather solitary affair.

My next plan was to catch a bus to Lagos, a place brimming with activities I was eager to dive into. I arrived in Lagos with enthusiasm, staying at a hostel highly acclaimed for its hospitality. Lagos proved to be a picturesque coastal destination. Upon my arrival, I found myself with a few hours to spare, so I headed straight to the beach. There, I basked in the warm sunlight and relished the tranquillity of having the entire beach to myself. Seizing the opportunity, I captured some stunning drone shots, the absence of any other people making the scene even more captivating.

As I strolled back, an unusual sight caught my attention – a bus from America! It was intriguing to think that someone was travelling in a converted school bus. This unique encounter added an unexpected touch of adventure to my day. Later, I made my way to the hostel, where I received a warm and friendly welcome from the staff and fellow travellers alike.

During my time in Lagos, I explored the area, taking leisurely walks and soaking in the sights. It was nice to know that I already had some friends here whom I knew from Faro. My favourite area to explore was the coast which had awesome cliffs which were around the beach like nothing I had seen before. The cliffs had so many different colours and each one was unique.

The hostel owner invited everyone for drinks on the rooftop and I was more than happy to join in. The atmosphere was sociable and relaxed. It was quite a delightful coincidence to discover that I also knew two individuals from the other hostel I had stayed at in Faro. With Christmas just around the corner, the hostel staff had prepared a special Christmas drink for everyone, a gesture that was both kind and complimentary. This added a warm touch to the evening. We then embarked on a pub-hopping adventure, which turned out to be quite fascinating. The pubs had a distinctly surfing-themed ambiance, likely since many surfers frequented the area. Although the place was relatively quiet due to the season and the ongoing impact of Covid-19, there were enough of us to have a fun night.

One of my memorable outings was a visit to the Sagres Castle, an impressive fortress jutting out into the ocean. I opted for a bus ride to reach the location, a journey that took approximately two hours. After purchasing the entrance ticket, I had the privilege of exploring the castle's remarkable grounds. The castle's setting was nothing short of enchanting, perched dramatically over the ocean's expanse. A notable feature was the abundance of birds in the area, a consequence of their migration to the warmer climes of the south of Portugal

During this visit, I had a bit of a drone-related adventure as well. While attempting to capture a stunning shot of the castle, I encountered a gusty wind that made it difficult for my drone to come back to me. The return journey was equally challenging, with the wind resistance slowing down my drone's progress and depleting its battery at an alarming rate. With each decreasing bar on the battery indicator, my concern grew. Thankfully, the drone managed to return just in the nick of time, with a mere 8% battery remaining. It was a tense moment, but the experience added an element of adventure to the day.

Lisbon is an incredible city, offering a great range of activities. Armed with a map and a spirit of adventure, I embarked on my plans to explore the city's diverse attractions. The efficient transport system made getting around a breeze, allowing me to traverse its corners with ease. Lisbon boasts a thriving café culture, which I eagerly embraced, sipping my way through its charming coffee spots.

One of my most adventurous days was when I journeyed to Sintra, a location north of Lisbon renowned for its enchanting castle - a UNESCO World Heritage site. The day commenced with an early morning bus ride to reach this destination, followed by a hike up a substantial hill to reach the top. Many tuk-tuks and tour guides run this route, catering to those disinclined to walk. Various spots were marked where the drivers paused and I, too, halted on foot to savour the views. Though continually beckoned by taxi offers like a famous person, sheer determination propelled me forward, unwavering in my determination to conquer the ascent. Some fellow passengers even egged me on to accept a ride, yet the drivers wouldn't entertain passengers without payment. While I could have paid, where's the adventure in that?

At one of the most breathtaking viewpoints, I approached a passerby to capture a photo of me, oblivious to the fact that they were a persistent driver. He positioned himself and me for what I anticipated to be the perfect shot, my anticipation growing. Imagine my chagrin when it turned out to be one of the worst photos I've ever encountered. Well, at least that snap has a comical tale attached... sigh...

The following day, I set off for Europe's westernmost point and a hidden beach. A bus ride posed an initial challenge due to my lack of cash, but a kind driver waved me on for free. The western point had a flag and a view stretching out to the vast sea. My next destination, the hidden beach, involved a perilous descent down a rugged path, complete with rope-climbing sections. It was a thrilling challenge and upon arrival, the serenity was awe-inspiring. With only the sound of waves breaking the silence, I witnessed a group practising yoga amidst the rocks. Drone in hand once more, I captured some of my most stunning shots, illuminated by the magical golden hour. My return to Lisbon was resolved with an Uber ride, as my cashless predicament continued.

Amidst my Lisbon adventures, I visited Portugal's purported best bakery, a spacious establishment offering both table service and takeaways. I was pleasantly surprised by the reasonable prices and indulged in their famed 'de nata', a delightful, sweet cream tart that lived up to its reputation. All conveniently available on the digital menu.

My final Portuguese stop was Nazaré, renowned for its colossal waves, some of the biggest on the planet. However, during my visit, the town felt more like a ghostly enclave, perhaps due to the offseason. Still, I explored its cafes and witnessed impressive waves, while plotting a return when they'd be even grander. What stood out most about Portugal was the trust woven into daily interactions.

A café's understanding gesture of allowing me to fetch cash and pay later exemplified the country's warm and welcoming spirit.

Italy

Nora, whom I had the pleasure of meeting in Greece had initially planned to accompany me on a journey to Budapest. However, the unpredictable course of COVID-19 disrupted those plans. Undeterred, we devised an alternative adventure – we'd meet in Rome, eager to explore the city together.

My flight from the UK to Rome was marked by a harrowing landing, as I descended through a storm. The flight had moments of stomach-churning turbulence, like a thrill ride at an amusement park. The unsettling part was the unpredictability of these drops; you never knew when or where they would occur. The best strategy was to stay calm and avoid tensing up, as that seemed to exacerbate the sensation. Despite the turbulent welcome, I arrived at our Airbnb before Nora, as her flight was delayed due to the storm.

Our choice of accommodation was good, located just outside the bustling heart of Rome but easily accessible via a local tram. When Nora finally joined me after several months we caught up and reminisced about our past adventure in Greece, where we had contributed to turtle conservation efforts. Armed with a carefully curated list of must-visit places in Rome, we were eager to immerse ourselves in the city's rich history and culture.

One of Rome's unique features that I discovered was its advanced public transportation system. The buses were equipped with real-time tracking systems, allowing passengers to monitor their location and proximity to the next bus via smartphone apps. As we rode the bus, passing by centuries-old buildings, I found myself poring over my map, eager to identify these historical landmarks, I couldn't wait to explore on foot.

The walking tour embarked near the iconic Piazza Venezia, a central square in Rome known for its grandeur and historical significance. It's home to the imposing Altare della Patria (Altar of the Fatherland), a monument dedicated to Italy's first king, Victor Emmanuel II. This colossal white marble structure dominates the square and serves as a symbol of Italian unity and freedom.

During our tour, our guide shared intriguing anecdotes about the square. The most captivating was the fact that from the balcony above, Italian leaders and kings often delivered important speeches, addressing the nation from this prominent location.

As we strolled through the ancient streets, our guide regaled us with captivating stories of the Roman Empire's different kingdoms. Our journey led us to the Forum, a sprawling archaeological site nestled in the heart of Rome. This was once the vibrant hub of ancient Rome, a place of political, social and commercial activities. However, the Forum eventually fell into decline and disrepair, primarily due to a combination of natural disasters, including earthquakes and the ravages of time.

One interesting aspect we learned was that the marble from these deteriorating structures was often repurposed. It was used in various construction projects throughout the city, demonstrating the practical recycling practices of the ancient Romans. The marble's legacy lives on in other architectural wonders of Rome. Our next stop was the awe-inspiring Colosseum, one of the most iconic symbols of Rome. This colossal amphitheatre, once used for gladiatorial contests and public spectacles, stood before us in remarkably well-preserved condition.

Our guide shared intriguing details about the Colosseum's history, including the speculation surrounding how it was once flooded for epic naval battles. Despite extensive research, the exact method by which they filled it with water remains a historical mystery. Some theories suggest it may have been connected to a nearby river through an intricate system, such as a trench.

Regrettably, due to the aftermath of Brexit, I had to contend with substantially higher admission fees to enter this historic site. Nevertheless, our visit to the Colosseum was an unforgettable experience, fuelled by our knowledge of its captivating backstory and its enduring presence in the heart of Rome.

The following day, Nora and I decided to do some exploring on our own. Nora had mentioned a famous set of stairs she was eager to see, the 'Piazza di Spagna'. We wandered around the area, keeping an eye out for these renowned steps, yet we weren't entirely sure of their exact location. After some strolling, we decided to take a break and sat down. To our amusement, a security guard soon approached us, chiding us for sitting on the very stairs we had been seeking! It was quite comical how we unwittingly found ourselves right where we wanted to be.

Rome's bus drivers certainly have a reputation for their bold manoeuvres. Exiting a bus often felt like they were in a hurry to offload passengers, sometimes only slowing down briefly and expecting passengers to leap off! This led to a humorous incident when Nora alighted first and the bus doors abruptly shut in my face before it sped away. We exchanged amused glances, smiled and waved our funny goodbyes, knowing I would need to walk back to meet her.

During our visit to Rome, we had our sights set on the renowned Vatican City, conveniently located nearby. It was amusing to observe many people dancing in the streets with headphones on, prompting us to wonder what music they might be listening to. It felt like a scene from a video game, with individuals dancing to their own rhythms. We encountered one street performer, an older gentleman who I joked was my dad. We saw him on two separate occasions in different parts of the city.

Rome was also home to a large population of starlings, which would majestically fill the sky. Witnessing these graceful displays in the sky was a breathtaking sight, as they moved in synchronized harmony. One evening, as the sun set, we noticed a lengthy queue of people gathering near a wall with a peculiar hole in it. Intrigued, we joined the line and made funny speculations about what people might be so eager to see. After a rather lengthy wait of about 10 minutes, we finally got a chance to peek through the hole. To our delight, it offered a stunning and perfectly framed view of St. Peter's Basilica.

Our next adventure took us by train to Pompeii, a destination I had been eagerly looking forward to exploring. We had booked another Airbnb and embarked on a journey to this ancient village. Pompeii is a small and tranquil place, with a few restaurants and a church that we had the opportunity to explore. It was sad to learn about the tragic history of Pompeii and to walk amidst the well-preserved ruins. The level of detail in the artwork and architecture was astonishing and the sheer size of the site made it impossible to see everything in one visit. In a humorous turn of events, while waiting for Nora to use the restroom, I had the audio guide hanging around my neck, leading a few people to mistakenly believe I was a guide!

On another day trip, we ventured to the Amalfi Coast, renowned for its stunning landscapes and picturesque villages. The skills of the bus drivers navigating these treacherous coastal roads were truly impressive, often manoeuvring within centimetres of other buses—a nail-biting experience to say the least. The weather wasn't perfect when we arrived, with gusty winds, but we managed to hike to several viewpoints overlooking the charming coastal villages. It was remarkable to see how the houses were ingeniously designed into the rugged mountainside terrain.

One rather embarrassing moment on our journey occurred when I may have had a bit too much wine and ended up feeling unwell in our Airbnb restroom. Unfortunately, the toilets in Rome weren't the most advanced and the one I used became clogged. Our plan was to leave discreetly before the host discovered what had happened. We meticulously cleaned the restroom and made it look presentable, at least until it was flushed. To our surprise, the host arrived earlier than expected and the first thing he did was flush the toilet, resulting in a rather embarrassing situation when everything came back up. It was an amusing mishap, but I couldn't entirely claim responsibility.

After bidding farewell to Nora, little did we know that our paths would cross again sooner than expected. My last few days before my trip to Egypt were spent in Naples, a city that felt reminiscent of a scene from the Grand Theft Auto video game series, albeit for a brief visit.

Egypt

Having ventured solo to a handful of destinations, I was now seeking to challenge myself and delve into some tricky situations. A ridiculously affordable flight from Naples to Egypt caught my eye – an opportunity too good to pass up. The allure of chasing the sun was strong, considering how infrequently it graced the UK. Of course, my preparations included thorough research on Egypt's safety situation, which had me ready for the worst. Online accounts painted a grim picture, citing danger and a prevalence of scammers. I'm usually cautious about taking everything online at face value, but this time, caution seemed prudent. I wanted to arm myself with knowledge and one topic that kept cropping up was Egypt's tipping culture. It seemed that tipping was expected for every service, even for simple assistance from strangers on the street. Little did I know just how challenging this trip would turn out to be.

The chaos began even before I stepped onto the plane. I was taken aback by the sheer number of passengers refusing to wear masks amidst the ongoing pandemic. It came to light that many anti-vaccine/covid sceptics were flocking to Egypt due to the absence of strict restrictions. Upon disembarking, I was struck by the sight of airport staff openly smoking indoors – a cultural norm in Egypt. Procuring a visa proved to be no straightforward task either. Thankfully, a helpful staff member assisted me with the process, though he conveniently skipped returning my change. In the grand scheme, it wasn't a significant amount, but the incident set the tone for my Egyptian adventure – not even getting change back at the airport.

Exiting the airport felt like emerging from a bunker, a sight etched in my memory. Stepping out of a narrow corridor onto a debris-strewn parking lot, the surreal contrast to Egypt's tourism image was stark. I had envisioned a more built-up environment upon leaving the airport, but reality surprised me. A horde of individuals bombarded me, vying to get me into a taxi. I had prebooked a taxi through my accommodation and I managed to locate the driver holding a sign with my name.

Initially expecting a private transfer, I was taken aback by the subsequent hour-and-a-half wait for other passengers arriving at the airport. A camel might have delivered me quicker. But such was the essence of Egypt – a country that moves at its own pace. The first fellow passenger, emerging after about thirty minutes, was an Englishman named Mark. I was relieved to find company, though less thrilled that he happened to be a non-believer in COVID-19. Nevertheless, our conversation flowed and he shared his extensive travel experiences, enlightening me about Egypt and addressing my concerns and queries.

My first destination was a place called Sharm El Sheikh. I had booked a charming wooden cabin just a stone's throw away from the beach. The prospect of making new friends and unwinding had me brimming with excitement. My arrival happened under the cover of night and after a chat with the receptionist about how much of a discount I wanted for the delay, I was led to my accommodation. The cabin came complete with a comfortable bed, a bathroom and even a mosquito net – a crucial detail in these parts. Having been travelling during the chilly grip of winter, I was eager to bask in some warmth.

I set an early alarm for 6:30 AM and as if by magic, the morning light broke through. Stepping out onto the cabin's porch was a surreal experience. The sky was a canvas of the bluest blue and the calm splashes of the sea against the shore felt like a serene melody. I truly felt like I had stepped into paradise. I strolled down to the restaurant, where a complimentary breakfast awaited. I must admit, it might have been the strangest-tasting cereal I've ever had and everything seemed oddly different, but I chalked it up to needing time to adjust to the local flavours. As the sun gradually ascended, its warm rays on my face marked a wonderful start to the day. Playful cats frolicked about and I indulged in the simple pleasure of tossing them bits of food. Ah, yes, cats were part of the Egyptian backdrop too!

I was quite satisfied with the resort's offerings, especially considering the value. A salad and pasta would set me back about £4 – a fair deal. The common relaxation and dining area had a distinct vibe. Low sofa seats, a customary feature in Egyptian culture, adorned the space, while vibrant textiles abounded, prompting the customary removal of shoes. It proved to be an idyllic spot to get work done or study, all the while savouring a meal and gazing out at the sea.

On my first day, my strategic plan revolved around the sunbeds, naturally. I struck up a prolonged conversation with Mark, a seasoned traveller with a treasure trove of captivating stories. One anecdote stood out – his daring jaunt to Australia on a one-way ticket, armed with insufficient funds for a return journey. Ingeniously, he turned to selling jewellery, an easily portable commodity to fund his globetrotting escapades. Now, that's the spirit of problem-solving in action. Reassured by Mark's words about the safety of the local town, Soho, I decided to embark on a 25-minute walk to explore. Stepping outside the resort was like stepping into a wholly different realm – a single road amid vast stretches of sand, a landscape unlike any I'd encountered before. The initial stretch was a bit disheartening due to the litter strewn along the roadside, but then things started to change for the better as I approached the town. The once-bare expanses transformed into a landscape peppered with resorts under construction, a clear testament to the burgeoning tourism industry's ambitions.

Venturing into Soho required passing through a security checkpoint, a reminder that this oasis of tourist activity existed within a larger cultural context. Soho itself was a revelation – pristine and bustling with activities catered to visitors. However, as I discovered, this luxury came at a price, quite literally. A slice of cake set me back about £3, an affordable sum by Western standards but a relatively steep indulgence in the Egyptian context.

A few days later, Mark extended an invitation to explore the old market, which he aptly described as a slice of quintessential Egypt. This seemed like an ideal opportunity to ease into the Egyptian experience under his guidance. To reach our destination, we hailed a taxi and I couldn't help but notice Mark's masterful bargaining skills that whittled the fare down to 200EGP, approximately £5. Price negotiation is paramount, as unregulated spending could easily burn a hole through one's pocket. As I settled into the backseat, it became apparent that seatbelts weren't in vogue here. The unexpected auditory assault from a speaker in the boot – cranked to maximum volume – had me resorting to earbuds for protection against deafening soundwaves. The taxi's driving style was an exhibition in itself, with one hand on the wheel and the other choreographing a dance in the air. At one point, he even tried threading like a needle between a lorry and a car on a two-lane motorway. By the time we arrived, my ears were still ringing with echoes of the auditory ordeal.

However, reality didn't quite meet Mark's anticipation; the old market turned out to be not so old after all. Instead of the historical charm he envisaged, the market was a blend of new shops, police presence and even familiar brands. Amid this modern backdrop, Mark took on the role of a guide, imparting invaluable insights about Egypt and its culture. Naturally, a culinary adventure was also on the agenda. Determined to make my mark, I entered spirited bargaining for the return taxi journey, emerging victorious with a fare of 150EGP.

One of the factors that drew me to this particular resort was its affordability and the added bonus of having its own accessible coral reef right off the beach. Considering I was travelling light with just my hand luggage, I lacked the necessary snorkelling gear. Thankfully, Mark came to the rescue, lending me his snorkel equipment so I could give it a whirl. It was a bit of a struggle to set up initially, my first rendezvous with a snorkel, but after a few trial runs in the water, I eventually got the hang of it. The day itself was a tad overcast and I found myself to be the lone aquatic explorer in those waters. Fellow beachgoers, passing by, had given me a heads-up about the potentially chilly water, but as an Englishman accustomed to frigid seas, I wasn't fazed. Sure, the initial immersion was a bit nippy, but once past that brisk jolt, the water felt rather tolerable.

Below the surface, a vibrant underwater realm unfurled before my eyes. Schools of fish, as diverse in colour as they were in shape and size, meandered around the coral. It was an otherworldly sight, unlike anything I'd ever encountered before. This spot turned out to be a perfect introduction to the underwater world for me. The array of hues amongst the fish was staggering and they seemed just as intrigued by me as I was by them. A few even swam right up next to me, an experience that filled me with wonder. My lack of footwear kept me cautious around the coral, as I'd been forewarned about its razor-sharp edges. Despite the overcast conditions, the visibility was impressive – I could peer all the way down to the reef's floor, several metres below the water's surface.

Gaining a bit more confidence, using the snorkel with the safety of the ladder never too far away in case my initial nerves resurfaced. It was a remarkable experience to be part of this underwater universe, even on a cloudy day. Interestingly, coral reefs are not only stunning natural wonders but also incredibly vital ecosystems that support around a quarter of all marine species, making them essential to the health of our oceans.

Amidst the tourist hub of the area, a range of activities awaited and I decided to dip my toes into a couple of them, eager to immerse myself in the authentic Egyptian experience beyond the resort's cocoon. My first escapade led me onto the back of a 4x4 bike, venturing into the desert with a promising stop at the famed Echo Valley. The day's itinerary was set for a 9 am pickup, so punctually, I stationed myself outside my resort at the appointed time. Or so I thought. After half an hour of waiting, I finally managed to get through to them via message, only to discover they had managed to pick the wrong resort to collect me. Another 10 minutes stretched into eternity before they assured me another driver was en route. Yet another hour later, a car finally pulled up. In hindsight, lounging at the resort until I had a confirmation of the driver's arrival might have been a wiser choice than partaking in the waiting game. This incident was my introduction to the intriguing concept of Egyptian time, where 10 minutes could easily morph into a leisurely 2-hour stretch.

Initially, I anticipated being chauffeured straight to the quad bike track, but my driver had other plans. He kindly offered me a cigarette (which I politely declined) and veered off on a mission to locate an ATM. Our pit stop materialized at a fuel station, where I found myself entrusted with his phone while he replenished both the vehicle's tank and his wallet. Service with a funny twist, something you would not encounter back home in the UK! Eventually, we reached the quad bikes and without much time to waste, I was straddling the 4x4 machine. The ground rules were straightforward: stay obediently behind the leader, no overtaking. A tad disappointing, given the sluggish pace we were relegated to. Along the way, our trip paused at 'Echo Valley,' a place where vocal enthusiasm led to a delightful reverberation lasting several seconds. Even shouting my name! Another halt was at a village where a cup of tea treated my taste buds to delightful taste. Setting the stage for my downfall into overpriced photography and eager to secure the snapshots taken, I ventured a fee of 250EGP after the vendor's initial demand of 300EGP – a good effort, I thought. Though later humbled by the realization that my bargaining needed a bit more fine-tuning, but fear not, for this lesson served as a beacon of wisdom for my ensuing adventures. Onward!

I had another tour lined up, a decision that almost wavered due to its rather brief 8-hour duration. Considering the journey to the destination took a solid 2 hours, I was sceptical about the promised experiences fitting within the time frame. Mark raised his eyebrows in doubt, suggesting I might want to cancel, deeming it too good to be true. But I thought, why not? After all, a quirky tale often springs from an adventure that feels a bit off-kilter. This escapade involved a trip to Dahab, an Egyptian coastal town to the north of Sharm. The day's agenda promised a rendezvous with a vibrant valley, snorkelling escapades and a camel ride. With a shrug, I decided to give it a shot – for the story.

Unlike previous instances, this time the timing was on point. I found myself ushered into a van. Attempting to strike up conversation, I quickly realized I was the lone English speaker amidst a sea of Russian voices. Being the odd one out, grappling with the feeling of being misunderstood, made for quite the surreal experience. The minibus itself was far from comfortable; the absence of air conditioning coupled with windows that stubbornly refused to budge turned the drive into a sweaty ordeal. If that wasn't enough, the icing on the cake was the hour-long hold-up at the Sharm security checkpoint – a bit of a chaotic nightmare.

The journey finally got underway, revealing a straight road framed by imposing boulders, offering a glimpse into Egypt's distinctive terrain. Midway, we pulled into a roadside store – but the prices were nothing short of highway robbery, even my most enthusiastic bartering efforts yielded no results. Just when I thought the situation couldn't deteriorate, a young girl's stomach disagreed vehemently with the bus's motions, resulting in sick everywhere. Eagerly, we disembarked upon arrival, greeted by the stunning sight of crystal blue waters dotted with water sports enthusiasts.

Our initial stop was the valley, which did manage to impress. Traversing between towering cliffs, I captured some cool snapshots to remember the occasion. The tour guide, in his element, embarked on a lengthy discourse – but not in English – talking about the area's history. Unfortunately, my grasp of the local language left much to be desired, but a fellow English speaker (the sole one, it seemed) kindly relayed a summarised version of the guide's words, highlighting the essentials of what I was missing.

The prospect of snorkelling beckoned and our second port of call was a shop proffering rental gear. The guide advocated for the full kit, citing the chilling waters. Sceptical, I recalled my dip in the waters just yesterday – perfectly fine and within the realm of comfort. His suggestion seemed like a subtle financial nudge, a classic 'extra layer for extra money' tactic. Yet, confident in my swimming prowess, I deemed myself sufficiently prepared without the extra layers.

After this equipment interlude, we embarked on another short drive, ending at the coastline where the snorkelling was set to unfold. As I immersed myself in the water, it quickly became evident that a strong current was coursing along the shoreline, exerting its powerful influence. This realization prompted a swift decision to alter my course and head back prematurely. Lacking any specialized gear, it seemed the prudent choice, for venturing further could have proved unnecessarily challenging.

What ensued was a battle, a swim against the relentless forces of nature. Progress was frustratingly slow. The direct path back to the beach was rendered impassable by the coral lurking beneath, posing the threat of painful cuts and an even more precarious situation. Thus, my strategy shifted; I had to swim in parallel to the shoreline, hoping to find a way to navigate the waves.

The task was monumental, perhaps one of the most arduous swims I've ever undertaken the water pushing strongly. The shore seemed agonizingly distant and out of reach. I persevered and gradually the distance lessened. It was a testament to the sheer willpower it sometimes takes to triumph over nature's force.

Eventually, after an ordeal that had pushed both body and mind to their limits, I made it back. Every breath was a victorious gasp, a celebration of having battled the elements and emerged victorious. As I walked back to the rest of the group, little did they know I had just struggled with nature's power. An epic tale of the day I turned the tide... almost literally!

In a shift of pace, I indulged in an activity that felt far removed from the sea's embrace – a camel ride. It was an amusing event, sharing company with these majestic creatures. The finale for the day was a communal dinner, a moment of shared camaraderie over food and tea.

After bonding with a bunch of fellow adventurers during my Dahab escapade, it was time to explore the nightlife. This club wasn't just a club; it was a beachside paradise. I could practically taste the summertime vibes radiating from its very core. Surprise, surprise, the DJs were pumping out some wicked Western house/EDM beats that got my feet itching to groove. But hold on to your wallets, because this experience came with a bit of a price tag shocker. The entrance fee clocked in at around £10 (thank heavens for my local insider, who got me in free) and don't get me started on the drink prices – a whole £10 for a simple vodka and coke. Very steep for Egypt.

Next my plan was to go to Cairo the capital. I got off the bus and it was so hectic. My hostel was a mere 10-minute stroll away, so I figured, why not soak in the local vibes and walk? Now, I'm no stranger to dodging traffic, but Cairo's roads were in a league of their own. It was like frogger game on steroids, except instead of frogs, it was me navigating this automotive obstacle course. I swiftly learned that crossing alone was a mission. So, I did what any savvy traveller would – I piggybacked on a group of locals' road-crossing skills. You'd think they were choreographing a dance routine as they zigzagged through the traffic and I gamely joined their traffic tango.

Let's talk about the cars – they have this whole "stop or slow down for pedestrians" hidden under a rock. The result? An adrenaline-pumping rush with speeding vehicles while trying to cling to the white lines of safety. The soundtrack to this spectacle? A symphony of constant honking horns, like a terrible orchestra adding to the chaos. The bonus? I got a firsthand taste of Cairo's notorious pollution – a fog of smog that adds a whole new dimension to the phrase "city aroma."

But hey, I made it to my hostel in one piece and the friendly faces of fellow travellers erased any memories of road-crossing trauma. Fast forward to the afternoon – stomach grumbling in protest – and my taste buds were in for a treat. I followed the locals' recommendation and hit a modern-looking fast-food joint nearby. Earphones plugged in, I dived into a wrap while catching a movie. Just as I polished off the last bite, the universe decided it was time for a twist in the plot. A dude from Saudi Arabia, my neighbour at the next table, struck up a conversation. As per Arabian tradition, he extended an invitation to share a meal. Now, keep in mind, I was stuffed, but he went all out, ordering a feast of Egyptian delights. My taste buds were in for a cultural whirlwind and the best part – it was all on the house! We parted ways, contact details swapped and even though he never hit me up later, I walked away with a heartwarming tale of a spontaneous foodie connection. Most encounters aren't about hidden motives – they're just about a shared meal and some friendly banter.

Later that evening, one of my temporary roomies at the hostel tossed out an invitation to hit a bustling market. Now, I had half a mind to attempt the whole market scene – the attention, the relentless sales pitches, the feeling of being a walking wallet – you know the drill. But then again, this guy seemed like a seasoned traveller and if there was ever a moment to dive into the market hell, it was now.

So, off we zipped in an Uber taxi, the city's rhythmic chaos harmonizing with my rising anticipation. As we landed at the market, it was like stepping into a lively video game with NPCs in full force: "Step right in, mate! Best prices in town! Just for you, friend!" And the timeless classic, "Lovely jubbly!" It was a cacophony of commerce, a symphony of sales pitches. Oh and here's a bonus – the locals' knack for handing out creatively inaccurate directions just to keep you delightfully lost amidst the shopping labyrinth. Strategic roadblocks in the form of friendly folks parading their wares right in front of you – a tactic I had to admit was quite ingenious.

I strolled, I bartered, I dodged and I shopped – every twist and turn unveiling a new treasure trove of narrow streets packed with stalls manned by locals hustling for their daily bread. For all the chaotic commotion, it was a genuine glimpse into the city's heart and soul.

Amidst all the haggling, food was on the agenda, but here's the kicker – we weren't exactly aiming for the touristy eateries with wallet-thinning prices. No sir, we had a mission: find the local haunts where flavours are authentic and prices don't play tricks on your wallet.

Easy, right? Not quite. Turns out, getting a straightforward answer about where to eat was like finding a needle in a haystack. We ventured into a couple of local cafes, only to be fed blatant fibs about food availability. Oh well, onto the next! Finally, after some exploration, we stumbled upon a humble food stand that seemed to have a decent online reputation. We snatched up a couple of seats, placed our orders and braced ourselves for a local culinary adventure.

The feast laid before us was a carnival of flavours, a symphony of aromas. Various pots of sauces and meats sizzled on the barbecue, right beside our makeshift dining spot. Every bite was a delightful dance of spices, an invitation to indulge in Egypt's culinary secrets. Oh, but there was a little something extra in the air – pollution and noise. Yep, the soundtrack to our dinner was a medley of honking horns, chatter and the pulse of a city that never seemed to sleep. But hey, that's the Egyptian way, right?

The following morning, as I nibbled on my breakfast which was much better than the flavourless cardboard resort breakfast, a fellow traveller and I struck up a conversation. Little did I know that this encounter would trigger my first-ever case of coincidence. After exchanging Instagram handles, we discovered that we had a common friend on the platform – a girl I'd met in Portugal and he'd crossed paths with her in Budapest during different chapters of our trips! The world sure is a tight knit place.

My next venture was to the famed Egyptian Museum. Armed with the knowledge that it was colossal; I dedicated an entire day to navigate its depths and secrets. Passing through security, I stepped into what felt like a mammoth storage room – a treasure trove. It was top to bottom full of artefacts. The grand statues that greeted me at the entrance were huge. Regrettably, there was an absence of detailed information about the exhibits and the fact I couldn't afford a guided tour for myself, since they didn't do group tours. I wasn't too sure what I was looking at. So, my strategy was to whip out my phone and Google any artifact that caught my eye. Some objects were self-explanatory, like the mummies, but others left me scratching my head in wonder.

The museum sprawled across two floors, crammed with relics from floor to ceiling. I intentionally paced myself, wanting to absorb every inch of history. Amidst this immersive experience, an unforgettable moment occurred. A young Egyptian girl, around 8 years old, dashed up to me, blurting out "Selfie!" in adorable English. I grinned and obliged and with swift precision, she captured the snapshot and darted back to her parents. I often wonder where that photograph resides now.

While the museum housed a wealth of artifacts, some were conspicuously absent due to the delayed opening of a new museum which nobody seemed to know when this would happen. Ascending the stairs to the upper level, I stumbled upon rooms with English explanations sprawled across the walls. Naturally, I delved into every line, soaking up intriguing historical insights.

After this, my plan was to return to the hostel. To get back, I had to navigate a very bustling road. I often walked alongside the locals, but on this occasion, someone kindly waited and assisted me in crossing. He struck up a conversation and I inquired about the best places to eat. However, he cleverly led me to his shop, from which I promptly exited. If I wanted to shop, I would have ventured into a store; there's no need to push it on someone. I discreetly observed him from a distance, only to realize he was waiting for more tourists, despite telling me he needed to pick up his children from school. Even in the most unexpected situations and places, there are individuals seeking to capitalize on your presence. It can be mentally exhausting. Indeed, after encountering so many experiences like these, it's easy to become wary of anyone who approaches you with offers of help, as it often feels like everyone has their hand out for your money.

Afterwards, I took a leisurely stroll and sought out one of my favourite smoothie spots that Mark had recommended to me back in Sharm. Then, I made my way back to the hostel. I didn't spend too much time on the streets, as they weren't the most pleasant places to be. Most of the time, I preferred the comfort of my hostel.

Although, now getting exhausted from the city of Cairo, the next day, I had ambitious plans to visit the iconic pyramids, one of the main reasons I ventured to Egypt. Initially, I intended to go with a group from the hostel, as there's safety in numbers and vendors tend to hassle you less. However, my morning got off to a sluggish start when my alarm failed to wake me. I decided to do it solo and hopped on an underground train to Giza, the closest station to the pyramids.

While on the train, I was somewhat amazed to find that the carriage I was on was predominantly occupied by women. It later dawned on me that I had unwittingly boarded the women-only carriage, a practice in Egypt to help prevent sexual harassment. Upon exiting at Giza, I was immediately inundated with folks trying to sell taxi rides and other services for which I had no need. I skilfully brushed off the barrage of hawkers.

However, one man and his young son, perhaps around five years old, caught my attention. They approached me and inquired if I'd like to share a taxi to the pyramids. I figured there was no harm in it, so long as we agreed on the fare beforehand. We settled on 25 Egyptian pounds, a reasonable price for a taxi to the pyramids. The man kept emphasizing that I was his "Egyptian friend" and that I'd receive a special "Egyptian price," which struck me as odd since we were simply sharing a taxi. I began to suspect something was amiss.

The man claimed he worked at a school and wanted to show his son the pyramids. As we drove along the highway, the road opened, offering a clear view of the pyramids. Even the man's child exclaimed, "Wow!" We arrived just outside the pyramid village, the taxi departed and it was just the three of us. He led me to a waiting area and by this point, my suspicions were on high alert. So, I handed over my 25 Egyptian pounds and prepared to leave.

Moments later, a horse-drawn carriage arrived and the man persisted in urging me to board, promising me the "best price, Egyptian price, my friend." However, when I pressed them for the cost, they were ignoring the question. Finally, they disclosed the fare: 200 Egyptian pounds, roughly equivalent to 50 British pounds. This was exorbitantly expensive and I neither had the funds nor the desire for such an overpriced carriage ride. I decided to walk towards the pyramids instead.

For the next two to three minutes, the man continued to trail me, steadily lowering the price as I distanced myself. It was a well-orchestrated scheme targeting unsuspecting tourists at the pyramids. Fortunately, my wits were about me and I didn't fall victim to their ploy this time.

Using Google Maps to navigate my way to the pyramids, I found myself relentlessly pursued by people offering horse rides and other unnecessary services I had no interest in. Some individuals even offered directions to the entrance, but I disregarded them, suspecting they might lead me into their shops. It was an incredibly stressful experience and I chose to ignore them all. Unfortunately, as a 19-year-old Englishman, I seemed like a prime target and they swarmed around me like persistent flies.

One man followed me for several minutes, even down an alley, prompting me to start recording him, which finally convinced him to leave. Upon reaching the entrance, I was bewildered to find it consisted of little more than a high fence and a small building with a single entrance. For one of the last remaining wonders of the world, the lack of a grand entrance was surprising and it strongly hinted that the primary concern here was money. Several people continued to hound me, attempting to sell me tickets away from the entrance, but I brushed them off. I was perfectly capable of purchasing a ticket on my own. My strategy was ignoring everyone as rude as it seemed.

After verifying the entrance through Google Maps and after much manoeuvring through the crowds and passing through security, I thought I had finally escaped everyone. However, just as I entered the pyramid complex, I was "greeted" by "government officials" – workers employed by the government to enhance tourists' experiences but who often did quite the opposite. One of them complimented me on my skill at ignoring people, which briefly built some trust and I began to think he might be genuine. That was my first mistake. This man followed me closely, spoke impeccable English, shared some interesting facts and I couldn't shake him of – mistake number two. Repeatedly, he assured me, "You don't need to tip me" and "I'm just here to help," but as it turned out, that wasn't the case.

Suddenly, I found myself at a camel and although I hadn't particularly wanted to ride one, I reluctantly negotiated a somewhat reasonable price and mounted it. I later realized I'd tipped the guy way too much because he conveniently didn't give me any change. This put me in a foul mood. I was genuinely angry but couldn't do much as I was on the camel. I tried my best to enjoy the ride, but after the past hour, I felt utterly used and objectified. The man leading the camel took some photos and then asked for a tip. I didn't give him a single penny, having paid more than enough already.

After dismounting the camel, I explored the area, with persistent people watching my every step. I was ready to confront the next person who tried to scam me. All of this made my visit to the pyramids far from enjoyable and I felt rushed. Even reflecting on this memory now stresses me out. I paid extra to enter the King's Chambers, which was a unique experience within the pyramids and provided a welcome respite from the incessant hassle. The climb up was surprisingly warm, but it was awe-inspiring to think I was inside one of these ancient structures. Remarkably, one of the individuals attempting to sell me something even waited for me outside the pyramid, greeting me with an unsettling, "Ah, my English friend." He wanted a tip for doing nothing but making my experience more unpleasant. I laughed in his face and walked away. I'd had enough. All of this led me to leave the pyramids much earlier than I had intended.

Upon leaving the pyramids, I decided to demonstrate what I'd been through, so I played the role of a clueless tourist and discreetly recorded the mess around me on my phone. In the span of just one minute, about five people approached me, attempting to sell me a taxi ride or some plastic trinket. My intention was to walk back to Giza, as it was still daylight and the weather was beautiful. I followed

Google Maps down some truly local streets, ones that rarely saw tourists, judging by the curious stares I received. However, these locals, although initially startling, didn't bother me and the experience felt incredibly traditional. I even walked past some children playing football on the road who waved at me. It felt a bit unnerving at first, being so far from other tourists, but as I got used to it, I realised no one meant any harm. Eventually, I found myself on a busy road and became a bit disoriented, so I hailed a taxi to the station, which surprisingly cost me only around £2!

Back at my hostel in the morning, I met an English girl called Yasmin travelling solo around Egypt. She was strikingly beautiful and notably didn't wear a hijab. We had a conversation about how she coped with the attention, given that as a white woman with blue eyes and blonde hair, she attracted a lot of interest from Egyptian men. She explained that she ignored them and didn't react to the attention. I found it interesting to meet someone like her.

I also asked her and another guy I met at breakfast if they wanted to check out another museum, a new one focused on mummies and filled with informative text. It was a train ride away, so we all headed to the underground and took the train. It was a relief to travel with other people, as it allowed me to let my guard down a bit with more eyes around. Upon reaching the station, we began the 30-minute walk to the museum. You'd think they would place such an attraction somewhere more accessible. Walking along the road was nothing short of surreal. It felt like being a celebrity. Cars would slow down and the drivers would ask us to get in. Some residents even opened their doors, inviting Yasmin for tea. Cars slowed down so that the men inside could unabashedly stare at us. Any men passing us on the street would make comments and try to impress the English girl. I certainly wouldn't want to be a solo female walking down that road.

When we finally reached the museum, it was a strikingly modern and unique building and we were relieved to have arrived. The museum had two floors: the lower one was filled with the stories of remarkable mummies and the upper floor was a treasure trove of history. We explored the lower floor first and it was astonishing to see how well-preserved the mummies were. Often, you could even see their hair still intact and you could imagine how they must have looked in life. The best way to describe it was as if they had been placed in an oven and then shrivelled up. Sadly, we weren't allowed to take photos, but it's a place I'll never forget.

On our way back, we coincidentally ran into another girl from our hostel who happened to be heading to the same museum. That evening, we had a little party at the hostel with drinks. It was a welcome break as Cairo's Egyptian culture can be overwhelming at times and it felt nice to have a more Western style gathering.

At this point, I had a decision to make. I had booked a flight from Hurghada about two weeks later, which meant I had two more weeks to explore Egypt. Many people recommended heading south, which made sense considering my flight was departing from there. So, I decided to embark on a very long train journey to Aswan, known for its more relaxed atmosphere compared to Cairo. I opted for a cheap taxi to the station, as it would have been a hassle to drag my luggage all the way there. Outside the station, it was complete chaos: cars incessantly honked, people shouted and it was just mayhem. I navigated my way through the commotion and entered the station, making sure I had everything I needed.

The train ride was expected to last about 13 hours, so I chose a night train to save on accommodation costs. Getting a ticket proved to be quite a challenge since only one person at the ticket counter spoke English. I had to go to each counter, attempting to find someone who could help me. It was a stressful ordeal and Egyptians are not known for their patience. At one point, about five people were trying to translate for me, but we eventually figured it out. I decided to splurge on a first-class ticket, partly out of curiosity about what first class on an Egyptian train was like and partly for a touch of luxury during a 13-hour journey. It was relatively inexpensive, just a few more pounds than the standard ticket. However, luxury was far from the reality of these trains. The seats were dirty, uncomfortable and smelled of human sweat. Inside the train, the conditions were the worst I had ever experienced. I couldn't help but wonder how bad the standard seats must be.

The train departed approximately an hour late, setting us back from the start. My plan was to try and sleep to pass the time, but fate had other ideas. Just across from me, a man snored louder than I had ever heard in my life - it was utterly maddening and I was tempted to throw something at him. This prevented me from sleeping throughout the entire journey, making it incredibly uncomfortable. There was no way I was going to get any sleep. To make matters worse, the train frequently stopped for about 30 to 60 minutes at a time and we were making painfully slow progress. I began to doubt whether this journey would really take just 13 hours or if it would drag on longer. At one point, when I felt I was almost half asleep, we stopped AGAIN, right outside a mosque, where the 4 am prayers began. Just when you thought that was enough, some passengers started playing the prayers on their phones. It was pure chaos and sleep was a distant dream that night.

Seeing the sun rise in the morning brought a glimmer of hope that I would reach Aswan today, but I was still very far from my destination, despite being 10 hours into the journey. I hadn't brought much food with me, but luckily, there was a trolley with meals on board, ensuring I had something to sustain me. The meal included a roll and a sweet snack and wasn't too expensive. When the man finally stopped snoring, it felt like a sign of hope because that constant racket had made the journey twice as torturous. I was so exhausted that I didn't even have the energy to work or watch a movie, so I just sat there, gazing out of the window. We passed by villages and many farms, which offered a fascinating glimpse into rural life. Time seemed to crawl and 22 hours later (10 hours later than planned), we finally arrived in Aswan. Stepping out and inhaling the fresh air was incredibly refreshing, as I felt grubby after a full day on the train.

I had booked a hostel that was conveniently located just a short walk away from Elephant Island. This island held historical significance as a trading hub in ancient times. After my long train journey, I was quite hungry and decided to treat myself to a restaurant overlooking the Nile. The view was breathtaking and the food was simply amazing. The restaurant was also conveniently close to the ferry that would take me to the island where my hostel was situated.

That evening, I found myself sitting near a group of fellow travellers and one of the guys kindly invited me to join them. Naturally, I accepted the offer and it was nice to have some spontaneous company. They suggested an excursion to Abu Simbel, which is the southernmost point in Egypt. Regrettably, the cost was a bit steep for me, so I had to decline the offer.

The ferry ride to the island cost about 50 pence and took just five minutes to cross the river. Despite its small size, the island exuded a local charm and felt far removed from the touristy hustle and bustle of Cairo. This contrast was particularly evident in the behaviour of the local children, who didn't ask for money but rather offered high fives and invited me to play with them. Despite the language barrier, we managed to engage in some fun games. One of their favourites was a high-five game where I'd try to dodge their hand. They absolutely loved it and their smiles were infectious.

My hostel had a fantastic view overlooking the Nile, which was a delightful sight to wake up to each morning. I had a few activities planned but mainly wanted to spend a few days unwinding and relaxing. While there were a few other travellers around, I didn't particularly connect with anyone.

One day, I decided to take a boat to the nearby desert, just beyond the island. It was a warm and sunny day, perfect for exploring the unique landscape. The desert boasted intriguing buildings and hills to wander through. Climbing up one of the hills offered a panoramic view of Aswan, which was truly spectacular. Despite being far from the city, there was an unusual stillness and I could hear the distant sounds of cars and people shouting. I had some food with me, so I savoured a peaceful moment, eating while taking in the view.

The desert was unlike any climate I had experienced before, with sand and black rocks scattered all around. It was an incredible sensation walking on the warm sand beneath my feet and it easily brushed off. I also ventured into a few abandoned buildings, which was an awesome and solitary exploration in the middle of nowhere. It was a moment of complete harmony and I relished every second of it.

Exploring Aswan felt like stepping into an Egyptian town, minus some of the more overwhelming aspects of tourism in Egypt, such as constant approaches from people asking for money, although it did happen on occasion. On my second night at the hostel, a group of people I had met in Cairo joined me. It was a welcome addition, providing both company and the opportunity to explore together. We found a cool, budget-friendly bar not too far from the island where we were staying. There, we enjoyed a few drinks while sharing stories and experiences. I also had the chance to meet an English guy who was working in Egypt. Our conversations delved into culture and how he found living in this unique place. He mentioned that often he would simply respond in Arabic, saying, 'No, I'm local,' which tended to deter people from hassling him.

One memorable night, we discovered an incredibly affordable food store selling local dishes for about 0.5-2 pounds. It made us feel like kings. As we strolled past a shop, the shopkeeper used a line that caught our attention. He asked, 'Where are the tourists?' It felt like a genuine cry for help and we couldn't resist talking to him. Our conversation ranged from COVID-19 to the challenges facing Luxor, which were evidently substantial. It was one of the few times I genuinely felt sympathy for someone here, although I couldn't help but wonder if I was being naive or if he was just trying to make a sale.

Another friend from Cairo, who was staying at a different hostel in Aswan, messaged me about a trip to Abu Simbel with a group of fellow travellers. The offer was remarkably affordable and I felt like it was an opportunity I couldn't pass up. We collectively hired a private driver for the day and it was an incredible experience to see eight solo travellers come together from various parts of the world and different hostels to plan an adventure. We co-ordinated pickup times and brought cash and everything went smoothly. Everyone was punctual and we embarked on our journey to Abu Simbel.

The drive took about three hours in a minibus, which highlighted why Abu Simbel was challenging to reach. There's only one bus per day and it prioritises locals. Despite the early hour, conversations flowed. When we arrived, it was pleasantly quiet, allowing us to leisurely explore the magnificent monuments. They were truly awe-inspiring, especially when you consider that they had to be moved higher up and relocated due to the rising waters of the Nile. Learning about the preservation efforts for Abu Simbel was fascinating, involving the efforts of hundreds of archaeologists and funding from various countries due to the high cost. I couldn't fathom how they worked there during the scorching summers, where temperatures easily reach 45 degrees Celsius. We took some group photos and arranged our return transport. It was one of the most spontaneous and enjoyable days I had experienced and many from our group were also heading to Luxor, which would be my next destination.

Following my time in Aswan, I decided to make my way to Luxor. It had been highly recommended to me due to its rich historical significance and being so close, it seemed unwise to miss it. I boarded a train, which, thankfully, didn't take too long - just about 6 hours, which felt like a breeze compared to my previous journey.

Upon arriving at the hostel in Luxor, I was absolutely astonished by the number of familiar faces. It turned out that many of the people I had met on the Abu Simbel trip were also staying here, along with someone I had encountered in Cairo. The odds of everyone selecting the same hostel were incredible. Instantly, I felt at home, knowing I was acquainted with nearly half of the hostel's occupants. Moreover, I had booked a private room that included complimentary breakfast, all for the incredibly reasonable price of about £6 per night. The hostel's location, just off the main street, was ideal, putting me near shops and food stores.

However, there was one significant downside to the area - the pervasive sense of desperation for tourism. I had never been in a place where I felt like an object and Luxor was no exception. At every turn, I was followed and relentlessly pitched to buy various items. It was a constant battle to protect myself from these persistent sales pitches.

Despite this, Luxor had a lot to offer in terms of historical sites, including Karnak, temples, the Valley of the Kings and experiences like hot air balloon rides. Given the plethora of attractions, I decided to spend several days here and I had my own room and enjoyed complimentary breakfast each morning.

During my stay, I encountered a fascinating individual in the hostel - a man who was pedalling his bicycle around Egypt! Every morning, the police in several vehicles would knock on the hostel door to ensure he was still there and hadn't left without their permission. Their daily visits were quite comical. The only part of his journey where he wasn't allowed to cycle was between the checkpoints, for his own safety. In these cases, the police would drive him to the next checkpoint. He mentioned that when he was cycling, they would always follow him, urging him to hurry whenever he took a break. On his final day at the hostel, he had to inform the police. Around two police cars and one tourist car arrived that morning to ensure he was properly escorted. It seemed like overkill, but perhaps they couldn't afford to risk more terrorist incidents, since tourism makes up 10-15 percent of the economy.

In Luxor, I spent the first few days in the company of a group of people I had met along the way. We decided to visit the Karnak temple, where we hired a guide.

Having a guide proved invaluable as they provided a wealth of information and insight into the historical significance of the site. It enhanced our experience as we explored the temple complex, allowing us to truly appreciate its grandeur.

Our next excursion took us to the Valley of the Kings. To reach this archaeological treasure, we initially planned to walk, which would have taken about an hour along the road. However, taxi drivers at the starting point offered amazing rates for the journey. Despite our initial intention to walk, the persistent taxi drivers eventually offered such a low price that we couldn't refuse, so we decided to take a taxi to the site and walk back to our hostel later.

The Valley of the Kings was an awe-inspiring experience. We hired a guide once again and the level of detail inside the chambers was truly remarkable. We explored approximately four of the chambers and each one left us in awe of the ancient craftsmanship and history preserved within. As we exited the site, we encountered a few vendors whose shops were closing for the day. Feeling hungry, I inquired about the price of an ice cream, but the initial quote was quite high, around £5. I chuckled and walked away, but the vendor followed us, repeatedly lowering the price. Eventually, my friend bought two ice creams for just £1. It appears the vendor was struggling to make sales that day and his persistence almost resembled begging.

We were among the last tourists to leave the Valley of the Kings that day. As we walked back along the dark road, we noticed a police car approaching. To our surprise, it pulled over and the officer gestured for us to hop into the back. It was an unexpected and exciting experience to ride in a police car in Egypt and we were relieved that it was for a positive reason. In the back, we didn't have seats and we could see the driver watching a movie on his phone through a small window. This incident was a testament to the unique experiences one can have while travelling.

We then found a local pizza shop where the pizza was only about £3 and was amazing! We also tried some ice cream which they made. However, walking back to the hostel proved to be a somewhat risky endeavour. The road was dimly lit and cars often didn't use their headlights to conserve fuel and keep their eyes adjusted to the brightness of the road. This practice made it dangerous for pedestrians like us, as drivers sometimes couldn't see us in the darkness. I discovered that Egyptian drivers use a flashing light signal to acknowledge each other on the road. To test this, I flashed my iPhone's light at an oncoming car and sure enough, it flashed back, indicating that it had seen us. This communication helped us feel more secure on the road.

Nonetheless, the walk remained treacherous, as some drivers even travelled in the wrong direction on the road to reach a nearby petrol station. Egypt's lax traffic rules and practices contribute to the high number of accidents on its roads.

Additionally, I often wore a face mask to protect myself from the pollution caused by passing cars and the blowing sand, which was prevalent in the area. The pollution was quite severe and although my mask might have provided only minimal protection, it offered some peace of mind in that regard.

One of my most cherished spots in Luxor was a delightful restaurant with a view of the temples. I noticed that it attracted both locals and tourists, creating a pleasant mix of clientele. The restaurant also offered very reasonable prices, making it a favourite haunt. On some days, I couldn't resist going there twice, especially for their incredible chocolate cheesecake slice, which was not only delicious but also the largest slice of cake I'd ever seen. The view of the temple from this vantage point was truly exceptional.

One evening, as I dined with a group of fellow travellers, we gazed out the window and witnessed a troubling sight. Skinny horses pulling carriages passed by and the treatment of these animals was distressing. On this night, the situation escalated to a horrific level as we witnessed a horse collapse from exhaustion and starvation. Its owner responded by kicking and pulling at it in an attempt to get the poor animal back on its feet before anyone noticed. I reached a breaking point, unable to tolerate the scene any longer, I stormed downstairs and confronted the owner. Although I knew my actions might not bring about immediate change, I felt compelled to speak out against the cruelty I had witnessed.

Another popular activity I observed in Luxor was the hot air balloon rides, which offered breathtaking views of the city and its historical sites. The cost was surprisingly affordable, around £30, so I decided to book a ride for the following morning. I teamed up with a new friend from the hostel and we set our alarms for an early 4 am start, aiming to arrive just before sunrise.

We were picked up in a van and transported to a boat, where we enjoyed complimentary tea. The boat ferried us across the river to the hot air balloons and the scene was nothing short of spectacular. It resembled a bustling operation, with countless white transport vans lining the road, each filled with passengers from various hotels and hostels in Luxor.

Upon arrival at the site, we had mere minutes to spare before some of the early risers were already soaring above us in their hot air balloons. The entire field was a mesmerising display of colourful balloons inflating in unison. We were divided into groups and instructed to wait while our balloon was prepared. The process of inflating the balloon was a remarkable spectacle, akin to a perfectly orchestrated balancing act.

We were then loaded into small pods, but considering the reasonable price we paid, I couldn't complain about the cozy quarters. Our tour guide also served as the driver and spoke excellent English. He provided descriptions of the landmarks we passed as we embarked on our magical journey.

As the sun began to rise, the experience became increasingly enchanting. The sky was adorned with a multitude of hot air balloons and I estimated there were about 25 aloft at once. The morning's minimal wind allowed our driver precise control over our route. At times, we descended close to archaeological sites, almost within arm's reach. Then, we ascended high into the sky, giving us a panoramic view of Luxor.

One striking observation was the pollution that blanketed the city, a stark reminder of the air quality issues faced by the locals. Nevertheless, the sight from our vantage point in the hot air balloon was breathtaking and I managed to capture some of the best photos of my travels.

After approximately an hour, the skilled driver expertly landed the balloon in the exact spot from where we had taken off. Accompanied by two cars that had followed us throughout the journey. We all had to go into the brace position, but the landing was so gentle it felt like we hadn't landed at all. Six strong men steadied the balloon to ensure a smooth touchdown. This type of landing was humorously referred to as the "Egyptian landing," and it was unlike any other landing I had experienced. The minimal wind and perfect planning made it a memorable end to an incredible journey. The hot air balloon ride over Luxor was a breathtaking adventure and one of the most unforgettable experiences of my travels.

On one of the days in Luxor, I visited a smoothie shop to enjoy one of my favourite smoothies. Little did I expect what would happen in the next few hours. The gentleman who served me appeared very friendly; I always like to give people the benefit of the doubt, so I engaged in conversation with him. He offered me a complimentary smoothie as a sample. He expressed his desire to show me around Luxor and show me to the 'best' of the city, while also cautioning me about potential scammers in Luxor. I pondered whether this man might be genuine. I even offered him some money to test his intentions, but he declined. He inquired about my whereabouts and as I was staying in a hostel, I shared this information. Additionally, he introduced me to his family, which I didn't think much of at the time. Later, he kindly offered me a lift back on his moped, an experience I couldn't resist trying. We exchanged contact details when he dropped me off and everything seemed fine.

The plan was to explore Luxor together the following day after he finished work. However, the messages I received that evening took a rather creepy turn. He sent messages such as 'I want to get to know you better,' and I felt that he was making advances. Furthermore, he bombarded me with 40 photos of himself (none inappropriate), which was rather peculiar. I decided to stop responding to his messages, thinking that would be the end of it.

The next day, I decided to go for a walk and upon returning to my hostel, I was startled to learn that six men had come looking for me by name. This was rather alarming, as it appeared that this individual was not giving up on his pursuit. I instructed the receptionist to inform anyone who came asking that I had taken a train to Cairo in the hopes that they would cease their search. Fortunately, I was leaving the following day anyway.

Later, when I came downstairs, I discovered eight more men arrived inquiring about my whereabouts. Despite the potentially dangerous situation, I wasn't overly concerned. I believed that they needed tourism and, therefore, had to be cautious in their treatment of tourists, as any negative incidents could harm their country's reputation. This is one of my favourite stories to share because it sheds light on some of the less favourable aspects of the country and how some individuals may persist despite receiving a clear 'no' as an answer. I learned a lot from this encounter, underscoring the importance of remaining vigilant, as some people will attempt to take advantage of any lapse in one's guard.

I left early the following morning and boarded a bus bound for Hurghada, my final stop. Hurghada, much like Sharm El Sheikh, is a highly touristy destination and I had been advised to skip it. I had a few hours to spare before my flight back to the UK, so I took a reasonably priced taxi to the beach for some relaxation. Later, I realized that I was supposed to pay for access to the beach (of course, in a tourist area in Egypt). Hurghada boasts numerous beaches and is not a typical traveller's destination. I randomly chose a beach near the airport, found a spot overlooking the water and soaked up some sun.

To my surprise, within minutes of settling down, a friend I had made in Cairo walked right past me! We spent the next few hours discussing our respective adventures. It's incredible to think that if either of us had chosen a different spot on the beach, we would never have known the other person was there. It was a remarkable coincidence and I still can't quite believe it. In a city with a population of over 250,000, our paths crossed within 30 minutes of my arrival. It was a wonderful and relaxing way to conclude the trip and I felt ready to leave.

Once again, I hailed a taxi to the airport, which was surprisingly quiet for an airport. I passed through security, where they conducted multiple searches and bag checks. Perhaps it was because the airport was quiet and they needed something to occupy their time. Additionally, I had to "sign in" my laptop on a piece of paper, although I couldn't fathom the purpose of that. Egypt had been an adventure that taught me valuable travel and life lessons. I do hope to return someday, but I'll limit my visit to the places I missed and won't plan on lingering.

Budapest again...

After my time in Egypt, I wanted to fly back to the UK for a few days to visit family and friends. Since flights into the UK are often quite affordable, it didn't cost much to return home briefly before flying out again. On my final night in the UK before leaving, a famous DJ named 'James Hype' was performing at my local club. I was eager to see him, so I went clubbing, got only 2 hours of sleep and then embarked on a drive to the airport, my dad kindly took me.

My parents have always been incredibly supportive of my travels. Whenever possible, I make an effort to get to the airport/home on my own, but there are instances when it's simply not feasible due to train strikes or inconvenient flight times. In these situations, my dad has been exceptionally kind and reliable. He always steps in to drive me getting to or from the airport, ensuring that I have a smooth start or finish to my journeys. It's a tremendous relief to have such a supportive and caring family when it comes to my travel adventures.

To reach Bulgaria on a budget, I had to make a stop in Budapest. Since Budapest is one of my favourite destinations, I thought, "Why not stay for a few days?" To ensure I didn't get too carried away and miss my flight, I opted to stay in a budget hostel. It wasn't a party hostel, but it did offer free breakfast. Upon arrival, they insisted on cash payment, which was a bit annoying, so I had to head straight to an ATM. Furthermore, the receptionist seemed rather impolite and often ignored greetings. Great! It turned out to be the perfect hostel for my needs, as I knew I wouldn't want to linger with such customer service.

That evening, there was a pub crawl and I was the only person from my hostel attending. It was my first solo night out, but having done it once before, I felt a bit more confident. When I arrived, I met several cool Americans, about 12 of them, who were on a big trip together. It sounded more like a nightmare than an enjoyable holiday, but regardless, they were very open and easy to get along with. I also met a few other people that night. They were fascinated by my travel stories and one American girl named Audrey, who becomes relevant later in this narrative and I got along particularly well. It was a great night despite having had only 2 hours of sleep.

The following day, I ventured out with three English people I had met on the pub crawl and we visited the famous Roman outdoor heated baths. To my surprise, we stumbled upon an entire room that I had missed during my previous visit! The water was at a toasty 38 degrees Celsius, creating a peculiar sensation as your body wanted to sweat, but you were submerged in water. We also discovered a sauna and an ice bath, which was fun to alternate between. That evening, we went for a few drinks and found a student bar where you could even pour your own drinks, a testament to the trust the establishment had in its people. I never expected to have so much fun after just a few days, but Budapest never fails to entertain, which is why it remains one of my favourite destinations. This is partly because it's full of tourists and since I already have some knowledge of the city, people often like to tag along and I enjoy showing them around.

Bulgaria

Shortly after my trip to Egypt, my family friend Chris extended an invitation to join him for some snowboarding in Bulgaria. I was absolutely up for the adventure, especially considering I had never tried snowboarding before and was eager to give it a shot. Given Chris's experience and skill in snowboarding, I couldn't have asked for a better person to accompany me on this trip. As it was during a busy season, Chris managed to secure a shared room with two beds, which wasn't an issue for me since I was accustomed to sharing accommodations.

The lift pass cost £150 and equipment rental came to only about £80, so I was able to enjoy this experience quite affordably compared to other snowboarding resorts. My journey began in Sofia and I had about a week to explore the city on my own before meeting up with Chris in Borovets. My initial impression of Sofia was that it appeared somewhat dirty, dimly lit and not particularly inviting. However, over the course of my stay, I grew to appreciate and even love this city. It was the first time I had ever felt so at home in a city after just a week of being there. Let me elaborate.

The hostel I stayed in was quite good, although I was the youngest guest and there weren't many people my age, so I often ventured out on my own. I did find it a bit challenging to fill my days because it seemed that there were limited things to do in Bulgaria and I had arrived during the off-season in Sofia, meaning that some activities and attractions were closed. Despite these initial challenges, I made the most of my time by taking a trip to a nearby mountain, participating in a free walking tour and exploring the city's sights. I also went out a few times to bars with fellow hostel guests.

As I spent more time in Sofia, I developed a strong connection with the city. It was the first time I had ever felt so comfortable and at home in a new place so quickly. To put it in perspective, I was taken aback by the city's size, both in terms of its physical footprint and its population. For instance, I frequently visited a local bar where I often recognized familiar faces. This level of familiarity was something I hadn't experienced to this extent before. I believe part of this was due to the relatively low number of tourists during my visit, which meant that I frequently encountered the same people. Additionally, most of the people I interacted with were from other countries and had decided to move to Sofia because they had fallen in love with the city and appreciated the lower cost of living. I could genuinely envision myself making such a move in the future. I was also pleasantly surprised by the cost of living in Sofia. For example, you could enjoy a soup and a drink for around £1.5 at a soup cafe and a slice of pizza cost just £1.

A hilarious incident occurred at the hostel when conversation turned randomly to a crazy English girl who had recently arrived from Budapest. I couldn't help but recall a few eccentric characters I'd come across during my first time in Budapest and decided to show an Instagram photo of a girl from my hostel whom I suspected was the same person. Amazingly it was the same girl!! It turned out I wasn't the only one who thought she was a bit crazy.

One night, I decided to go clubbing at a place called 'EXE,' which I was told was the best club in the country. To my amazement, it surpassed all my expectations and is, to this day, the best club I've ever been to. The place was packed, creating an incredible atmosphere. What set this club apart was the strict no-mobile-phone policy, which encouraged everyone to fully immerse themselves in the party. The club was decked out with lights on every wall, creating a mesmerizing visual experience and the DJ's performance was flawless. Just reminiscing about it makes me want to return. Prices were like those in the UK, which I had anticipated. I left Sofia with a deep affection for the city and a desire to return someday.

I then took a bus to Borovets, where I met up with Chris later that evening. We went out for some food and despite the peak season and tourist location, I was pleasantly surprised that prices were not exorbitant. We woke up early the next morning, had a hearty £5 English breakfast and headed to the slopes. We started on an easy, low slope and Chris did a great job teaching me the basics. I couldn't believe how quickly I got the hang of it and managed to maintain my balance quite well. To allow Chris to have his fun, I decided to stick to the smaller slope. However, walking up the slope each time, combined with the blazing sun, proved to be quite tiring. We met at a local shop for a recharge and some food. Later that day, when the slopes closed, we had dinner and decided to check out the nightlife in Borovets.

Borovets was renowned for its wild party scene and it certainly lived up to its reputation. The first bar we entered featured a rather large, topless English man spinning around on a pole. It was like a large chicken on a stick at a supermarket. However, the most shocking part was the price of the drinks. A double coke and vodka (equivalent to a triple in the UK) cost around £2, signalling that this was going to be one crazy night.

It seems like every night in Borovets was a memorable adventure. The place was bustling with people and a good number of them were on stag parties, including a lively group of about 15 Irish guys who were out partying every night, even if they were hitting the slopes during the day!

During one of these wild nights, I had a close encounter when one of the Irish lads picked me up and started spinning me around. It was a dizzying but funny experience and I felt like I could fall at any moment! The topless men jumping onto tables was another sight to behold. They were so intoxicated that it was almost comical to watch and I couldn't believe that nothing got broken during their antics. That night, I even stumbled upon a half bottle of Jägermeister hidden on a seat, which ended up in my drink. Chris, who wasn't known for heavy drinking, also let loose that night and paid the price the next day when he felt very ill. His family and friends were very surprised to hear that he was drinking! In short, it was a night of chaos, but also a lot of fun. The pubs in Borovets had some of the best atmospheres, each offering its own form of live entertainment and bringing people together. There was always something happening.

On our way back to the accommodation every night, we had to pass by the "Titty bars," which were essentially strip clubs. These places always had people outside trying to entice passersby to come in. Their sales pitches were often quite humorous and meant to grab your attention. One particularly funny incident occurred when one promoter was showing a group of lads some adult content on his phone right outside one of these bars. They joked around but ultimately didn't go inside. However, he then turned his phone toward an elderly man out of the blue, saying, "Look, old man! Are you interested in these girls?" The old man was visibly horrified and the shocked look on a girl's face who happened to be walking by was priceless. It felt like watching a live prank unfold and we couldn't help but laugh. It seems they have their own ways of entertaining themselves.

I also had my first ever solo night out in Borovets, one that wasn't part of an organized pub crawl, as I had an extra day to myself. I didn't expect much, so I started with a solo meal. I had to sit at a 6-seater table as there were no other available tables. A family joined me later since there were no other seats available. They were a friendly English family and I shared stories about my travels and my Amazon selling venture with them. They were very impressed and we discussed various topics, including the news and everyday life. After our meal, the parents invited me for a drink. I accepted and it was beginning to feel like a great night. They insisted on buying me every single drink, which was incredibly kind. We went to a bar with live music and the atmosphere was fantastic. After bidding them farewell, I decided to stay out a bit longer. It wasn't that late and I had been incredibly lucky so far. I always find it easy to blend in with people on the dance floor and if you look like you're having a blast, people naturally gravitate toward you. I ended up chatting with a group of people around my age who were sitting at a table behind me. It was unbelievable when we discovered that they lived just a 5-minute drive away from me back home! That sealed the deal and I had made some friends for the night. Once again, I found myself with free drinks coming my way. We partied until the early hours of the morning, having a blast. On our way back to the accommodation, the strip club promoter tried to pick me up and put me into the strip bar. It must have been quite frustrating for him that his tactics weren't working previously, so he went to his last resort!

It was a fun week and although not too good at the snowboarding I enjoyed it and can't wait to give it another go again. I now was back to solo and wanted to explore more of Bulgaria.

In response to the locals' recommendations, I decided to make Plovdiv my first destination. I hopped on a train to Bulgaria and found myself engaged in a conversation with a fellow passenger who, as it turned out, was also headed to Plovdiv. To my surprise, even the train inspector joined in the conversation, although he occasionally forgot to carry out his duties. He proudly showed me his ageing equipment, which he mentioned hadn't changed since the tracks were laid. His English was very good since he used to work in London. It turned out to be an unexpectedly sociable train journey.

Despite my weariness from travel, I was sorely tempted to settle in with some Netflix, but I didn't want to appear rude. I soon discovered that Bulgarians are incredibly friendly people and it was an excellent start to my trip. I came across a hostel in the old town of Plovdiv that had exceptional ratings. What intrigued me most about it was that the old town had a no-car policy, allowing only essential vehicles. I booked a stay there, intrigued by the prospect of living in such a unique environment. The hostel exuded a classic charm with its old-world appearance and it even offered complimentary breakfast. As a nice personal touch, there was a large whiteboard at the entrance, welcoming me by name.

Plovdiv, I found, struck a perfect balance between vibrant nightlife and rich historical heritage. Little did I know that it boasted the longest shopping street in Europe at the time. Strolling down this street felt like walking on history itself, given that it was once a grand Roman arena. Some parts of this historical relic were still visible as I explored the area. The lively atmosphere on Fridays and Saturdays, with bright lights and bustling crowds, even reminded me of Lisbon.

I decided to venture out for a solo night in Plovdiv, though it proved a bit challenging as most locals were in their own groups. I didn't stay out too late, but I was glad I gave it a try.

Travel often brings you into contact with people who are unique, for better or worse. In my hostel, I met a French guy called Roman who was residing in Bulgaria illegally due to an expired visa (over 90 days). He was quite the character. He mentioned that he used to work as a drug tester, which paid handsomely.

Unfortunately, one of the drugs he tested had tragic consequences for another tester, resulting in ongoing financial compensation for him. He used this money to sustain his life in Bulgaria, given how affordable it is to live there.

What stood out most about this guy was his extraordinary alcohol consumption. He'd start his day with vodka as if it were water and was drunk most of the time. His behaviour in public could be quite embarrassing, as he tended to cling to me like an over enthusiastic puppy. Fortunately, I had the company of a Canadian guy called Steeven who was also staying with us. Despite the French guy's quirks, he proved to be rather entertaining and I ended up spending time with both of them. Travel has a way of introducing you to truly one-of-a-kind individuals. I don't think I could have been with this French man for long if it wasn't for the normal Canadian guy. We ended up travelling for a while together.

Some amusing anecdotes about him come to mind. I remember him finishing someone else's meal at a bar once after they left; the people at the neighbouring table found it absolutely hilarious and he didn't seem to have a shred of shame about it. He also shared an interesting story about his past - he claimed to have been a stripper who would strip down and dance on stage during rock concerts. We initially thought he was pulling our leg, but he proudly showed us a video of his performance that was surprisingly still on YouTube.

He also told us stories about how he had been banned from numerous hostels in the area due to his behaviour. One particularly wild tale he shared was about a time when he had to visit a police station to retrieve his bag. But perhaps one of the most extreme stories he told us was about how he had managed to shut down a train station in France simply because he had 'spat on the floor' during the coronavirus pandemic.

During my stay in Bulgaria, I happened to be there on a special day called "Martenitsi." This delightful tradition is deeply ingrained in Bulgarian culture and serves as a symbol of renewal and hope for the arrival of spring. People exchange red and white bracelets, known as martenitsi, as tokens of appreciation and gratitude for their friends and family. These bracelets are more than simple accessories they ensure good health and luck. The tradition involves hanging these bracelets on the first sunny day, typically on a blossoming tree or a branch. I received one such martenitsa from the hostel receptionist, which was a heartwarming gesture. In return, I embraced the tradition and gave martenitsi to some of my newfound friends during my stay.

One night, I ventured out to experience the Bulgarian club scene for the first time and I was genuinely astonished by the impressive lighting and special effects - it was nothing like I expected from Bulgaria. What struck me most about Bulgaria was its rich traditions. For example, during club nights, it's normal for people to toss numerous napkins into the air, creating a cascade of white that blankets the dance floor. Additionally, there were individuals with drums moving through the crowds, adding rhythmic beats to the music. Bulgaria also has a unique music genre called "chalga." It's a type of music I had never encountered before - it's characterized by its fast pace, heavy drumming and spirited singing. It's challenging to describe, so I recommend checking it out online to get a feel for it.

One of my most enjoyable days was when I joined a free walking tour; amusingly, the French guy had done it about three times before, which I found rather comical. He had initially planned to do it again but changed his mind upon seeing the tour guide 'wearing a mask'. One can only wonder how he behaved on those previous tours. It was a fascinating experience to stand in places with such deep historical roots and absorb all the knowledge shared. Plovdiv truly captivated me, enveloping me in its rich history. Given my previous trip to Egypt, which had left me somewhat wary of people, I was initially hesitant when invited to have soup with a fellow tour participant. In my mind, alarm bells were ringing, but, there was no cause for concern. I ventured to the soup shop with a friendly young Bulgarian I had met on the walking tour, where we enjoyed some delicious £1.5 soup with bread. It was a bit surreal coming from Egypt, given my previous experiences; I almost needed to relearn how to trust people. The soup shop, as I was told, remains open 24/7 since many young people visit after a night of revelry to sober up with a warm bowl of soup.

From there, I made my way to Veliko Tarnovo, another destination that had come highly recommended. I took the train with the French guy and the Canadian guy and their contrasting personalities made for some amusing moments. The French guy was a bit tipsy, which added to the entertainment with his unpredictable antics. I preferred this lively company over travelling alone on the train. When we arrived at the station, we faced about a 30-minute walk to reach the city. We opted for walking over a taxi, although it proved to be a challenging and arduous journey with all our luggage. In hindsight, taking a taxi might have been the more sensible option, considering how affordable it would have been when divided among us.

Upon reaching the hostel, we found only one other person there and the atmosphere felt unusually quiet. I inquired with the receptionist about the lack of activity and he explained that it was due to both the winter season and the impact of COVID-19, which had deterred many travellers from coming to Bulgaria. It's disheartening to think that the hostel used to be bustling with activity and even had staff members living on-site, which speaks to its previous popularity before the pandemic. Now, it stood nearly empty, hosting only a handful of guests. Given my limited plans in the area, I didn't intend to stay for an extended period.

The French guy was the walking plot twist of our trip. With his unpredictable behaviours, he could have easily been a character in a reality TV show. Every day felt like a new episode. One night he also caused a huge argument with one of the other guests for a reason I can't remember but it wasn't important. Every day was a drama with this guy and always kept it interesting.

The town boasted a grand castle and little did I know, it was the eve of an anniversary celebration that drew the entire town together for a mesmerizing light show. Unaware of this event, I owe my thanks to the hostel receptionist who clued me in. The display was nothing short of spectacular, accompanied by music and a symphony of lights. It easily ranks as the most impressive light show I've ever witnessed and I couldn't have timed my visit better. The entire castle was bathed in radiant hues and a cascade of captivating effects.

The following day, my friends and I explored the castle in the day and paid for a small entrance fee. It was awe-inspiring to behold, bearing in mind its tumultuous history and the remnants still evident in the ground. In an inexplicable turn of events, the French guy, perched on a tower, decided to engage in some questionable behaviour by spitting off the top of the tower. Little did he know that there was a staircase below and his projectile came very close to a young girl. Imagine trying to get out of that one. Ew…

But that's not where his eccentricities ended. He wished ambitions of becoming an Instagram sensation and made a daring plan. Picture this: him holding his trousers and pants open, while we unleashed a colossal snowball aimed right at his nether regions. Without a hint of hesitation, the Canadian guy crafted a massive snowball with uncanny precision, hitting the target dead-on while I recorded. The French guy's reaction, a blend of shock and panic, was priceless as he scurried to a corner, frantically attempting to rid himself of the snow, inadvertently creating a rather dodgy act. The bemused reactions of other visitors were priceless.

On that same day, we embarked on an excursion to a swing. But this was no ordinary swing; it offered an unparalleled view of the entire town. Locating the entrance proved to be a challenge, yet once we did, we embarked on an incredible cliffside walk. The view from the swing, overlooking the entire town, was nothing short of breathtaking, making it one of my most cherished photographic memories.

Staying in hostels exposes you to a diverse array of characters and regrettably, we had the misfortune of sharing our room with an English fellow who turned out to be quite a handful. He not only invited himself to join us for drinks but also attempted to drag us into bars owned by his 'mates,' which wasn't part of our plan. His mood soured when we opted for a different pub instead. He also ordered drinks on our table but didn't pay, leaving me with the unexpected bill. He was the last person I would buy a drink for. Although the town was undeniably picturesque, it lacked the vibrant energy we sought. However, fortune smiled upon us one night when we chanced upon an underground bar hosting live music, infusing the evening with a lively atmosphere. Many remarked on our luck in finding it, as it seemed to be one of the few bustling spots around.

It's not every day that you encounter such an eccentric cast of characters while travelling, but this particular mix felt like a recipe for potential disaster. That fateful night, the English guy's peculiar behaviour was very twisted when he began kissing his phone and acting utterly bizarre. Fortunately, the French guy, known for his frankness, didn't hold back words and promptly told him to 'shut up,' all while sprinkling in some witty remarks. It was as if I had stumbled into a spontaneous comedy show.

The morning after that peculiar night, the room stunk from the English guy, emitting an unpleasant odour. We had no choice but to throw open all the windows in a desperate bid for fresh air. The French guy, never one to hold back, would occasionally make exaggerated "eww" sounds when in close proximity to the English guy, not-so-subtly hinting at the unpleasant stench that lingered.

Faced with the unbearable situation, we decided that the English guy needed a shower and fast. Yet, even after this refreshing interlude, the room's aroma still left much to be desired. In the end, the French guy took matters into his own hands, literally and figuratively, moving the bed and opting for a night of slumber in the communal area.

After a series of eventful days, it was time for me to return to Sofia. I secretly hoped to leave before the French guy could latch onto me again. However, as fate would have it, his plans coincidentally aligned with mine and he ended up joining me on the train back to Sofia.

During the train ride, he was erratic and started berating the locals for wearing masks, which made for an uncomfortable atmosphere. I decided to distance myself from his antics and ended up striking up a conversation with the locals, finding solace in their company while subtly venting about the French guy's behaviour. Upon arriving in Sofia, I quickly lost sight of him and to be honest, I wasn't particularly eager to meet up with him again after that train ride.

With about a week left before my flight back to the UK, having explored all the destinations on my list, I found myself pondering what to do next. It was then that a friend I'd met in one of the hostels in Egypt messaged me, announcing his impending arrival in Sofia. The timing couldn't have been more perfect. I suggested we consider booking an Airbnb, as the cost wouldn't surpass that of a hostel by much. We stumbled upon a superb apartment situated near the nightlife scene and on the opposite side of the city from where I'd previously stayed. It promised fresh adventures. Remarkably, we secured this Airbnb gem for less than £10 per night, an absolute steal. It was a delightful departure from hostels, offering a touch of luxury. My plan for this final leg of my Bulgarian escapade? To revisit missed attractions and, of course, revel in the nightlife!

We embarked on our first night out in Sofia and headed to Bar Friday, a renowned spot frequently visited by tourists. Upon our arrival, it was relatively quiet, but we struck up a conversation with two German lads who were also in town for a few days. Later in the evening, a lively group of Bulgarians joined us and their warmth led to an unexpected invitation for a night of clubbing. We found ourselves in the Uni district, teeming with local students and clubs lining the entire street. It was like stumbling into a slice of Dubai with its dazzling lights and electrifying atmosphere. However, as it was a workday, the crowd was thinner than expected, so we decided to call it a night relatively early.

To add to the adventure, we had one of the German lads crash on our sofa since his mate had left early and wasn't responding to calls!

One of the recommendations on Google I had received was to visit a rock museum. Initially, it sounded a bit boring, but as it was an inexpensive activity, I thought, why not? Perhaps I'd stumble upon some unusually fascinating rocks. When we arrived, it seemed like we were the only visitors in the entire building. With low expectations, we began our tour, but to our surprise, it was genuinely captivating. The museum showcased various crystals and rocks in colours and shapes I hadn't imagined. Some rocks displayed a stunning range of features like rainbow hues, stair-like formations, glassy textures and a dazzling shine. These unique combinations made them rather spectacular. I took my time, wandering around, trying to absorb as much information as possible. We ended up spending a few hours there and even created some humorous social media posts to share our experience.

Afterwards, we took a stroll and I showed my friend around the city. By sheer chance, we discovered that we were just a short walk away from the starting point of the free walking tour, so we decided to join in. It might not have been the wisest idea after a late night out, making it challenging to absorb all the information, but the parts I did remember were genuinely intriguing.

I also had a few solo nights in Sofia, which turned out to be incredibly enjoyable. It sometimes takes a little while to get into the groove, but I learned to keep my phone aside, put on a friendly smile and people would naturally gravitate towards me. One night, I began at a bar with a lively club atmosphere and then headed to one of my favourite spots, Bar Friday. There's a unique sense of being a "celebrity" when you're travelling solo and open to meeting new people. Since I had gone out for a few nights in a row, I began recognizing familiar faces in the bars, which fostered a sense of belonging. This quick integration into the local scene made me fall in love with Bulgaria even more and it had only been about a week since I arrived. Remarkably, I even spotted a few guys in the club whom I had met during my stay at the hostel about three weeks ago! Bar Friday, a mix of tourists and locals, was relatively quiet when I visited, but I cherished the opportunity to get to know people better in its laid-back atmosphere.

It was a real bonus that my mate wanted to join me for a night at EXE, unquestionably the best club I'd encountered in Sofia. We teamed up with the friends we'd made on our very first night in the city and we let loose. I had an early morning flight to catch the next day, so I couldn't afford to stay out too late, but we managed to party until around 4 am. This place regularly hosted top-notch DJs and their events sold out rapidly, a clear indication of just how popular and happening it was.

Nice

Originally, I had planned to spend a fortnight in the UK before embarking on my next adventure. However, fate had other plans. Both Audrey (who I met in Budapest) and I unexpectedly found ourselves with some free time during that very week I was in UK. Without much to do, I booked a flight and just three days later, I landed in Nice! How spontaneous! To save a few bucks, I opted for a flight to a nearby airport and then hopped on a bus to reach Nice since it proved to be a more cost-effective choice.

This had been one of my most spontaneous moments. After all, I had hardly spent any time with her and all my friends thought I was crazy. But I figured, what is the worst thing that can happen?

Nice hadn't been high on my travel wish list initially, mainly due to its reputation for being a rather expensive destination. However, the luxury of free accommodation and the intrigue of exploring a new place proved irresistible. Upon arrival, I was pleasantly surprised by the warmth of the weather and the astonishingly clear, crystal-blue waters. It was an unexpected gem that took me by surprise.

Audrey was deep into her studies during my visit, affording me lots of downtime to study and explore. During my stay, I met with her university friends and as is often the case with students, our evenings typically involved some pre-drinking, a dash of games and then off to the parties we went. For those brief days, I truly felt like a local and I've come to believe that this is one of the finest ways to truly immerse oneself in a new place. Pre-drinking was a must, given the rather steep prices - I recall shelling out a whopping £14 for a simple gin and tonic, an amount that could cover two nights' accommodation in Egypt or even a budget flight!

We even embarked on a mini-adventure to Monaco, a mere 40-minute train ride away. This day trip not only added another country to my checklist but also offered a unique experience that could be squeezed into a single day. Wandering the streets of Monaco, I couldn't help but notice the abundance of supercars and luxurious boats, truly living up to its reputation as a millionaire's playground. We concluded our excursion at the one and only McDonald's, as it was one of the few places our wallets could afford. 1 in 3 people are millionaires and I would always wonder how much money the person next to us had.

On my final day in Nice, I embarked on a hike to one of the city's hills, which rewarded me with a magnificent viewpoint overlooking the entire city. I was particularly impressed with the strategic placement of the airport, making it easily accessible and surrounded by water on both sides. In total, my spontaneous trip to Nice spanned about four days and was brilliant.

Greece again...

My old friends from England and I hatched a plan to rent a spacious villa in Zante for a week. This villa boasted 8 rooms and a refreshing pool and it was conveniently located near the lively Lagunas strip, which was a bonus. For this trip, I had quite a bit of gear in mind to bring along. Surprisingly, I managed to squeeze my laptop, drone and a second pair of shoes into my hand luggage, alongside my clothes. My journey began with a flight that touched down in Athens, a full 9 days before my rendezvous in Zante. To my surprise, there were a substantial number of solo travellers around during this period and I had the pleasure of meeting quite a few of them.

During most of my days in Athens, I found myself exploring the surrounding hills, offering splendid vistas of Athens and its surroundings. I also took time to delve into museums and I was struck by how deeply connected their exhibits were to Egyptian history.

Athens, despite its compact size, appears high when viewed from some of its taller hills. I opted for a 30 Euro pass, which granted access to many of the city's significant historical sites. As I wandered, I listened to an Athens podcast, which served as an informative and entertaining companion. Over the next few days, I made the most of my pass, visiting various archaeological sites and landmarks. Additionally, I embarked on a pub crawl, which proved to be great fun and offered opportunities for pool games and socialising.

However, the experience took an odd turn when a rather crazy American individual moved into my room. He espoused extreme views and made outrageous statements, which prompted me to report his behaviour. Surprisingly, the owner seemed to blame his behaviour on alcohol and no action was taken. This unsettling behaviour continued and I'd never encountered anyone quite like him before. I was more than relieved to part ways with him.

Fortunately, I met some wonderful people on this trip. In particular, I formed a connection with two South American girls residing in the Netherlands, as our vibes matched perfectly. Another fellow traveller named Tom, an Aussie and I got along splendidly. The hostel also had a pool table and I spent a lot of time playing pool. I started considering future trips, possibly to their home countries as they were keen to host me.

Following my time in Athens, my next destination was Meteora, a place that had been on my bucket list for quite some time. Essentially, Meteora is home to several monasteries perched atop massive rock formations that were shaped millions of years ago during dramatic climatic shifts. These monasteries were built as protective sanctuaries during times of war and only six remain active today. I took a train from Athens, which proved more challenging than anticipated due to the absence of clear platform signage indicating the train's destination. Towards the end of my train journey, I noticed a young woman of similar age who appeared to be a fellow traveller, asking others about our stop. I struck up a conversation with her and we agreed to grab some food later that evening, along with the Aussie Tom, who had also journeyed from Athens. We enjoyed a meal and a few drinks, marking a lively start to our new destination.

The following day, I decided to embark on a hike to three of the monasteries. Unfortunately, one was closed, but the other two were awe-inspiring and well worth the $3 entry fee each. The scenery was truly otherworldly, with the colossal rock formations dominating the landscape like candles on a cake. I also had some fun capturing drone footage, as the weather was remarkably calm, allowing me to venture a bit further than usual. However, that evening, news broke that Greece was going on strike the following day. While Tom had to depart, I decided to stay an extra day, bracing myself for over 10 hours of travel, which I originally planned to split over two days. On that evening, with Tom gone, Julia and I ventured out for dinner. We opted for some budget-friendly gyros and had a hilarious encounter with two dogs, who decided to engage in a fight! In the chaos, Julia flipped the entire table, ensuring we didn't get bitten. After the commotion settled, we couldn't help but laugh at the absurdity of it all. Julia had made friends with some fellow travellers at her hostel, so we joined them later for a few drinks.

I made a promise to Julia that I would capture some drone shots, so the following morning, me and a few others who were keen to join, woke up bright and early for a hike to the summit. This time, we opted for a different route that I hadn't explored before. It proved to be more challenging, as it didn't follow the road but rather consisted of winding paths, offering some hidden gem views along the way. Along this route, we encountered two monasteries I hadn't visited yet; they were quite substantial and provided impressive vistas.

Continuing our hike, we followed the road until we stumbled upon a lost mobile phone at the roadside. We paused for a couple of minutes, deliberating on what to do, when suddenly, the phone began to ring. It was a Bulgarian man who had lost his phone and then he managed to track us down. He expressed his gratitude and just as he was about to leave, I mentioned that we were trying to reach a monastery before it closed (as a possible reason for a lift). My plan worked and he kindly offered us a lift in his car which saved a long walk on the road.

Zakynthos

My next destination was Zakynthos, a Greek island where I would be meeting up with eight friends flying in from the UK. Due to the strike, I had to complete all my travelling in a single day, which took more than 11 hours and involved trains, buses, ferries and taxis. However, I had endured longer journeys in the past and it was the only way to reach Zakynthos.

We had rented a spacious house and it was going to be a lively week. Our first day happened to be one of the girls' birthdays, so we decided to celebrate by renting two boats and exploring the beautiful island of Zante. It was a fantastic experience and I managed to avoid a nasty sunburn, which was a bonus. This trip was refreshingly unplanned, allowing us to spend our days lounging by the pool, sipping cocktails in the sun and enjoying a different type of holiday.

Despite the relaxed atmosphere, I still embarked on a few solo adventures. While all my friends went to the beach, I was eager to hike to a vantage point to watch the sunset. I decided to stick with my plans and set off on a roughly 1.5-hour walk from the villa. The journey wasn't the easiest; it was hot, uphill and I was following Google Maps. As I walked down a single-lane road, a car approached and stopped. The occupants kindly offered me a lift. It was a British couple on vacation with their family. I explained my destination and they informed me that this road was on private property. Clearly, Google Maps had led me astray. They kindly offered to take me back to the main road.

First, we drove up to the top of the road to check on their children, who were looking after some animals. There they noticed a local woman tending to the animals and she informed me that the restaurant I intended to visit was closed. This was disappointing, as all indications suggested it was open. The couple then drove me all the way back to the villa, which was an incredibly kind gesture. I was very grateful and they must have enjoyed our conversation so much that they went out of their way to help me. This marked my first solo hitchhiking experience, albeit a short one, but it was certainly a memorable and positive one.

During our first attempt to reach Shipwreck Bay, which is one of the most famous Greek beaches due to the presence of a shipwreck, the winds were too strong to safely reach it by boat. The story behind this shipwreck is that it was carrying illegal items and the Greek government trapped it in the cove. Many people visit Zakynthos specifically to see it and we were determined to do so. We decided to hire a larger boat and a driver for the day, ensuring we could sail safely in the windy conditions. Along the way, we explored some of the coastal caves before making a quick stop at Shipwreck Bay. It was a breathtaking sight and we captured some fantastic, unique drone photos with the shipwreck nestled in the cove.

Afterward, we asked the driver if he could take us to the top of the bay, where a short walk would allow us to look down onto the cove. The view from the top was stunning and on our way back, we stopped for a group dinner, capping off an incredible day of exploration.

After my time in Zakynthos, my next destination was the UK, as there were no direct flights to other destinations apart from Athens. I had originally planned to stay in the UK for about five days before my next trip. However, getting back proved to be a near-impossible task. It was Good Friday and many services were not operating. Trains were not running either. To get home, I would have had to spend the night at Stansted Airport and arrive home late in the afternoon. Almost all the buses were sold out.

Fortunately, my dad showed incredible kindness by driving to pick me up from the airport. It was a considerable effort on his part and I was grateful for his assistance in making my journey back home much smoother.

Netherlands

I promised Sonique and Tamryn, the two South Africans with whom I got along nicely in Athens, that I would come to the Netherlands and two weeks later, I was there! I flew in the evening, which was nice as I didn't need to stay overnight at an airport. My plan was to take the bus and then Sonique would meet me at the train station.

While I was waiting for the bus, I noticed a funny sign that said, 'Kiss and ride.' I thought it was funny, but it turns out 'Kiss' means a quick drop-off in the Netherlands. I arrived at the train station and it was great to see my friends again. We couldn't quite believe it. When I got picked up it was the best pick-up ride I have ever been on! A very modern Mercedes which could partially self-drive, had LED lights inside and was so smooth. The reason is that their jobs included being Nannies for a very high-class family. This meant they could use everything and live in the house. I was lucky enough to go inside one of the houses and it was amazing. Everything blew me away, even the tap. This tap was no normal tap; it had four settings: cold water, hot water, boiling water and sparkling water. The house also had a gate, a robotic hoover and grass cutter, outside heating and lights, all controlled with the phone.

The house I was staying in was just across the road. The plan we had for the next day was to go to one of the theme parks nearby, some say it is like Disneyland! As a bonus, we were kindly given free tickets from the hotel (which the family owned), which saved a lot of money.

When we arrived, it was very magical. We went to a restaurant in a jungle setting with magical creatures all around. I don't really like rides, but I wanted to push myself and try something new. We found a roller-coaster that wasn't too twisty but picked up a bit of speed. I always feel like such a wimp on rides, as I always see children going on with their families and it makes me feel a bit silly. The ride was fun and when I relaxed and embraced it, the ride become a lot more enjoyable.

We also went into a spinning house, which was very confusing. The seats moved and the walls moved. I couldn't tell if I was upside down or just on the side. It was a very fun day and brought out my inner child.

On Sonique's last night before she left for South Africa, a party was hosted to celebrate her farewell. It was a bit challenging for me because everyone was speaking Dutch and I didn't want them to switch to English just for my sake.

However, as the night went on, more people began to speak English and I had a few conversations, which was nice. They were fun and I also enjoyed listening to Dutch music, which I must say I really liked and added to my playlist. That was my last night. It felt both short and long at the same time because we did so many things. We said our goodbyes the next day and went our separate ways.

My next plan was to visit Nora who I met in Greece; she had invited me to Germany some time ago but I hadn't had the chance to go until now. I had about one week spare before visiting, so I decided to go to Amsterdam! Initially, my plan was to stay for only one night, but I had a few friends there and had heard about King's Day. King's Day is the biggest holiday in the Netherlands, marked by huge celebrations. Everyone goes on boats and parties are held everywhere. This year, it was expected to be even bigger since it was the first event in two years due to COVID, so I decided to extend my stay.

Amsterdam is known for being quite expensive, so to keep costs down, I booked three hostels over four nights. Strangely enough, this turned out to be cheaper than booking continuously. In the first hostel, I met some cool people and we exchanged contact information. It was great because they could be potential companions for King's Day festivities.

The city itself is very pretty and clean. The canals give it a unique charm and the bike lanes create a calm and peaceful atmosphere. I had never been anywhere quite like it and I thought it could be a great place to live. People were generally very friendly, despite warnings that not everyone likes tourists. Most people seem to think that Amsterdam is only about drugs and the red-light district, but it's so much more than that. I did see a few people on drugs, but it wasn't as common as you might expect. The main issue for me was the cost, as Amsterdam is quite expensive, from food and drinks to accommodation.

In the second hostel, where I stayed for two days, I met a lot of friendly people. I also met up with my friend Julia, whom I had met in Greece. She showed me around the city, giving me an insight into the day-to-day life of a local. Students in Amsterdam have free public transport throughout the Netherlands, which is a fantastic idea and encourages people to study and work in Amsterdam. Julia also took me to see the world's most beautiful theatre. Afterward, we visited 'Ripley's Believe It or Not! Museum.' I didn't know what to expect, but it turned out to be very enjoyable. It featured a lot of famous items, such as the world's longest fingernail and the social media dress that nobody could agree on the colour. We also walked through the red-light district, which was a unique experience, as very few places have such areas.

During my time in Amsterdam, I had the chance to experience King's Day, which is a massive celebration in honour of the King's birthday. I had high expectations, but the day exceeded them. It all started with pre-drinks at my hostel, where I met a lot of people. From there, we split into groups and I joined my friend from another hostel. The entire city was incredibly busy, with all the pubs and restaurants packed. However, we struck up a conversation with some locals who invited us to join them in a queue.

The music had a distinct Dutch flavour, but the crowds were overwhelming, so we decided to explore further. We stumbled upon a street party with a DJ playing from a window. Everyone was smiling and people of all ages came together to sing and dance. It felt like being at a festival right in the heart of the city. I got back to my hostel around 2 am, knowing that the next day was going to be a big day of celebrations.

I had chosen my next hostel because it was only a 15-minute walk away, making it easy to move all my belongings. My plan was to explore and see what King's Day was like during daylight. Even at 11 am, the canals were full of boats packed with people, from the front to the back. I had never seen anything like it. Normally, such boat traffic wouldn't be allowed in the city, but on this day, rules were relaxed and it seemed like everyone had gone a little crazy. People were setting up impromptu stages with DJs outside their homes, often on stairs or balconies.

Next, I decided to head to the main area where all the boats congregated. As I walked in that direction, I could hear the music growing louder and the view over the water was breathtaking. There were about 100 boats filled with people having parties. I really wanted to get on one of those boats, but it was a challenge due to the sheer number of people trying to board them. People typically rent boats with a group of friends or family, so finding a spot wasn't easy.

Back on my own, I wasn't sure what to do next. I walked back to my previous hostel to use the internet when some people walked out and invited me to join them. Since I had nothing else planned, I happily accepted. Some of the people in the group were familiar with King's Day and knew all the best spots. We strolled along the canals, which, at certain points, were like a boat traffic jam. We also went to an area where the canals formed a T-junction and both sides were filled with ravers. People were releasing flares, smoke and even had confetti onboard. The only downside of being in a large group was the waiting for people to take smoke breaks or use the restroom (which wasn't easy with so many people around).

Eventually, we walked to the other side of the city and took a free public boat to an island. However, I didn't find it as exciting as expected, so I left the group at that point and decided to return to the hostel for a quick break. As I was walking back, I stumbled upon a lively party on a street corner. Despite being alone, I felt like joining in. Just at that moment, almost magically, a guy tapped me on the shoulder and said, 'Ollie!' It turned out he was from my previous hostel and recognized me because of the distinctive hat I was wearing. In a city with so many people and places, the chances of him seeing me were incredibly slim. I was thrilled and he told me he was also travelling solo. I went back to my hostel to use the restroom and we continued partying on the street corner. We were even lucky enough to stand on the stage, which was a lot of fun!

Later, we hopped between different street parties until we struck up a conversation with a young Dutch couple. They were friendly and we ended up going clubbing with them and a few new friends. The club had a fantastic atmosphere and I didn't get back until 4 am. I had to wake up at 9:30 to check out and catch a bus to Germany.

Germany

My intention was to spend a couple of days in Frankfurt. The journey there proved rather stressful, as I accidentally boarded the wrong train, which whisked me away to an entirely unfamiliar town. Compounding the difficulty was my mobile phone declaring a lack of a functional SIM card, rendering me unable to access the internet or contact anyone. Thankfully, a kind gentleman at the station offered me a hotspot, allowing me to reach out to my parents, with considerable difficulty. After grappling with phone issues for approximately ten minutes, my device finally decided to cooperate. I used it to navigate my way to the hostel, arriving roughly two hours later than planned. Due to the delay, I had missed both lunch and dinner, but fortunately, the hostel provided a safe haven. While the staff were friendly, I couldn't help but notice that the hostel fell short in several respects. Astonishingly, they didn't even provide bed sheets, a rather unhygienic oversight. Thankfully, my stay was limited to just two nights. Another noteworthy drawback was the placement of the "working area," situated right next to the children's play zone. The resulting noise level made focused thinking near impossible.

Frankfurt boasts some attractive areas, characterized by towering skyscrapers, rendering it a unique destination within Germany. Additionally, the city features an old town where historical buildings have been meticulously reconstructed to their post-war appearance. Walking through these streets was a distinct pleasure, allowing me to immerse myself in a bygone era rather than just imagining it. However, it was surprising to encounter a considerable presence of drugs and unsavoury elements just beyond the touristy zones. I found myself traversing some rather dodgy streets, keeping my phone discreetly tucked away. Witnessing groups of individuals using needles for self-injection was a little unsettling. The transformation of the street scene in mere minutes was astonishing. I'm relieved that my stay was brief, as one can experience much of Frankfurt in just a single day.

My friend Nora, whom I first met in Greece, resides in Germany and kindly offered to host me for a few days, which was generous of her. To reach her place, I had to take a bus and a train, after which Nora would pick me up from the station. Apart from disembarking at the train station a bit prematurely, I managed the journey without any hitches. Upon my arrival, Nora treated me to a delicious dish called Käsespätzle, which I suppose can be described as noodles with cheese.

Our plan for the evening was to go clubbing in Heidelberg with one of Nora's friends, which turned out to be great fun. The cost was somewhat steep, on par with prices in the UK, but the club offered a diverse range of music and the people were friendly. We didn't return until around 5 am, with the sky starting to take on a blue hue, prompting us to grab some much-needed sleep.

The following day happened to be Labour Day in Germany, a special occasion when everyone takes to their bikes and enjoys beer – precisely my kind of day! In the midst of lush forests, little buildings offered food and drinks and it was incredibly crowded as it was the first such gathering since COVID. I borrowed Nora's brother's bike and we pedalled for about 20-30 minutes to reach our first stop, where I had the pleasure of meeting Nora's parents. They were lovely, reminiscent of my own parents and they kindly treated us all. The queue was quite long due to the high turnout, but we were fortunate to receive table service from some wandering staff members. The atmosphere was wonderful, with a live local band providing entertainment.

Afterwards, we headed home and cycled to the next stop, which was a bit farther away. There, we encountered Nora's friend Nina, who worked at the bike stop and generously offered us some complimentary food. It was an experience I wouldn't have had if I had stayed in hostels. We slept early that night, still tired from the previous evening's adventures.

Nora's parents were incredibly kind and prepared a lavish breakfast the following morning, complete with meat, bread and cereal. It was a delicious and a perfect way to kickstart the day. Our plan was to visit Heidelberg, renowned as one of the most picturesque cities in Southern Germany, with a river meandering through its heart and a wealth of historic buildings. Interestingly, during the war, it was one of the few places spared from bombings.

Upon our arrival, we were greeted by its breathtaking beauty as we strolled through the city. Heidelberg also boasted a castle where I unexpectedly encountered the world's largest wine barrel. This barrel was so immense that it had steps leading to its top, forming a platform where one could walk. The panoramic views from the castle were equally stunning, offering vistas across the entire town and far into Germany.

Afterwards, we returned to Nora's granny's house, where she prepared a traditional meal. This dish was typically reserved for special occasions due to the meticulous preparation required. To determine when it's perfectly cooked and to prevent the bottom from scorching, you must rely on your senses of smell and sound. We complemented the meal with soup, which we could dip our food into and it was delicious. I also had the opportunity to try some homemade wine as Nora's family owned land with grapevines. I sampled both the wine and the drink and they were exceptionally tasty, though somewhat challenging to describe the flavour.

Nora then drove me to a hilltop to observe the surrounding farms, as the area was known for producing a significant amount of alcohol. We watched the sunset on that clear day with few clouds.

The following day held exciting plans, including a visit to a small town followed by a meal and a walk around town with Nora's friend, Nina. The town was small but charming, featuring numerous shops and cafes. After patiently waiting for Nina, we enjoyed a meal (I had a pizza) and then proceeded to the park. It happened to be a day when many students had finished their studies, creating a lively atmosphere. People were playing music and there was a game called Spikeball involving hitting a ball on a trampoline and the opposing team having to return it using the trampoline without letting it touch the ground. It looked like great fun. However, the weather took an unexpected turn – to the left, we had sunshine, while to the right, a menacing dark cloud loomed, accompanied by distant thunder. Moments later, heavy rain began to fall, prompting us to retreat to the car. Subsequently, we met another of Nora's friends and headed to a pool table room brimming with tables. It was an enjoyable day filled with closely contested matches.

I was immensely grateful to Nora and her family for hosting me. It was a privilege to feel like part of their family for a few days and to truly experience German hospitality. As a token of my appreciation, I brought them some chocolates and candles plus extended an invitation for them to visit Britain anytime.

My original plan had been to travel to Morocco, but due to Frankfurt having two airports and both Nora and I being unaware of this, I unfortunately missed my flight. The airport was located quite a distance from Frankfurt, necessitating a two-hour drive. While I wasn't overly concerned about the financial aspect, as I hadn't spent much on the ticket, it was frustrating that my plans had gone awry. I checked for alternative transportation and found a bus headed to Prague. So, £30 later and after an eight-hour bus ride, I found myself in Prague.

Prague

I opted for a hostel a bit on the outskirts of town to save a few quid, but I didn't mind the extra walk. Considering the ongoing war in Ukraine at the time, there were quite a few Ukrainians bunking at the hostel. It made me ponder how long they'd be seeking refuge there, but I reckoned I'd encounter more of the same as I got closer to Ukraine itself.

On my first day in Prague, I set out for a stroll and exploration. I was quite surprised by how compact Prague was compared to the likes of Budapest, which left me wondering if I'd planned too many days here. During my wanderings, I stumbled upon one of the world's oldest functioning clocks and the tiniest house in Prague – a mere door and a wee frame!

What had me most excited, though, was the nightlife – the very reason most folks flock to Prague. I linked up with some fellow hostel dwellers and hit a few bars before venturing into a club. Sadly, the choice of club wasn't mine and it turned out to be a proper tourist trap. It felt more like a night out in the UK, which certainly wasn't what I'd travelled all the way to Prague for. Fortunately, I'd already marked a few promising clubs on my map a few days prior and I was determined to give them a shot.

The following day, I decided to join a walking tour, which turned out to be so much fun. It was one of the best tours I've ever experienced, taking us through the charming old town. I soaked in a wealth of historical knowledge, particularly about how Germany used political manoeuvrings to annex the Czech Republic, effectively using Prague as a gateway to the rest of Europe. Remarkably, Prague, untouched by the war, boasted original architecture, making it one of the most picturesque cities I've ever explored.

During the tour, I struck up a conversation with a friendly British chap and we decided to check out a train pub I had marked on my map. The concept was rather nifty – a train delivering food and drinks right to your table. We sat there, eagerly awaiting our order as the train zipped by and stopped at the tables to deliver their food. I couldn't help but think I'd have been over the moon as a kid in a place like that! I placed an order for some chips and a pint and it was a unique experience watching the train pull up next to us. We had to retrieve our grub from the train before it chugged along to the next order. It didn't break the bank either, setting me back about £5.

That evening, my main goal was to hit a techno club and immerse myself in Prague's music scene, which was one of the key reasons for my visit. I popped over to the hostel, hoping to round up some partygoers and ended up with about a dozen blokes all keen on hitting the club. Not a bad turnout, really. It's always good to have a lively crew.

Once we made it to the club, it was a completely different vibe. Techno nights are more of a marathon than a sprint, so it's no surprise that folks often resort to various substances to keep the party going all night long. Personally, I stuck to sobriety and didn't partake in any of that stuff. The night started off slow but gradually filled up with revellers as the hours passed. Everyone was absolutely grooving to the music and there were no cliques – you never felt alone. Every single person was moving to the beat. The club even had a smaller room, but it wasn't as bustling. As expected, there were quite a few offers of recreational substances, but hey, it's a techno club in Prague, what else would you expect? I called it a night around 4 am, which wasn't too shabby, but some folks went all out and partied until the early afternoon. Take Zak, for instance – he went to a rave nearby and rolled back in at 1 pm!

My plan for the next day was to join another walking tour, this time focusing on the castle area of Prague, which I hadn't explored yet. I managed to drag myself out of bed around 11 am, grabbed a shower and had a spot of lunch before heading out. I had a few hours to spare before the tour, so I hiked up to a viewpoint overlooking the entire city. I also spotted the TV tower, which is famously touted as one of the ugliest buildings and I could certainly see why, especially from up high. I eventually made it to the tour and it was great to discover parts of Prague I hadn't encountered during my earlier strolls.

My time in Prague was a blast. The city, in terms of the number of tourists and general atmosphere, felt a bit like Budapest, but the nightlife was on a whole different level. There was music to suit every taste and the city seemed to be constantly buzzing with events and parties at any time of day or night. Prague sure knows how to throw a party! My initial plan was to head to Poland next for a few days before moving on to Morocco. However, a friend who was also in Poland, doing some hiking in a certain location, suggested I join her. It seemed like a fantastic way to wind down after all the partying in Prague. I hadn't set a strict schedule for when I'd head to Morocco and I was loving this carefree style of travel with no concrete commitments. The only hiccup was the pesky 90-day rule, thanks to Brexit, which meant I couldn't stay in Europe for too many weeks. Nonetheless, Poland beckoned and I was looking forward to a change of pace and some hiking.

Poland

I arrived in Zakopane, Poland after a long journey involving three buses and a train, but thankfully, I didn't encounter any issues along the way. I made sure to ask fellow travellers if I was getting off at the right stop. To my pleasant surprise, the prices here were quite reasonable. I grabbed a portion of chips for about £1.5 and stocked up on some food at a local shop for around £1. It was a refreshing change after spending so much time in expensive places.

Today, I reunited with Yasmin, a friend I had made during my time in Egypt. I got to the hostel around 8 pm, but unfortunately, nothing was open for a late meal. Feeling tired, we called it an early night after making a rough plan for the next day's adventures.

The following morning, we set our alarms for around 9 am and enjoyed our basic but free breakfast – can't expect much more for £5 a night, right? Our initial plan was to hike up the green path leading to the mountains and it took us a few hours to reach our destination. We had to be cautious and stick to the designated paths due to the presence of potentially dangerous bears and snakes if we strayed too far. Although the weather was mostly cloudy, it didn't rain, except for a brief shower. When we reached the summit, we were treated to a splendid view of the town below, a truly picturesque sight. However, it turned out to be a bit of a dead-end, so we retraced our steps and considered it a trial hike. We then plotted our adventures for the next two days, given the sunnier weather forecast.

The hostel itself was the cosiest I've ever stayed in. It was filled with fellow hikers, which created a fantastic atmosphere of people united by their love for trekking. The house rules required everyone to wear socks or slippers indoors, thanks to muddy shoes, which kept the place clean and pleasant. The hostel offered affordable laundry facilities, free breakfast and board games that brought everyone together.

The next day, Yasmin planned a challenging hike that would likely take us the whole day to complete. We left the hostel a bit later than intended, as it was a struggle to get out of bed, but we hit the trails as soon as possible. Once again, we stocked up on food from the local shops since there would be no stores high up in the mountains. We ascended a rocky path to reach the forests and began our journey up the mountain. The hike was tough due to the uneven terrain, but as we gained altitude, the trees gave way to breathtaking views of the surrounding mountains. We also had a clear view of the trail we had conquered the previous day, which now seemed tiny in comparison to the one we tackled today.

We took an early break to lighten our backpacks, making it easier to carry them during the hike. As we neared the summit, we encountered patches of snow and the landscape became increasingly picturesque. Along the way, we passed through some enchanting areas with streams crisscrossing our path, requiring us to hop from rock to rock. The water was so fresh that we even sampled some and it tasted cool and pure. The higher we climbed, the fresher the water became. Eventually, we reached an area with benches and a few people milling about. We noticed a sign pointing to a viewpoint about a 10-minute walk away, so we decided to check it out. This viewpoint perched on a massive rock offered a stunning 360-degree panoramic view of the town and the towering mountains all around. It was a sight to behold and a highlight of our hike.

Afterwards, we retraced our steps, making the long journey back down the mountain. It was a challenging descent, but the reward was worth it – we reached a spectacular waterfall. We took some fun photos and found a spot next to the waterfall where we skimmed rocks into the water. By the time we returned, our legs were trembling from the exertion. We headed straight to a restaurant and treated ourselves to a well-deserved hearty meal. We had initially planned a big hike for the next day, but we decided to opt for some relaxation at the natural baths nearby instead.

Well, that night started out as your typical evening, but boy, were we in for a surprise! The bloke in the bunk below me was emitting an aroma and it was horrendous. Yasmin picked up on it too, so we hatched a genius plan to build a fortress of towels around him. We hung them from the bunk rails, attempting to quarantine the offender. It was like a comedy routine and we couldn't hold back our laughter. In fact, we found it so amusing that we had to make a quick exit from the room since others were asleep.

The stench was so pungent! But oh no, the moment I stepped back in, that unmistakable odour smacked me right in the face and I burst into laughter once more. I even resorted to using a freshly cleaned towel as a makeshift gas mask to protect myself. Meanwhile, Yasmin took refuge by opening the window and sleeping with half her body dangling outside.

We had planned to sleep in the next day, but our room mates had other ideas – they were making a racket, slamming doors and making it impossible to get any rest. Fed up, we decided to move to an eight-bed dorm, which was a welcome escape from the odour. After getting settled, I teamed up with one of the guys from our hostel to visit the natural warm baths, a must-do experience in Poland.

The water originates from deep within the earth, making it warm and rich in vitamins beneficial for the body. The weather was also splendid, unexpectedly allowing us to enjoy some bathing. The pool cost about £12 for a three-hour session and included hot tubs, slides, various pools and even sports facilities. It is a great place to spend a full day with friends.

Later, I grabbed some meals for just 40p, thanks to a half-price reduction at the store and joined everyone at the hostel to socialise in the evening. It was during this time that I received a message from a friend I had met in Amsterdam (who was now in Italy) informing me that she had just met another friend of mine. It turned out to be a Canadian chap I had met in Greece during a pub crawl about a month prior. The odds of two friends randomly encountering each other, selecting the same hostel, going to the same destination and being there at the exact same time were quite astounding!

The next day marked a significant adventure as we set out to visit Morsie Oko, one of the highest lakes in all of Poland. To reach it, we took a bus from the hostel, which dropped us off near the end of the road leading to the lake. The only way to reach it was via a two-and-a-half-hour walk or by taking a horse-drawn carriage. We grabbed some food from a nearby café and embarked on the hike. This route was well-trodden, being quite popular and it was fully paved, making for easy walking. Along the way, there were restroom facilities and rest stops, providing ample opportunities to take a break. Initially, we noticed a lack of snow, so we assumed the lake wasn't frozen.

However, at one point during the ascent, we experienced a sudden drop in temperature and the landscape became increasingly snowy. When we finally reached the summit, it was well worth the hike. The lake was completely frozen over, except for a small area where ducks were happily swimming about. There weren't too many tourists around, which made it easy to explore and take photos. I had never seen water so blue and clear, surrounded by pristine white ice.

Despite the snowy conditions, Yasmin and I decided to see how far we could go around the lake. She was even wearing trainers instead of hiking boots, which made it a bit more challenging for her. We followed the paths left by other hikers and though it was a bit slippery, it was manageable. At one point, we encountered a steep, slippery section that would have led us straight into the water if we had slipped. We contemplated turning back but both wanted to venture a bit further. Fortunately, we observed other hikers overtaking us and noticed their technique. Instead of stepping forward, they moved sideways like crabs, facing forward. This way, if they slipped, they would hit the wall rather than end up in the lake below. We adopted this technique, which proved much easier and took our time. There was no rush and we carefully placed each foot on the snowy terrain, eventually making it to the other side.

We found a fantastic rocky outcrop leading into the water and sat down to enjoy some food. I had never seen ice on the water, so we had some fun breaking it apart by throwing rocks and trying to pick up the ice. I even spotted a fish and marvelled at how it survived in a lake so high up. A bit further along, there was a fresh mountain stream where I refilled my water bottle since it was drinkable. The water was cold, crystal clear and tasted just like chilled water from the fridge. I started with a small sip and I continued drinking it during the descent. It was reassuring to know we always had access to drinkable water nearby.

The hike back was strenuous and our legs felt increasingly heavy, but it was all downhill. We managed to return within a reasonable timeframe. After enjoying a meal at the restaurant, we headed straight back to the hostel and promptly fell asleep – we were utterly exhausted!

I couldn't believe the string of coincidences and reunions I experienced during my trip. I hardly felt solo at all because I was constantly meeting new people or catching up with old friends. It's truly incredible how vast the world is, yet you're never far from familiar faces and friendly encounters. It's like the world has this magical way of bringing people together.

Krakow

The following day, we took it easy before catching a bus to Krakow, where we had reserved a spot at a lively party hostel. My friend Yasmin was also with us for just one night before heading off to Slovakia. As we disembarked from the bus in Krakow, we were greeted by a bustling scene, teeming with people, including a significant number of Ukrainians. Inside the bus and train station, we noticed makeshift sleeping areas where people were resting and it was heartwarming to see numerous volunteers tending to their needs. We also passed by a food tent where Ukrainians could receive complimentary meals. Witnessing this on the ground was truly eye-opening.

Our hostel, though slightly on the pricey side, offered complimentary breakfast and dinner. Upon our arrival, we couldn't resist the allure of a cat cafe – a place filled with charming cats, just as the name suggests. Inside, we encountered about five cats, either playing or lounging about. We had to make a reservation for our dinner and upon returning to the hostel, we eagerly indulged in our meal. To our astonishment, it turned out to be the finest dinner I had ever experienced at a hostel. There were pizzas, burgers, pasta and everything was of exceptionally high quality. It was a real treat to enjoy such delicious food without an extra cost!

Later, someone from the hostel informed us that it was a free museum evening, during which nearly every museum in the city was open to the public at no charge. Unfortunately, it was already quite late and we were determined to head out for the evening, so we decided to forget the museums. Strangely, the hostel seemed rather subdued for a Friday night, so we ventured to a few local pubs and then made our way to a club. As we strolled through Krakow, it was hard not to notice the city's liveliness, with people everywhere, ready to revel in a festive atmosphere. We opted for a local techno club, which was enjoyable, although it did seem somewhat quieter than we had expected. We returned to the hostel at 3 am and to our delight, there was still some leftover pizza on the table – a perfect late-night snack.

The following day, I decided to take a leisurely stroll around the city, intending to visit some of its attractions. It was incredible to see a multitude of Ukrainian protesters and signs at nearly every corner, a clear indication that many Ukrainians had sought refuge in Poland. Some of the speeches I witnessed were deeply moving, with the speakers' emotions palpable as they stood right before us. As I explored more of the city, I couldn't help but feel a bit unenthused. It seemed like any other European city, with its churches, castles and shops. It was challenging to fully appreciate its beauty due to its familiarity.

I resolved to start planning my trips a day in advance to have more structured and purposeful explorations. I was growing eager to leave Europe and venture somewhere a bit different. That evening, two Ukrainian girls who had just been in Kiev joined us in our room. Speaking with them was an incredible experience. They shared how they had been in Kiev throughout the war and had recently managed to leave, which was no easy task. The first few nights had been extremely difficult for them, but they eventually adapted.

That night, I went clubbing again and found myself in the best techno club I had ever experienced. It was located a bit outside the city but had a vibrant student crowd and a strong local vibe. It was a refreshing change from the touristy clubs and I particularly enjoyed how they seamlessly mixed techno with some current tunes.

The following day, I decided to visit an underground museum showcasing the ruins of the town's historical past. The ticket cost about £5 and I couldn't help but feel a bit disappointed when I learned that entry was free on Tuesdays – I should have timed my visit accordingly. Subsequently, I opted to visit places where I could gain free admission.

The underground museum was relatively new and featured interactive exhibits that provided insight into the town's history, allowing visitors to imagine what life was like in the past. It primarily served as a bustling trade hub and you could see the areas where traders were centuries ago. From there, I ventured to the national museum, but I found it somewhat lacking, particularly since some of the items were from Egypt and I had already seen similar artifacts before. I was relieved that I hadn't paid for entry, as it might have been a bit disappointing. Following this, I made my way up to the castle. I returned to the hostel with the intention of having a relaxed evening, as I was scheduled to visit Auschwitz the following day.

The next morning, I woke up early and headed to one of the clock towers, where I could enjoy a panoramic view of the city for free. My plan was to then take a bus to Auschwitz, where I had a tour booked for a more immersive experience. However, I encountered an unexpected hurdle as the bus only accepted cash and had limited departures each day. Regrettably, I missed the bus, which was exceedingly frustrating. I spent the rest of the day searching for remote job opportunities on my computer in the hope of getting lucky.

The following day offered a number of free museum options, so I purchased a 24-hour tram ticket, got an early start and first attempted to visit a bunker (though it was unfortunately closed, as I had suspected). I then took a leisurely stroll through a park. Along the way, I stumbled upon the Graduation Tower, a structure designed to extract salt from water naturally, creating an environment with air quality akin to sea air. It was a refreshing change from the pollution of Krakow and evoked memories of the seaside. I also visited an aviation museum located in the other square, which featured a collection of vintage planes, helicopters and old war vehicles – a real treat for me.

Later, I explored an art and technology Japanese museum, but to my surprise, there wasn't much technology on display; instead, it was filled with artwork and cats. In the evening, I decided to join a pub crawl, as I had been relatively low-key for the past couple of nights. It turned out to be a blast and I was part of a fantastic group. I was taken aback by the number of Scots in the group; it seemed like nearly a quarter were Scottish. Interestingly, I also learned that the leader of the pub crawl, known as "Jeep," had met someone named Han, my close friend whom I had also encountered during my travels in Egypt and Sofia, Bulgaria! It was uncanny how many coincidences were occurring on this trip, as it seemed both of us were extensively exploring Europe. The next morning, I woke up at 9 am to check out and grab some breakfast.

With no specific plans for the remainder of the day and feeling a bit weary, I ended up watching a movie and working on my laptop until around 3 pm. Then, I took a tram and train to the airport, arriving with a comfortable two-hour buffer before my flight. However, I encountered unexpected delays during the border check. The officer scrutinized my passport meticulously, spending nearly ten minutes on it and consulting with a colleague and making phone calls. He eventually informed me that I had exceeded my allowed days in Europe by six days. Due to Brexit, I was only permitted to stay in Europe for three months within a six-month period. I was certain I had calculated my stay correctly and showed him my app, which indicated I had 11 days remaining. He scrutinized it further with me and I pointed out that Bulgaria, not being in the Schengen area, shouldn't count toward my 90 days. He reviewed it again and finally stamped my passport. It was a nerve-wracking moment, as overextending one's stay in Europe could lead to severe consequences, even a ban from re-entering. Fortunately, I had managed it correctly. Afterward, I embarked on a smooth flight to Liverpool, where I had to endure a nearly 10-hour layover before my flight to Romania. During this time, I spent most of it in the airport, working on my computer.

Romania

I chose Romania as my next destination because it is not part of the Schengen area, which meant I could stay for up to three months without the pressure of having to leave. It was a pleasant arrival at 11 am to Sibiu, leaving the whole day ahead for me. I took the bus to the city, which cost about 34 pence, followed by a short walk to my accommodation. I had booked a place with a private room and a hot tub, but upon arrival, it didn't meet my expectations and lacked the promised hot tub. I wasn't pleased, especially since I had paid more than I would have for a hostel. I attempted to get a refund, but they refused, despite the false advertising. It was frustrating, but I decided to let it go.

Afterward, I took a much-needed nap and later went for an evening walk to explore the area. It was quite picturesque and reminded me of Italy, with old buildings featuring various vibrant colours. Romania has a unique architectural feature in some buildings – small slits in the attic for ventilation. However, Romania is a superstitious place and some locals believe that these vents are used for government spying! I visited the main square, which wasn't overrun with tourists, so the prices were reasonable. I treated myself to some incredible ice cream (the best I've ever had) and enjoyed a Napoli pizza. The ice cream stalls were lined along the street, offering a wide variety of flavours, presented in an impressive manner. I called it an early night after the walk, as I had plans to meet a new friend for a tour the next day.

My dad had messaged me about someone he spoke to who had a connection in Sibiu my current location. We agreed to meet up in the morning and she kindly offered to show me around the city and her favourite spots. We climbed the tower, which offered one of the best views in the city. I always enjoy seeing places from a high vantage point because it gives you a real sense of the city's size. Afterward, we walked for about an hour to reach an open-air museum, where traditional old houses had been relocated to one area to preserve them. Volunteers diligently cared for these houses, keeping them in excellent condition. There were over 100 unique old buildings, some of which you could enter to get a glimpse of what life used to be like. Most of the houses had small entrances and beds because Romanian people were historically shorter and I had to bend down to enter the rooms. The houses were also colourful, with different shades – I saw many blue houses. After our visit, we walked back and had a drink; I opted for a kiwi shake, which cost about £3. Later, I returned to cool off as it was a scorching hot day and then planned to meet a local German guy for a few drinks.

I had connected with him through Couchsurfing, an app where people can host you in their homes for free, allowing budget travellers to experience the local community. It's a fantastic concept and you can rate hosts for added safety by choosing those with good ratings. The app also has a feature for meeting up with locals, which was particularly useful since I wasn't staying in a hostel, making it harder to meet new people. When I arrived, there were four of us in total and we played some billiards (pool), which I enjoyed since it had been a while since I'd last played. The German man, Jan, was volunteering at a local church and the other two worked with the volunteers. Many Germans opt for this kind of experience as it's a cost-effective way for them to travel for an extended period. We then went to one of the local clubs/bars, aptly named 'Oldies Pub,' as there isn't much nightlife in Sibiu. It had a mix of ages and offered a good selection of music. It was kind of them to let me join them for the evening.

The next day, I had plans to go hiking, but the temperature soared to almost 30 degrees Celsius and it seemed too risky to spend the entire day outdoors in that heat. I decided to take it easy and work on my travel plans, along with some tasks I needed to complete. It was wonderful to have such warm weather again, but I felt like I had stayed in Sibiu for too many days and being in a private room limited my opportunities to socialize. I resolved not to make that mistake again.

My next destination was Cluj-Napoca, a popular location with plenty of direct buses and trains. In the morning, I visited the train station to check my options. To my surprise, it seemed like I would have to make two changes to reach my destination, which sounded a bit crazy since it was so near. I then headed to the bus station, but it was closed. Some locals informed me that buses needed to be pre-booked, leaving me with no choice but to opt for the train. I wasn't thrilled when I saw the train – it was covered in graffiti and quite run-down. However, I had encountered similar conditions in Eastern Europe, like Greece and Bulgaria. The train journey took six hours, whereas a car ride would have taken only two, but on the plus side, the ticket was a mere £4. I was determined not to make any more mistakes on this leg of the journey, as I had already experienced enough mishaps during this trip.

Navigating the train system was challenging because there were no station names or platform numbers. Google Maps also didn't work well due to the remote areas we passed through. This meant I had to ask fellow passengers on the train and go from carriage to carriage to find someone who spoke English and could tell me if I was on the right track. At one point, I had a layover of just six minutes, which was quite stressful, but I followed a man who led me to the correct train platform. I also saw the train inspector walking along the tracks, highlighting the different rules in this part of Europe compared to other regions. My second layover was only an hour, during which I bought some juice for about 50p.

During the train ride, I was busy planning my return to the UK since we had some family events and my birthday was approaching. It was a challenging task because the flights for the dates I was considering were quite expensive. I also wanted the freedom to travel without the pressure of a looming flight deadline. It was a tough decision to make, especially since I was also interested in heading down to Turkey. Eventually, I decided to book a reasonably priced flight to London a bit earlier, just to have the option available and it wouldn't be a problem if I missed it due to having so much fun and wanting to continue my adventure here. As I gazed out the window during the train journey, I noticed mostly hills, farmlands and quaint villages. Some of the train stations were incredibly small, likely serving only a handful of passengers each day.

Eventually, I managed to reach Cluj-Napoca on time, around 6 pm. It felt like a bit of a wasted day, but it was manageable. I booked only two nights at my hostel as I didn't want to stay too long and potentially get bored. Cluj is known as one of the student hubs in Romania, so I hoped to find some good nightlife, even though it was a Sunday. Upon arriving in Cluj-Napoca, I was eager to explore the nightlife despite it being a Sunday. I went out with two people I met at the hostel and we headed to the area known for its nightlife. Surprisingly, it was quite quiet and we struck up conversations with some locals. They seemed a bit puzzled by our presence as they didn't often encounter many tourists. I realized it had been a while since I had heard English being spoken so well. It was enlightening to chat with them and they mentioned that university accommodation costs as little as £18 a month, making it essentially free. We continued our evening by walking through a park where we stumbled upon some students celebrating their completion of medical studies. The celebration was disrupted by security at one point, but the party soon resumed before we all got chased off. People must have wondered why there were random individuals from Britain, Australia and Germany at their student gathering – it was certainly an unusual sight. The next day, I had planned to visit a church, but it was closed for renovation. Instead, the three of us from the previous night decided to go to the salt mine. I had missed the opportunity to visit one in Poland, so I was eager to explore one here.

We took a taxi, which turned out to be quite affordable when split among the three of us and it took about half an hour to reach the mine. The entrance fee was just £9, which I found to be very reasonable. The journey began with a long corridor surrounded by salt walls. At the end, there was an elevator that took us down to the lower levels. The view was stunning, showcasing the vast expanse of land that had been excavated for salt. There was another area even further down with boats and a large pool of water. We wandered around the upper level, where they had a Ferris wheel, table tennis, a pool table and even a bowling alley. We were eager to explore further down, so we took a second elevator. It was amazing to see all the salt formations on objects and we even rented a rowboat. I took the oars and it turned out to be more challenging than it looked to get the technique right. Afterwards, we snapped some photos and returned upstairs to play some table tennis, which was a fun activity after a long break. We managed to catch a bus back and the fare was less than £2, making it an economical trip. I had hoped to go out that night, but my companions were too tired to join in the evening's festivities.

I had a flight to the UK booked from Bucharest because I wanted to visit friends and family and celebrate my birthday with them. However, I was keeping my options open and if I found a hostel I really liked along the way, I would stay and celebrate my birthday there instead. At this point, I was a bit pressed for time to explore Romania by the 31st, so I planned to spend just one night in some towns to reach Bucharest for Friday and Saturday. This faster pace would also reduce waiting around time.

I was contemplating my next destination and feeling that Europe was becoming a bit repetitive. I was considering taking a break and volunteering at a hostel for a few weeks or perhaps venturing somewhere further away. I was also looking forward to going to the UK to see friends and family, have a reset and planned to sign up for a gym membership to give me something else to do during my stay.

On my last morning in Cluj, I planned my trip and visited some gardens, which were a bit disappointing compared to others I had seen. Maybe it was the season, but they seemed quite empty. I then took a 6-hour train journey to Sighisoara, where I planned to spend just one night. Everyone had recommended Sighisoara but also mentioned that there wasn't too much to do. So, my plan was to stay until 2 pm, then catch a train to Brasov.

Sighisoara was a town built around and within an old castle and I was impressed by how they managed to preserve its traditional feel while making it a liveable space. The houses were very colourful and the roads were paved with bricks. I explored the town and climbed up to the "Church on a Hill," which involved going through a little tunnel to reach the hill. On top of the hill, there was a good view, a school and a church. The school was quite noticeable because there were many students around. I decided not to climb the tower or explore the museums, so I got some tea and enjoyed people-watching.

I walked to the train station, where I caught a train to Brasov, a city many people had recommended because there's lots to do in the surrounding area. The train ride took about 3 hours, during which I looked out the window and watched some Netflix to pass the time. In Brasov, the city centre felt quite commercial, but it was affordable and had a good atmosphere as I walked around. My hostel was located just off the main street in an excellent location, only a minute's walk away from everything I could need. I arrived in the late afternoon and there was no one in my room. I grabbed some cheap fries and garlic sauce for about £1.5 and they were tasty. I was hoping to meet more people in Brasov. I did hear some people talking in the hostel, so I approached them and the two guys were very friendly. We went out for dinner. To my surprise, I had the entire four-bedroom dorm to myself that night, which was a first for me. I couldn't believe there weren't more travellers in this city.

The next day, I really wanted to go for a hike, so I planned to climb the massive hill overlooking Brasov. On the hillside, there were the words 'Brasov,' similar to the Hollywood sign. I embarked on the hour-long hike up, which offered amazing views of the small city, followed by the descent. While I didn't encounter much wildlife, I did come across a woodpecker bird that was so loud it sounded like it was breaking the tree apart. It's incredible how strong their beaks are!

My next stop was the capital, Bucharest and I was hoping for a refreshing change based on my previous experiences in Romania. However, things took an unexpected turn. On the bus from the train station to the hostel, there was a guy arguing with the ticket inspector and the traffic was chaotic. The atmosphere just felt off.

Upon arriving at the hostel, I had to check in at the hostel bar, where there was shouting and arguing going on. I was told by one of the guys working there that there was a late delivery or something and he assured me that the woman in charge was not always like this. When she was finally ready to check me in, she still had a bad attitude. I had to pay in cash and I handed her a 200-note, expecting about 80 in change. She complained that the note was too big and went to the shops to break it, suggesting that I should be "kind" and "learn the currency." I didn't appreciate her tone at all and mentioned that maybe if they accepted card payments, it wouldn't be an issue.

During the hostel tour, she was very aggressive in her manner, even slamming doors. After about 5 minutes, she came back to me, realising that she had given me too much change and told me I should "count my money" as if it were my fault that she had given me extra. She took back the excess change, only to give me less than I was owed. I had to quickly chase after her to get the correct amount and I followed up with a comment about her needing to learn to count money. It was not a good start to my time in the city.

Thankfully, I had only booked two nights at this hostel, so if things didn't improve, I could move to a nicer one. This place had stood out to me because it had a bar and should have been an easy place to socialise, but so far, it seemed very quiet.

As I walked around the city, I noticed that it was very hectic and different from the other parts of Romania I had explored. People were staring at me and I had a few interesting encounters with locals, but I brushed them off. Unfortunately, I couldn't find anyone to join me that night, so I ended up just chilling.

The following day, I planned to do the free walking tour and the pub crawl to meet new people in the city. The walking tour was worth doing early as it gave me insight into the city's highlights and history. I tried to pace myself since I had a few days to explore. That night, I had intended to join the pub crawl, but bad weather with thunderstorms and rain made me reconsider, so I stayed in.

The next day, I was looking forward to leaving the hostel to go to a new one and tick off everything else I wanted to explore in the city. I dropped my things off at the new hostel, where I knew someone from my first solo trip in the Budapest hostel. It was a much better introduction compared to the previous hostel. I explored the city, taking in sights like the Communist parliament building and a couple of parks. When I returned to the hostel, I was pleasantly surprised by the number of people sitting around and chatting. I found a chair and started talking to soon-to-be friends. This new hostel was one of the best in the area and hosted numerous activities in the evenings to bring everyone together. Everyone seemed very friendly and I was looking forward to ping pong night scheduled for the following Monday evening.

After my leisurely stroll, I whiled away the entire afternoon and evening engaging in delightful conversations with fellow travellers. The atmosphere was incredibly relaxed, reminiscent of my first hostel experience in Budapest, a welcome escape from the previous establishment. Despite it being a Sunday, I had a feeling that there would be enough of us to paint the town. I was taken aback by the sheer number of people who were out and about and we stumbled upon a vibrant street party tucked away in an alleyway between two bars or clubs, complete with music that set the mood just right. There is indeed something magical about meeting a group of strangers mere hours ago, only for it to feel as though we've known each other for years. It's a sensation that's tough to put into words, but it's moments like these that fuel my insatiable wanderlust and make me want to continue this adventure indefinitely.

During this night, I crossed paths with two British chaps who, as fate would have it, hailed from a locale only a short 20-minute train ride away from mine. They had been wholly absorbed in the hostel's social scene, accruing a staggering tab of over £70, an impressive feat in Romania, where drinks don't come cheap. My good spirits took a hit when, that evening, my phone began to malfunction.

The screen exhibited an ominous blackness that slowly crept across its surface, resembling a spreading oil slick. Although it remained somewhat functional, I couldn't help but ponder whether I'd be phoneless by the end of my journey. My laptop offered a partial help and with just a few days left on my travel calendar, I needed to stay connected with newfound friends and ensure a smooth return journey home.

The following day, I was eager to explore the renowned aqua park and ended up being joined by Chloe, a fellow traveller who had been dedicating her time to childcare volunteering since October. We were also accompanied by two other hostel mates, although locating them proved to be a challenge as they arrived later than us. The aqua park entrance set me back about £20 for a full day of aquatic adventures and it was nothing short of incredible. The initial sight upon entry, featuring a large pool ensconced by palm trees and a swim-up bar, was genuinely awe-inspiring. The facility boasted an array of attractions, including various saunas, towering water slides, artificial waves and outdoor pools, an unparalleled aquatic playground in my experience. We made it our mission to conquer each and every slide, from the adrenaline-inducing steep drops that culminated in exhilarating splashes to the leisurely yet vibrant tube slides ending in gentle descents. Among the highlights was a slide that sent you upwards in a donut-like vessel, making it feel as though you could touch the sky before plummeting back to earth.

After our watery escapades, Chloe decided to treat herself to a relaxing massage, while I opted for more swimming before heading to the food hall to replenish my energy. The day was invigorating but also left us thoroughly exhausted.

On my final day in the beautiful Bucharest, I hadn't planned a particularly hectic agenda. My main objectives were to pack my belongings and ensure everything was ready for my return journey home. Unfortunately, my phone's screen was now completely black, with only a small corner barely visible. I spent my morning engaging in a friendly game of table tennis at the hostel, a delightful activity I hadn't partaken in for a week or two.

My evening flight back home was fast approaching, so I decided to pay a visit to the Parliament building and join a guided tour of its opulent interior. Although the exterior was rather austere, the grandeur and sheer scale of the interior took me by surprise. However, I must admit, the tour itself proved to be rather lacklustre as the guide's voice barely reached our ears amidst the massive chambers.

Returning to the hostel, the distant rumble of thunder signalled an impending downpour. Seeking shelter within the hostel's outside tent, I found myself trapped in an unrelenting thunderstorm, complete with colossal hailstones. These icy projectiles grew larger and larger, reaching up to 2cm in diameter, causing significant discomfort to anyone brave enough to venture outside. We were well and truly stuck!

In an unexpected turn of events, my phone alerted me with two emergency warnings, a stark reminder of the severity of the weather. This weather, I surmised, was likely a result of the daytime temperature reaching a scorching 31 degrees, which often leads to thunderstorms in the evening. As we sought refuge, a heartwarming scene unfolded: some of the volunteers from the hostel began dancing under the porch, celebrating the torrential rain with their rendition of "Singing in the Rain." It was a testament to the indomitable spirit of travellers who can find joy even in the most challenging circumstances.

After about 40 minutes, the rain finally relented, leaving a waterlogged ground in its wake. Some friends who were in town shared videos of cars navigating flooded streets with water halfway up their tyres. I was relieved that the rain had ceased since I had to catch a bus to the airport. Mentally, I wasn't quite ready to bid farewell to the adventures of this hostel, but I knew that I had to face the reality of returning home. My phone troubles served as a stark reminder that practicalities needed dealing with. It was heartening to reunite with friends and family, but my wanderlust remained unquenched and I was already contemplating where my next journey would take me. At this part in my journal, I still had concerns about the length of my travel book and wondered whether the Balkans could provide enough captivating stories and locales to fill its pages. Little did I know just how wrong I would be.

Turkey

I was after a destination that offered both warmth and an escape from the typical European landscape, I found Turkey to be the perfect candidate. I managed to snag an affordable flight into Sofia, Bulgaria, which served as my launchpad for this next adventure. Conveniently, I could catch a train from my home straight to Gatwick Airport, eliminating the hassle of multiple transfers.

As I contemplated sharing more of my journey beyond the confines of social media and my journal, I discussed the idea with friends and family. It was a slightly daunting prospect for someone who isn't particularly fond of putting their face online and who prefers living in the moment rather than constantly documenting it. However, I wanted to provide a glimpse into my travels, showcasing both the highs and lows, so I decided to film a significant portion of the trip for my Youtube.

My journey began with an overnight bus to Sofia, Bulgaria, where I'd then take a metro ride into the city centre before embarking on another overnight bus. Fatigued from a lack of sleep, I was nonetheless filled with anticipation and excitement about exploring a new destination. I savoured the early morning walk through Sofia, strolling past its key landmarks, an experience that felt somewhat surreal given that I had been there just a few months prior. While I held no concrete expectations, my thoughts occasionally drifted to Egypt, imagining that the experience might bear some similarities.

The eight-hour bus ride proved to be an adventure, especially as we navigated the border crossings. The presence of numerous police officers and the various steps required for clearance made the journey more intriguing.

Upon arrival in Turkey, I had booked a fantastic hostel with a rooftop bar that offered stunning views of the city. I eagerly anticipated exploring this vantage point. The sight of the sunset from the rooftop, casting a warm, golden glow over the city, was truly breathtaking. From this perch, I could also spot the distant silhouettes of mosques, an iconic feature of Turkey.

One aspect that struck me about the city was its sheer size. Istanbul was teeming with activity, yet it managed to maintain a sense of spaciousness, a unique blend of vibrancy and tranquillity. The city revealed a duality, as it straddled two continents, Europe and Asia, separated by water. This geographical division became increasingly evident as I ventured further east in Turkey.

On my first day in Istanbul, I wanted to get a feel for the city. My plan was to take a walk along the river, ending up at a mosque with the bridge as the backdrop. It was a perfect example of the city's contrast. Along the way, I tried a traditional dish, baked potatoes with filler. At first glance, I thought it was ice cream, but on closer inspection, I realized it was not ice cream but fillings made of cheese and carrots in small pieces. It was delicious and incredibly filling; I couldn't finish it all! On my way back to the hostel, I decided to stop at a park. It was a long walk back and I was pleasantly surprised by the locals chatting and playing games in the park. The park was enormous and one of the best I had ever been to. It even had some cool wooden bridges that crossed it, offering lovely views.

From Istanbul, I decided to skip the capital, as I had heard there wasn't much to do there and head straight to Cappadocia. Cappadocia had been a destination I'd longed to visit, mainly because of the hot air balloons that filled the skies each morning. You may have seen pictures online of these balloons at sunrise; they truly look amazing. The hostel I chose had a pool, which was refreshing given the warm weather. The area also offered hiking opportunities, including Love Valley, where the rock formations resemble male genitalia.

During this time, I had the pleasure of meeting Mariam, a Muslim resident of Egypt with aspirations of becoming a nurse. Engaging in conversations with her provided me with unique insights into the lives of locals in Egypt. Mariam and I, along with a small group of her friends, frequently embarked on hiking adventures. Her generous nature shone through on numerous occasions. I recall a particular incident where we stumbled upon $50 lying on the ground by the side of the road. Mariam was determined to give it all away and we decided to use the money to purchase dog food, feeding all the stray dogs in our town. This act of kindness was incredibly rewarding to know that the money went to a good cause. Meeting Mariam was an eye-opening experience. Despite hailing from a less affluent country, her generosity knew no bounds. Spending time with Mariam enlightened me and inspired me to be more compassionate and generous in my own life moving forward. Her kindness served as a powerful reminder of the impact one person's actions can have on others, transcending cultural and economic boundaries.

I also crossed paths with a young man named Declan, who was embarking on an incredible challenge. He was living on a mere £5 per day budget and cycling all the way from Greece to Georgia. Declan was equipped with a simple, inexpensive bike and his daily sustenance mainly consisted of nuts, chosen for their affordability and nutritional value.

On my last day in Cappadocia, I struck up a conversation with some English people who were headed to Isparta, which was very close to my next destination,

Antalya. They were driving and kindly agreed to let me join them. The group consisted of two brothers, a sister and a Turkish girl who was a friend and touring them around Turkey. We got along well and our plans changed as the trip went on. Due to the length of the journey, we decided to make a stop at Salda Lake, booking a room for the night. Upon arrival, we attracted plenty of attention from locals, as tourists were a rare sight. Our accommodation was incredibly cheap, around £4 each. After a few hours of sleep, we woke up to watch the sunrise. Salda Lake was used as a water reservoir and was remarkably clear. Although swimming wasn't allowed, it was a stunning sight. The beach had ground that closely resembled the terrain on Mars, leading NASA to conduct experiments there for future Mars missions. We hopped back into the car, had a quick meal and headed to Pamukkale.

Originally, I hadn't planned to visit Pamukkale because I couldn't get there via public transport, so I was grateful for the opportunity. It featured an archaeological site alongside the main attraction: terraces formed from the flow of warm mineral-rich water. The terraces stretched out for quite a distance, resembling a massive cascading water feature, with the city in the distance. I had never seen anything quite like it. We then embarked on a long and scorching walk up to the Roman amphitheatre, which was in excellent condition. From there, we had one more stop planned, the Sagalassos Archaeological Site. However, this was no ordinary archaeological site. They had discovered this location in a board game and decided to include it on their route. The drive offered breathtaking views as we ascended into the mountains, encountering very few people. We were free to explore the site with no barriers and I even ventured inside the amphitheatre, climbing all the way to the top. I captured a fantastic panoramic photo with the distant mountains and the entire building in the middle.

One of the most challenging tasks in Antalya was finding accommodation for five travellers. Most hostels had limited availability and could not accommodate all of us. However, we found one hostel with a room that had five beds, which was perfect for us. Antalya is a tourist hotspot and I wasn't sure what to expect. Upon arrival, I noticed numerous bars and restaurants and a clear contrast between the tourist and local areas.

Turkey was an amazing trip and I really recommend watching my YouTube videos to see a more detailed travel experience. I then travelled to Eastern Europe to explore some more countries.

Bratislava

Bratislava was meant to be a wild party experience, living up to its reputation as one of Europe's best party hostels. However, my arrival in the city came with unexpected expenses. With about 20 minutes left of walking to reach my destination, I decided to hop on a tram to save some energy under the scorching sun. After only five minutes on the tram, I realised I wasn't sure how to purchase a ticket. I approached one of the machines onboard with a contactless sticker and when it flashed green, I assumed I had paid for my fare. Many European transport systems operate this way. However, a ticket inspector approached me and asked for my ticket, which I couldn't provide as I had no proof of payment due to a lack of internet connection to show my mobile transaction. I tried to negotiate my way out of it, but he remained unfazed. To ensure he was an official ticket inspector, I even asked for his ID and he indeed was. He repeatedly threatened to involve the police, which I wished to avoid, not wanting to waste their time. Lacking cash, I reluctantly withdrew 50 Euros from an ATM and paid the fine. Reflecting on the situation, I was irritated at myself for my simple mistake. I could have just walked the extra 20 minutes or explained that I was "getting off at the next stop" while negotiating my case more convincingly. Nevertheless, life goes on and I proceeded to my hostel.

The hostel turned out to be quite cool, offering a warm welcome and a friendly atmosphere. It featured a kitchen, a bar and organised events. During the day, the hostel's volunteers arranged activities for guests to mingle and explore the city together. On that particular day, the event involved heading to the river for a few hours. It was an excellent opportunity to make new friends and discover some of the city's charm. Some adventurous folks even took a dip in the river, adding a refreshing twist to the day. One girl displayed her remarkable acrobatics in the water, leaving me in awe of her energy and skills. She shared that she used to practice acrobatics when she was younger and described the sensation as akin to flying, enabling her to perform astonishing tricks. Many of the hostel's occupants were students, seizing the opportunity to travel during their school break.

That night, I decided to join the pub crawl, this included stops at three bars and ended at a techno club. While I've experienced better-organized pub crawls, it's often the people you meet that make the experience memorable and this time was no exception. We ended up at a lively club, dancing the night away. The next day, I explored the city's landmarks, including a church, a bridge with a futuristic design reminiscent of a UFO and a stroll through the old town. Although many tourists visit Bratislava for its castle, I've seen my fair share of castles and felt no draw to it.

In a peculiar twist of fate, I crossed paths with a New Zealander I had met in Turkey while hiking in Cappadocia. It was surreal to encounter him again in Bratislava, thousands of miles away from our initial meeting. He shared his adventurous journey to Bratislava, which involved hitchhiking, bus rides and train journeys as he made his way to Poland to meet a friend. It was a pleasant reunion and we enjoyed catching up, especially since he had spent a significant portion of his life travelling full-time.

Despite waking up late the following day, I didn't have to wait long for the next hostel event. Since it was a Sunday, the event took place at the party hostel located nearby. The was hosted in the attic of the building and featured affordable drinks and an outgoing crowd. We engaged in card drinking games, filling the table with empty beer glasses. I appreciated that the hostel didn't pressure anyone into participating in activities they weren't comfortable with. For example, there was a "spin the wheel" game with various consequences, from free drinks to more daring challenges like the naked run – a testament to the hostel's wild reputation. While I wasn't particularly drawn to the crazier aspects, I enjoyed the conversations and meeting interesting people. I left the party around 3 am, but many stayed up drinking until the early hours of the morning. It was by far the wildest hostel experience I had ever encountered.

On my final day in Bratislava, I embarked on a day trip to Vienna, just an hour away by bus. It was another country I could cross off my bucket list. While Vienna boasted stunning architecture and a diverse crowd, I found it to be rather expensive and beyond my budget at the time. The city felt like a meeting point of Europe and I was excited for the evening event, a riverside party. We started at the wild hostel before marching to the river with a group of about 30 people. There, we made a bonfire and enjoyed the festivities, with one of the volunteers providing music via a speaker. It wasn't just about drinking; it was the atmosphere by the river which was really cool.

Zagreb

My journey to Zagreb, Croatia, marked the beginning of my exploration into the Balkans. The bus ride was intended to get me to Zagreb in the evening, but thanks to the sluggish border crossings that felt like they were operated by sloths, I ended up arriving much later than expected. This was frustrating, as many affordable hostels had become fully booked and I would miss my check-in time by just 30 minutes. However, I had been in touch with the hostel and they graciously waited for my arrival, which I appreciated immensely. It was my fault that I couldn't make the original check-in time, so their understanding was a welcome relief. I booked a two-night stay in Zagreb as I planned to take my time exploring the city over the course of two days.

Zagreb wasn't a top tourist destination, as it didn't boast an extensive list of attractions. Still, I was determined to delve into the city's offerings. One charming surprise I discovered was a miniature solar system within the city. It was a scaled-down version, starting with a two-meter-high representation of the sun and extending through the city to find the Earth and all the other planets. It was a delightful and educational concept that added a unique touch to the city.

During my stay in Zagreb, I had the opportunity to indulge in one of my favourite activities: a walking tour. These tours always provide a fantastic way to absorb the local culture and history.

I had initially planned to attend the Ultra Festival in Split, Croatia. However, when I checked accommodation options, I was astounded to find that the only available option was priced over £100. It was clear that this region, particularly the coastal areas of Croatia and Montenegro, had become quite expensive, even during what should have been a more budget-friendly travel season. This presented a dilemma, as I had hoped to explore the coastal towns along Croatia and Montenegro. Unfortunately, due to the high prices and limited availability, I had to abandon that idea. I was quite surprised by the cost, as I had expected these areas to be more affordable. Determined to continue my journey, I decided to head towards Albania, where I knew prices would be more reasonable, as fewer travellers ventured that far south. My next stop, therefore, was Bosnia, conveniently located along my route.

Bosnia and Herzegovina

My journey to Bosnia, particularly Sarajevo, was characterized by a lack of expectations and limited prior research about the country. I had heard stories about the relatively recent war in Bosnia and the persistent threat of landmines, but I was eager to witness first-hand how the country had evolved since then. My arrival in Sarajevo from Zagreb was an unexpectedly lengthy affair, largely due to the slow border crossings, which felt like they were being managed by sloths once again. We had to pass through both the Croatian and Bosnian sides, enduring two bus changes along the way. The initial change was necessitated by a bus breakdown, while the second was for us to board a smaller bus for the final leg of our journey. The overall trip took much longer than I had anticipated.

One amusing aspect of the long bus ride was observing the habits of the locals during our stops. Many of them would take advantage of these breaks to engage in some traditional practices. They would typically light up a cigarette, indulge in a shot or two of Rakija (a strong alcoholic beverage) and savour a robust cup of coffee. These rituals were not only a part of their daily routine but were also believed to have some health benefits. It was intriguing to witness these cultural traditions firsthand and gain insight into the local way of life while on the journey.

Surprisingly, I encountered a familiar face on the bus—an individual I had met in Istanbul, Turkey, at the beginning of my journey. We had shared several nights out during my time in Istanbul and to think that we would cross paths again over a month later on the same bus was nothing short of remarkable. The odds of such an encounter were indeed astounding.

Upon my arrival in Sarajevo, I opted for a budget-friendly Airbnb apartment, as I needed my own space after an extended period of staying in hostels. Fortunately, the apartment owner allowed me to check in early, which provided me with the opportunity to catch up on much-needed sleep. I had hardly slept during the bus journeys, constantly switching buses and enduring passport checks.

As I explored Sarajevo, one of the first things that struck me, aside from the bullet-riddled buildings I had noticed earlier, was the sheer number of structures that had been destroyed during the war. These damaged buildings served as haunting reminders of the harrowing events the city had endured. It was evident that the days ahead would be mentally taxing, given the knowledge of the horrific experiences this country had gone through. While the main city centre appeared to be in good condition, the signs of damage became increasingly apparent as I ventured into the outskirts of Sarajevo.

In my quest to learn more about the city and its history, I decided to join a free walking tour. Although my first choice of tour was cancelled, I quickly found an alternative just around the corner. The tour provided a wealth of information and historical facts. In simple terms, Bosnia had been part of Yugoslavia, a country that included some of the present-day Balkan nations. When Bosnia sought independence, the Yugoslav army, primarily controlled by Serbia, responded forcefully. This led to the Bosnian War between 1992 and 1995, during which brutal war crimes were committed. The city was encircled by surrounding mountains, which became the backdrop for relentless bombings and destruction over several years. Sniper attacks also posed a constant threat to the city's residents. Despite the adversities, the people of Sarajevo persevered and even organized theatre performances during this time, providing a temporary escape from the grim reality. The city itself was divided, with one side reflecting a modern European influence and the other side retaining a distinct Turkish architectural character. This contrast was evident in the buildings—look to the left and you'd think you were in Western Europe, while turning your head to the right would transport you to Balkan architecture. During the tour, I also heard a fascinating story about the City Hall. Originally, they had planned to construct it near the river, but a few houses stood in the same location. The locals were offered compensation to relocate, but one man refused. After a lengthy dispute, he eventually agreed to vacate the premises in exchange for a substantial sum and the condition that his house be dismantled brick by brick and rebuilt elsewhere. The building now bears his name and serves as a restaurant.

One of my planned activities in Sarajevo was a hike up a nearby mountain, partly because the summit offered an excellent view of the city and an abandoned bobsleigh track from the 1984 Olympics. Unfortunately, the track had been destroyed during the war by the military. The hike took about 1-2 hours and included abandoned buildings to explore along the way. At the summit, I had the opportunity to explore the bobsleigh track, walking its entire length and capturing some captivating photos. It was remarkable how quickly nature had reclaimed the track in just a few years. To descend, I took a chairlift back to the bottom. Sarajevo didn't boast much of a nightlife, but I did manage to find a good club. Additionally, I crossed paths with another English traveller during my time in the city, adding a social dimension to my stay.

The souvenirs in Sarajevo were unique and reflected the local culture. They were known for their love of coffee, so many shops offered coffee sets for purchase. Another poignant souvenir was small model guns that could be attached to keyrings, serving as a sober reminder of the region's troubled history. Throughout the city, one could spot the locations where mortar shells had struck buildings. To draw attention to these scars, some of the holes had been painted red to symbolize blood. The Museum of Crimes Against Humanity was a particularly powerful and sobering experience that I would highly recommend visiting.

After my time in Sarajevo, I received a recommendation to visit Mostar, which was renowned for its picturesque beauty. I took a bus to get there which offered some breathtaking views and while the bus followed a river for part of the journey, which was exceptionally blue due to minerals from the surrounding mountains. I was tempted to take a dip in its icy waters. Upon my arrival in Mostar, I found myself in one of the cosiest hostels I had ever encountered. The welcoming hostess prepared a fresh and healthy drink for me and the hostel exuded a homely atmosphere. It felt as though I was a guest in her own home and guests were expected to adhere to certain rules, such as eating only at the designated tables, removing their shoes and maintaining quiet in the evenings. This unique atmosphere was a refreshing departure from typical hostel experiences. The hostel also offered a complimentary local breakfast, fostering a social environment where guests could mingle. I was keen to explore the nearby lake, so I asked the hostel owner for a recommendation. She was very traditional and relied on a map and pencil to provide directions. The spot she suggested turned out to be perfect for a refreshing dip in the water. Even though the lake was one of the coldest in Europe, I couldn't resist the opportunity to submerge myself.

Mostar was famous for its iconic bridge, which stood over 30 meters high and spanned the clear waters below. Although the original bridge was destroyed during the war, it had been painstakingly reconstructed to closely resemble its predecessor. Visitors to Mostar were often treated to the sight of daring individuals leaping from the high bridge to entertain tourists and earn a living. These jumpers had specific financial goals to reach before taking the plunge. They also offered training for those who wished to experience the exhilaration of diving from the bridge themselves, though the activity was not without risks and required someone waiting below in a small boat. Mostar's streets were bustling, lined with numerous bars and restaurants overlooking the river. There wasn't an abundance of activities to engage in, especially considering that I had no SIM card to keep me tethered to my phone. This slower pace allowed me to fully appreciate my surroundings and I spent several leisurely days in Mostar. The hostel's friendly atmosphere facilitated social interactions and I often spent my days with fellow travellers. One of the guests at the hostel claimed to be a famous TikToker, a revelation that I initially found amusing but soon discovered to be true. He created travel content and ran a YouTube channel where he completed various challenges. Our conversations provided valuable insights into the world of social media and content creation. He also shared an amusing anecdote about attending Ultra Festival and being unable to secure accommodation, ultimately resorting to sleeping on a bench in Split, Croatia, all while partying with his luggage.

In Mostar, I embarked on what would become the hottest hike I had ever experienced. The temperature soared to about 32 degrees Celsius, which was considered relatively cool for the region at the time. I decided to hike up to a cross on a nearby mountain, accompanied by one of my fellow hostel guests. The heat was sweltering and I used my towel to shield myself from the sun's intense rays. However, the view from the summit made the challenging hike worthwhile. Despite the harsh terrain and the presence of landmines in the vicinity, we managed to stick to the designated paths for safety. Another intriguing site we explored was an abandoned bank building that had served as a sniper tower during the war. It was possible to enter the tower and explore its various floors, providing a glimpse into the city's tumultuous past.

Serbia

Choosing my next destination was a bit of a dilemma due to the high cost of bus fares and the fact that some popular places like Macedonia were out of my budget. After much contemplation, I decided to splurge on a bus ticket to Novi Sad, a city located north of Belgrade. My plan was to stay for just one night, as I had heard there wasn't a lot to do there. I boarded an overnight bus, which unfortunately was very full and left me unable to get any sleep. However, I was determined to make the most of my visit, even on limited rest and joined a walking tour in the morning.

The walking tour turned out to be quite informative and our guide led us around the entire town and castle, leaving me with a feeling that I had seen it all. While Novi Sad didn't offer a plethora of activities, it was still worth the visit to explore and gain insights into its history, especially regarding the war. During the tour, our guide shared an emotional story about his father, who had initially supported a political movement but later realised the grim reality and tragically took his own life. This narrative shed light on the ongoing challenges and denial associated with the war in some parts of Serbia.

Although Novi Sad itself had limited attractions, the people I encountered at the hostel made the experience interesting. In my dorm room, I met an Egyptian man who enthusiastically claimed to be a great singer. Initially, we weren't sure if he was joking or not, but we decided to test him. He began warming up and humming before launching into his song. His singing was far from impressive, yet he genuinely believed in his talent. We joined in, clapping and cheering him on, which turned the moment into a humorous one.

The atmosphere seemed lively, so I decided to join this fun group for a night out. We started at a posh rooftop bar, which, while a bit pricey, offered a fantastic view. However, the Egyptian man took out his own speaker and started playing loud Egyptian music, causing some embarrassment as people around us wondered why we had our own music. After convincing him to turn it off, we engaged in an intellectual conversation and learned about his rather unconventional perspectives on the world.

Our evening continued with visits to various bars, including a hairdresser bar where patrons could get haircuts while enjoying a drink. This unique concept aside, the Egyptian man, a non-drinker due to his Muslim faith, showed us that he could still have a good time. He danced to the music, balanced a glass bottle on his head and even engaged in playful sparring with another member of our group, inadvertently blocking the way for some irritated girls trying to reach their table. He was like a real life Mr Bean. Our final stop was a bar with live music where locals were enjoying a professional act. Our Egyptian friend suggested he could sing and with some persuasion, he approached the guitarist to ask if he could join in. Unfortunately, the guitarist shook his head and declined the request.

This Egyptian man truly stood out as a unique character and I couldn't help but hope for the opportunity to encounter him again in the future.

I opted for a swift and efficient train ride to Belgrade, the capital of Serbia. The high-speed train was a marvel of engineering, boasting tracks constructed by China, which allowed for such rapid transit. In just 30-40 minutes, I arrived in the bustling city. It had been a while since I had been in such an urban environment and the fast-paced atmosphere took some getting used to. My plan was to spend approximately three nights in Belgrade to explore everything it had to offer.

Upon my arrival in the evening, I was immediately captivated by the lively street scene. Belgrade is renowned for its street performances and artists and the city's streets were alive with activity. Street performers were doing Michael Jackson dances, group dances and even some bands were playing, all funded by donations from the gathered crowds. There were a considerable number of tourists around, as Belgrade is also well-known as a party destination. Although the hostels were a bit on the expensive side, I managed to find a place for around 12 euros per night. It was a decent spot, but it had a somewhat unusual atmosphere with many people making late-night phone calls in the common areas. However, I crossed paths with an older gentleman in the hostel, whom I had previously met in Sofia about seven months prior. I remembered him for his nightly ritual of enjoying a bottle of wine and one evening, he was quite inebriated, spouting off humorous nonsense, which became a topic of joking conversation in the room.

On my first night in Belgrade, I was eager to head out, but I found it challenging to find anyone to accompany me. Eventually, I connected with some people on Couchsurfing. The organizer of the group was a local, so we headed to one of the best local bars, a venue that was partly indoors and partly outdoors. Our group consisted of around 12 people and after some conversation, we decided to venture to a raft party, which was not a touristy spot and catered more to locals. The party was located on a wooden raft in the water and had a truly unique vibe. Because it was positioned quite far from residential areas, the party was allowed to continue until 7 a.m. I remember standing on the side of the boat, feeling a subtle rocking motion from the bass, which was an incredible sensation. There was also an upper deck where you could relax and sit down, a welcome respite after hours of dancing and partying. I was determined to stay until the sun came up, so I partied until about 6 a.m.

During the night I had a somewhat unsettling experience when a Serbian individual approached me around a corner and offered drugs. I declined the offer, which led him to ask where I was from. In hindsight, I should have lied, but I told the truth and mentioned my origin. This seemed to agitate him and he grew somewhat aggressive. His hostility stemmed from historical and political factors, such as the Kosovo issue and Western countries' support for Kosovo's independence, as well as NATO bombings in parts of Serbia. To defuse the situation, I quickly agreed with him, stating that I had come to Serbia to gain a different perspective on the news. He didn't seem entirely convinced, but I remained composed and managed to remove myself from the situation. It's possible that he was intoxicated or under the influence of drugs, which could explain his behaviour, but I didn't want to take any chances.

After a much-needed long sleep, that night I met a German girl called Vicky and I embarked on a visit to a renowned rooftop café with her, considered one of the best cafés in Europe. The café offered breathtaking views and had an impressive interior design. Adorned with art on the walls and equipped with board games, it provided a perfect spot to relax with a drink. For breakfast, I indulged in an iced coffee along with some fries – perhaps not the healthiest choice, but a tasty one.

Following this delightful breakfast, we decided to explore another area of the city, one that was reputed to be very different from Belgrade. We hopped on a bus and disembarked at a random point, choosing to wander towards the river. We followed a path that took us past houses and trees until we reached the water's edge. The rocky shoreline was littered with debris, but the scenery looked intriguing further up the river. We strolled along the beach and struck up a conversation with some locals who were in their front garden. They informed us that the beach was a dead-end, but out of curiosity, we continued further. This led us to an abandoned boat nestled in the forest. Although it was small, it was just large enough for me to climb inside and play pretend as the boat's captain. However, our exploration reached an impasse as we reached the end of the beach. Our choices were to turn back or attempt to find a way up from there.

Opting for further adventure, we ventured past the abandoned boat and discovered a set of rather sketchy-looking stairs that led past some old sheds. These stairs seemed to lead back towards the town. As we neared the forest, we encountered an irate dog racing toward us. Fortunately, the dog's owners were nearby and managed to call it back. They signalled for us to turn around, but when they realized we were tourists, I politely asked if we could pass through.

Thankfully, they kindly allowed us to walk through their garden and gate, providing us access to the town. It was certainly an unexpected adventure!

On our way back, we came across a wedding celebration. The music was incredible and the passion with which the songs were performed was awesome. We lingered around for a while, hoping for an invite, but unfortunately, that didn't happen.

We decided to continue our journey together since we got along so well and had a few planned destinations that we could explore. Our next leg of the journey began with a bus ride, but unfortunately, the bus was extremely crowded and we had to sit separately due to the lack of available seats. The bus was sweltering hot and I couldn't wait to depart as I was drenched in sweat from both the heat and lugging around all my luggage.

Before continuing our journey to Macedonia, we made a stop in the small city of Nis, located in the southern part of Serbia. It took a few hours on a crowded coach to reach Nis and our plan was to stay for just two nights since there wasn't much to see in this city. Nis was remarkably clean and featured a castle, which made for a pleasant place to unwind. One of the significant historical sites in the area was a Nazi concentration camp, which I hadn't been aware of before. Visiting the camp was a somber and eye-opening experience, allowing me to reflect on the horrors that had occurred there. After a brief two-night stay in Nis, we were ready to move on to our next destination.

Macedonia

My travel companion Vicky and I decided to explore Macedonia together, starting with its capital, Skopje. We had a hostel booked with good ratings and I had few ideas about what to expect other than for a few interesting facts I had gathered. For instance, Macedonia was the first country in the world to have phone signal coverage across its entire territory. Additionally, the country's mountainous landscape made many areas inhospitable for human habitation.

Upon our arrival, we had to endure a hot walk to reach the hostel. Once there, we discovered it had a pleasant café below where we could enjoy drinks and relax. It even had a balcony, which was a welcome respite from the scorching heat and offered a view over the city. In the evening, we decided to take a walk and explore the old town, which immediately reminded me of Turkey, though the locals here were not as pushy or focused on selling things.

During one of the most memorable walks, I've ever taken in a city, I encountered a multitude of statues. The government had erected over 200 large statues throughout the city, featuring famous and historical figures. While these statues were impressive to see, they also stirred controversy among the locals, who believed their government could have better spent the money, particularly considering that Macedonia is one of the poorest countries in Europe.

I felt an instant connection with Skopje, whether due to the people I met or the experiences I had. It's clear that this city is poised to become increasingly touristy in the coming years. The city boasts an old town with a bazaar where you can find items at local prices. A short walk across the oldest bridge in the Balkans takes you to the modern part of the city, where the statues never failed to amaze me. Some of the larger statues also functioned as water features, providing a refreshing spot to sit next to on scorching hot days. As always, I made a list of things to do and arranged my activities around the weather, which could sometimes reach a sweltering 40 degrees Celsius. On my first evening, I explored the old town and ventured into the modern area of the city, which took me by surprise.

The following day, we decided to explore the Matka Canyon one of Macedonia's natural gems, which required a bus ride. The canyon offered a pleasant walk, with the option to take boats for a fee or go for a swim. I was keen to check it out but we encountered a hurdle when trying to purchase bus tickets. The bus ticket station was closed and we were told it would open in five minutes. Unfortunately, the bus departed in that time, so we explained our situation to the driver. He communicated with someone and then simply let us on the bus, resulting in a free ride. The journey took around 40 minutes and upon arrival, we enjoyed a relaxing walk along parts of the canyon. The area had shops and restaurants, although they were a bit expensive due to the touristy nature of the location. Nevertheless, I opted for a healthy smoothie. Following this, I took a swim in the water but despite its coldness, it was refreshing and a great way to beat the heat.

On the way back, we managed to ride the bus without paying, as they didn't check tickets. That evening, there was a Couchsurfing meetup where locals and travellers gathered at a bar to socialize. We all met at an outdoor bar with live music and there were about 20 of us. I particularly enjoyed these meet ups, as they provided an opportunity to get recommendations from locals and chat with fellow travellers.

Afterwards, we went to a rock bar, but it was crowded and played music that wasn't quite my taste. I decided to walk back with some others from the hostel. Initially, I had planned to wrap up a few more activities and leave the following day, but I ended up extending my stay. I really liked this place; it was affordable and had plenty to offer.

During a Couchsurfing meet up, I spoke to various people who recommended that I visit Ohrid, located to the west of Macedonia. It's home to the deepest lake in Europe and around 3 million years old. I had already marked it on my maps, so their advice further fuelled my desire to go. I chose a budget-friendly hostel, costing about 7 Euros per night. The only drawback was that it lacked a kitchen and was around a 30-minute walk from the beach.

I took a bus to reach Ohrid since there were no trains available. The journey was scorching hot, as the bus was fully booked and lacked air conditioning, leaving me with just a hot fan blowing air onto my head, rather inefficiently, I must say. After a few hours, I arrived and the hostel was only a short 10-minute walk away. Due to Ohrid's elevation, it was a few degrees cooler than Skopje, making me feel that I didn't need an afternoon siesta.

Ohrid was surrounded by beautiful mountains, offering great hiking opportunities. However, the real hidden gem was the lake itself, so vast that you could easily mistake it for the sea. It plunged down to about 500 meters in depth. As I walked around the town, I was surprised by the number of people, mostly young Macedonians, who were on holiday in groups. The town's beach was divided into different sections and my favourite spot was near one of the famous churches. It offered both shade and sun, had a water refill point (the only one I came across) and was a bit quieter as people typically didn't venture that far for the beach. The weather was perfect; you'd get hot enough to break a sweat and then cool down with a swim in the crystal-clear lake, which felt just as warm as the Mediterranean.

Ohrid's combination of stunning natural beauty, a wealth of historical sites and a relaxed lakeside atmosphere made it a highlight of my journey through Macedonia.

On one of my days, I planned to visit the 'Old Bones Museum,' which was about a 20-minute drive from the town. To get there, I had to take a bus, which was straightforward after asking locals for guidance. The bus was quite crowded, but we eventually reached our destination. I was pleasantly surprised by the surrounding area, which featured breathtaking beaches with crystal-clear water and distant mountain silhouettes. The only drawback was the crowds. As I strolled along the beach, I stumbled upon an area known as 'Jungle Beach.' It had a bar, sunbeds and a DJ and it was less crowded. I ordered a drink and soaked in the energy and vibe of the place. It felt like an exotic Asian destination with bean bags, tables in the water and hidden spots for groups to relax.

To reach the museum, I had to leave the beach and walk along the road, which was a bit risky at times, but I had no other option. The open-air museum was a large wooden platform built on the water, with wooden buildings. It told the story of a small community that once lived on the water, allowing visitors to imagine what life was like in that setting. I was particularly excited to take photos, as the clear water and picturesque surroundings made it feel like a location straight out of the Maldives.

At this juncture in our journey, Vicky and I decided to bid each other farewell, choosing to embark on separate paths. My decision to extend my stay in Ohrid meant that our travel plans diverged, but we parted on good terms, cherishing the memories we had created together. Our shared adventures would always hold a special place in my travel experiences.

I was also pleasantly surprised by the nightlife in Ohrid. The streets were even busier at night than during the day, making it hard to move at times. Most people dined late, a trend I noticed as almost every restaurant was busy. Prices were slightly higher than in Skopje, but it was understandable given the area's popularity among tourists. Ohrid boasted several clubs and numerous bars to explore. Originally, I had planned to stay for only a few days, but I loved the place so much that I extended my stay to over a week.

I also learned that there was a festival taking place during my stay, which gave me another reason to extend. My only concern was getting bored, but my hostel had some cool people to hang out with during the day and night, which made time fly by. One of the artists performing at the 'Calling' festival was Vini Vici, a childhood favourite of mine and I had always dreamed of seeing him live. Now, while travelling, I had the opportunity to make that dream a reality. The 'Calling' festival was four days long and cost about £40, which was very affordable compared to festivals in the UK. The hostel was conveniently located only a 15-minute walk from the festival grounds, making it perfect for attending the event.

One of the things I liked most about Ohrid was the fact that it wasn't overrun by tourists from outside the Balkans. This sometimes made me feel like a celebrity. The locals often asked, "Why are you here?" To which I would respond, "I don't know, someone just told me to come here," which they found amusing. One evening, I was with an American traveller and we went to the end of a pier where many locals were drinking before heading to the clubs. We struck up conversations with some friendly locals who shared insights into local life. Eventually, a few more people overheard us speaking English and joined in. One of the guys invited me to go for a ride in his car around the city. I decided to go for it and as we drove around, we listened to music and he shared his life story. It was a short but fascinating ride and I learned that many young people in the area aspired to leave the country to seek better wages, so they worked hard when not partying.

Most of my days followed a similar routine: waking up late in the morning, having some breakfast, going to the beach and then heading out in the evening. I really enjoyed this laid-back lifestyle and everyone around me seemed to be in a great mood. The evenings were particularly lively, as the days could be scorching, causing many people to stay indoors.

While I was in Ohrid, I had the pleasure of spending a lot of time with my new Mexican friend named Tulum. He was an awesome guy and we truly enjoyed living in the moment and sharing our passion for music.

During our travels, we even decided to share a private room with two beds to save on costs. Tulum, with his musical talents, often composed music while he were on the move. It was incredible to bond over our shared interests and experiences. We had so much in common and I hoped to meet him again soon. To this day, we keep in touch and chat often.

On one memorable night, I joined a group of people from the hostel and went to a beach to have a few drinks and listen to music. We ended up connecting with a group of residents who were a bit tipsy and were having a party in the park. It made for an unforgettable evening.

My favourite beach was 'Gradsite,' which featured a DJ, food, drinks and, best of all, crystal-clear water that made it feel like you were at the sea. I nicknamed this place the 'Ohrid trap' because it was so hard for me to leave. The only buses out of town were in the morning and they were so early that I kept extending my stay for one more night, promising myself I'd catch the bus the next day. I ended up staying for over a week, which was quite a long time for this destination, but as long as I was enjoying myself, I didn't mind. I also indulged in one of the local delights, Buracks, a popular Macedonian snack. These are often enjoyed with a cup of yogurt or a cold beverage and are a must-try when visiting Macedonia, they were around £1 each and incredibly tasty. They were pastry parcels filled with cheese or meat and they were filling enough to keep me satisfied for half the day.

After spending two consecutive evenings hanging out with a group of locals. I decided it was time to leave. I felt that I had experienced so much and had made some incredible memories. The most challenging part was catching the early bus at 8 a.m., but fortunately, I managed to get a good night's sleep, allowing me to wake up on time.

Albania

Leaving the tranquil shores of Ohrid was sad but I needed to move on. I embarked on a bus journey that lasted approximately three hours, taking me downhill into significantly hotter temperatures. Unfortunately, the bus lacked air conditioning, leaving passengers sweltering in the heat. However, this journey allowed me to encounter fellow travellers, including my first meeting with an English traveller whom I had not seen for a while. I also shared the ride with two French girls, with whom I later split a taxi to the town to keep our costs in check. The oppressive heat made it less appealing to navigate public transport.

Upon arriving in Tirana, the capital of Albania, I checked into a six-bed hostel room, where I found myself sharing quarters with a British family of four. It was heartwarming to see a family travelling together, with one of their children as young as 15. August isn't an ideal time for budget travellers, but their presence in the hostel demonstrated that exploring the world as a family is indeed possible.

As I began exploring the city, I was taken aback by an intriguing detail at the traffic lights – the stands holding up the lights changed colours along with the signals. That night, I reunited with my Mexican friend from Ohrid and we strolled around the city. We attempted to enter a bar but were told we needed a reservation, though we had our doubts about the authenticity of that explanation. Along the bar district in Blloku, I was surprised by the ostentatious display of cars and the gazing/cat calling at women. However, this flashy scene coexisted with people begging, approaching cars in search of help. It was an unexpected contrast and it left me with mixed emotions. Unfortunately, I also witnessed a dog getting hit by a car, which was a somber moment. Fortunately, it appeared that the dog managed to escape without severe harm.

The following day, I participated in a free walking tour of the city, which proved to be informative and enlightening. I was astonished by the city's history and its preparations for war, which fortunately never transpired. Over 130,000 bunkers were strategically placed throughout the country and many of them still stand today. The guide also shared how the city was designed with a slight slope in the central open area. During the summer, this area could reach temperatures as high as 45 degrees Celsius. The slope allowed rainwater to be collected and pumped uphill, subsequently flowing down to help keep the area cooler.

One of the most captivating museums I visited during my time in Tirana was the bunker museum, which provided a remarkable glimpse into the preparations made in the event of war. Stepping inside the bunker was a truly fascinating experience as I explored its interior and discovered how it was designed to withstand various threats.

Inside the bunker, I had the opportunity to visit numerous rooms, each with its own unique purpose and significance. One of the standout features was the room where the general or high-ranking officers would stay in case of an emergency. The bunker's architecture was a testament to its purpose. Thick walls and sturdy doors in case the possibility of a nuclear attack, as evidenced by the bunker's construction.

Despite the historical insights gained from the tour, I didn't particularly warm to Tirana. It could have been due to limited interactions or communication barriers since English wasn't widely spoken. However, my less-than-enthusiastic experience in Tirana didn't dampen my excitement to explore more of Albania. With a cheap bus ticket that cost approximately £3, I looked forward to my next destination in the southern part of the country.

My journey through Albania led me to the historic town of Berat, a place where time seemed to stand still. Berat is known for its unique architecture and rich history, earning it the nickname "The Town of a Thousand Windows." The town is split into two distinct parts, each with its own character and charm.

The first part of Berat is Mangalem, a quaint and picturesque area nestled on the banks of the Osum River. What makes Mangalem so special is its collection of well-preserved Ottoman-era houses, which seem to cascade down the hillside, creating a stunning mosaic of terracotta roofs and whitewashed walls.

The second part of Berat is Gorica, located on the opposite side of the river. Gorica is a quieter and more residential area, with its own collection of historical houses and churches. The picturesque Gorica Bridge, which connects the two parts of town, provides a stunning view of the Mangalem quarter and is a popular spot for photographers.

During my stay in this small Albanian town, I had the opportunity to immerse myself in local culture in a truly memorable way. One evening, I ventured out to a local bar with an English friend I had met at the hostel. The town, being small, had a designated boardwalk where locals gathered and we found a spot at the far end, where the atmosphere was lively and inviting.

As we settled in, I couldn't help but notice the traditional dancing taking place around us. It was a captivating sight, with a DJ spinning music and people gracefully performing age-old dance moves. Intrigued and eager to join in, I struck up a conversation with an Irish gentleman seated nearby and extended an invitation to join us. Little did I know that this would lead to an unforgettable night.

Traditional Albanian dance, I learned, is distinctive in that it involves intricate hand and foot movements rather than the usual hip-centric dancing seen in many cultures. Admittedly, it was challenging to grasp at first, but with encouragement and guidance from the friendly locals, we managed to get the hang of it as the night progressed.

A lovely lady and her daughter, who were seated next to us, took it upon themselves to teach us the traditional dance. They patiently showed us the steps and motions involved. It was a humbling experience and we found ourselves in the centre of a circle, surrounded by locals who danced around us. To our surprise, they even recorded videos of our participation.

What struck me most about this experience was the warmth and openness of the locals. Despite being in a small, lesser-known town, they welcomed us with open arms and made us feel like part of their community. This genuine connection with locals is one of the reasons I cherish my travels to less affluent countries—they often possess a strong sense of community that wealthier destinations sometimes lack.

The Irish gentleman I met that night pointed out an interesting contrast: in wealthier countries, everything tends to be meticulously planned and organized, whereas in small towns like this one, everything flows naturally, fostering a sense of togetherness.

As the evening continued, we also met a trio of friendly French travellers and decided to extend the fun by heading to another bar for drinks. It was a delightful way to bond with fellow adventurers and share stories of our experiences. Little did we know that our paths would continue to intersect in the days to come.

The next day, I joined a free walking tour and then embarked on a journey with my new-found friends, all of us heading to the same destination—an iconic Albanian attraction known as the Blue Eye. However, little did we realize that our adventure was about to take an unexpected turn.

My visit to the famed Blue Eye in Albania turned out to be quite an adventure, albeit a frustrating one. It's a story that perfectly captures the unpredictable nature of travel in this part of the world.

The Blue Eye, a natural spring with crystal-clear blue waters, is one of Albania's most iconic attractions and I was determined to see it.

Initially, things seemed promising. I approached the bus driver and asked if he could stop at the Blue Eye. He nodded in agreement and I boarded the bus with high hopes. However, as the bus began to move, it quickly became apparent that something was amiss. We were heading away from the Blue Eye, not towards it. This unexpected turn left me bewildered, but I tried to stay optimistic, thinking perhaps we were making a detour through Sarande, a town just beyond the Blue Eye.

After an hour of travel, the bus came to a halt in Sarande. To my dismay, the driver declared, "Finish." This was far from the Blue Eye and I felt deceived. Reluctantly, I paid for my ticket, though I had no intention of accepting defeat. I knew I had to find a way to reach the Blue Eye and salvage the day.

The road ahead appeared chaotic, devoid of any sense of order. Amid the confusion, I noticed a man who seemed to be in charge of the situation. He told me to wait for an hour and so I did, despite the scorching heat and mounting frustration.

However, when I approached him again after the agonizing hour of waiting, he delivered a blow: "No Blue Eye, only you." It seemed that because I was the only passenger intent on visiting the Blue Eye, they had no interest in taking the bus on a route that would pass it.

Fuming and feeling as though everyone was conspiring against me, I decided to take matters into my own hands. I paid for another bus ticket back to where I came from. During the ride, I struck up a conversation with some Spanish travellers who felt sorry for me. Our journey took an unexpected twist again when the bus suddenly stopped outside a small village. This development raised our suspicions, but we all decided to exit the bus and see what was happening. To our surprise, two cars were waiting to transport us further.

I opted for one of the cars with my newfound Spanish companions, even though it meant cramming five of us into the back seat. The driver sped through the winding roads with reckless abandon, overtaking vehicles at breakneck speed. It was an adrenaline-pumping ride, to say the least. Upon arriving at our destination, the driver attempted to charge us an exorbitant fee for this journey. Despite us paying the bus ticket. It was clear that he wasn't a licensed taxi, but rather a friend of the bus driver. We refused to be taken advantage of and paid a more reasonable fare of 2 Euros before making our escape.

Despite the chaos and frustration of the day, I was grateful for the chance to meet my Spanish companions. I decided to make the most of the day by embarking on a hike to a nearby old bridge. The breathtaking views over the city offered a moment of solitude and reflection, reminding me unexpected detours can still make good stories.

The following day, I made my way to Saranda, with a stop planned at the mesmerizing Blue Eye on the way. The only hitch was that I had all my luggage and the Blue Eye was a good 30-minute walk from the bus stop. My spirits soared when I discovered that my bus was headed south, in the direction of the Blue Eye, indicating a scheduled stop.

Upon disembarking, I chanced upon a vendor selling plump figs. Politeness prevailed as I requested the vendor to keep an eye on my bag and kindly he kept it in the back. As a gesture of gratitude, I purchased some figs to savour on my walk. The bag which held all my valuables I kept with me, while a second bag contained my clothes.

The Blue Eye, a natural wonder, bustled with visitors, each required to pay a nominal entrance fee. This geological marvel is a freshwater spring that has been gushing from the earth for centuries, with its unfathomable depths of over 50 meters, yet only partially explored. A viewing platform awaited and I patiently waited for a clearing in the crowd to peer down into this aquatic abyss. The sight was akin to gazing into an alien realm, a world beneath our own. Some adventurous souls attempted to get over the gate's restrictions for a quick dip, but a vigilant attendant wielded his whistle to deter any boundary-crossers.

My curiosity got the better of me; I wanted to experience the cold 10°C waters firsthand, to test me. Upon my return from the viewing platform, I spotted a small enclave where a few hidden swimmers revelled. I put on my swimming trunks and waded in. The water, though numbingly cold, beckoned me deeper until it enveloped me up to my neck. I remained submerged until my feet began to go numb from the icy chill, which, admittedly, wasn't very long.

Returning to Saranda posed a challenge, for I knew that only one or two buses were scheduled for the day. I contemplated the idea of hitchhiking but thought it wiser to check if anyone else was returning from the Blue Eye and willing to split the fare for a taxi. After a spell of waiting, two young women approached me, seeking assistance due to their scooter running out of fuel. The nearest petrol station lay about two hours away by foot. Providentially, taxi drivers loitered nearby, offering them a ride to refuel. I endeavoured to negotiate a fair price with the taxi driver on their behalf, but his response was rather cryptic, "I'm mafia." I couldn't discern whether it was a warning or an explanation for higher charges, but I hoped the young women weren't being taken advantage of. Soon after, two groups of people arrived, also in search of transportation and together, we managed to secure a taxi for a fare slightly higher than the combined bus tickets.

My accommodations in Saranda were at a splendid hostel, characterized by a lively atmosphere and nightly events. The hostel's owner, an Australian, humorously explained how he had impulsively purchased the establishment during a night out. Adding to the charm, a delightful puppy graced the premises, although it had been taken by a guest from a bad character attempting to sell the pup off the streets

A night out was organized by the owner including an exhilarating midnight swim at the nearby beach. I was taken aback by the surprisingly warm waters for that time of night. While on the beach, we engaged in a rather perilous game. A can was stationed in the midst of our circle and participants took turns hurling rocks in a bid to displace the can from its position. The loser being the person to which the can was closest. The game, though brimming with risk, elicited peals of laughter. However, an unexpected turn of events abruptly concluded our amusement when a group of random youngsters began to fling large rocks recklessly at the can. One child even propelled a sizable stone perilously close to our heads. We promptly intervened and pondered the absence of their guardians, marking an unceremonious end to the spirited contest.

The next item on my agenda was a visit to Ksamil, a renowned tourist hotspot in Albania. Although I wasn't particularly excited about the idea, the captivating photos I had seen online left me with no choice but to explore it for myself. My journey got off to a rather rough start as the bus I boarded was incredibly crowded, the most packed one I had ever encountered. It was a claustrophobic experience, with barely any room to move and passengers squeezed in all around me. Albanian buses typically have two personnel on board, the driver and a ticket collector who collects fares. The ticket collector valiantly attempted to get passengers to move further down the bus, but the lack of space made it nearly impossible. I eventually decided to disembark a few stops earlier than intended just to escape the overwhelming bus environment.

My initial observations upon arriving in Ksamil were not entirely favourable. The shops appeared to be quite pricey and I learned that many visitors arrived from Corfu, which gave me some insight into the kind of non-budget travellers here must have. My first destination was Bora Bora Beach, renowned as one of the best beaches in the area. It did live up to its reputation, with golden sands and crystal-clear waters so pristine you could almost take a sip. However, every available sunbed was occupied and the water was teeming with people. I longed for a swim but had nowhere to leave my belongings since every inch of the beach seemed to be occupied.

Determined to find a quieter, free public beach for relaxation and a refreshing swim, I wandered further down the road and eventually encountered a couple of Italian people who were also in search of a public beach. I inquired if it would be ok to join them and they graciously welcomed me. We spent about an hour exploring, including a lengthy hike along a desolate path, yet every patch of sand we encountered seemed to be commercialized in some manner. Ultimately, we arrived at a rocky area where we could lay down and some of our group ventured into the water. The return bus journey was equally packed and I couldn't help but think that Ksamil might be a more serene destination during the off-peak season.

That evening, the hostel hosted a karaoke night. Situated in a residential area, the hostel also operated a nearby bar that could remain open late without disturbing any neighbours.

My next destination was Himare, another coastal town known for its less touristy atmosphere and superior beaches. I embarked on a bus with a scenic route along the coast, eventually reaching Himare. It was a small town where the primary attraction was undoubtedly the beach. I stayed at a delightful hostel, a mere two-minute stroll from the beach, but even this less touristy locale was bustling. The locals strategically placed umbrellas on the beach to reserve their spots, leaving little room for others.

However, I received a tip about a 'secret' beach that, as it turned out, wasn't much of a secret since many were aware of it. To reach this hidden gem, we embarked on an hour-long walk. Upon reaching the cliff's summit overlooking the beach, the sight of the crystal-clear, azure waters was an absolute delight. From here, we had to make our way down a path that presented a few challenges. Some individuals chose to turn back at the top after surveying the initial steep drop. As we descended, the path became quite steep and we had to rely on a rope to safely guide us down. If you slipped you could be in trouble. This added an element of adventure to our beach day. We brought along an umbrella to provide shade since the sun was scorching and we planned to spend most of the day here. It was great fun.

Following a rather busy day, I resolved to make the next one run like clockwork. I hopped on a bus bound for Shkoder, a journey that clocked in at about 3 hours but came with the delightful bonus of air conditioning – a welcome reprieve from the scorching buses I'd endured in the past. My chosen hostel, while a tad off the beaten path, boasted a garden teeming with fresh fruit trees and served up a mouthwatering homemade breakfast each morning. It was a delightful way to kickstart my day.

Moreover, a stroke of coincidence graced my stay in Shkoder. As I strolled through the hostel, my attention was drawn to a gentleman engrossed in his laptop. To my sheer amazement, I instantly recognized him from our chance encounter several months prior at a hostel in Greece. The serendipity of crossing paths with him once more in this remote corner of the world left me thoroughly astounded and thoroughly pleased.

Shkoder, upon initial inspection, may not seem like a treasure trove of attractions, but it did lay claim to a castle that offered up some decent views of the city. Uncertain about what lay ahead, I'd heard about a phenomenal hike in the vicinity that had piqued my curiosity. From Valbona to Theth. After some careful planning, it was an adventure I was eager to embark upon. I opted for an unconventional approach, deciding to tackle the hike in reverse, with the hope of encountering fewer fellow trekkers and hike towards my finishing point. My plan included a two-night stay in the initial mountain town, followed by a single night in the next stop along the way. Considering the hike spanned a substantial 8-10 hour. Fortunately, my hand luggage proved spacious enough and I was able to stash my main bag at the hostel for a nominal fee – all geared up for an adventure that promised excitement. To ensure a seamless journey to Valbone where I would start the hike, I took care to book my transportation well in advance. The journey comprised two buses and a ferry, a logistical puzzle that had been expertly pieced together.

Bright and early, around 6:15 am, a pickup from my hostel set my expedition in motion. We embarked on a bus ride that treated us to awe-inspiring mountain views. At times, the driver seemed to touch dangerously with the cliff's edge. After roughly two hours we reached the ferry port. The ferry itself perched high amidst the mountains, creating an otherworldly landscape that made me feel insignificantly small in the grand scheme of nature. Regrettably, the sight of litter strewn in the river below served as a stark reminder of environmental challenges.

Our next leg involved yet another bus, winding through the mountains, passing charming villages and shops, until we finally reached Valbone. Here, the journey dropped me off at my accommodation, a guest house with a dormitory. Coincidentally, Oscar my Mexican from Ohrid, was also staying here.

The hostel did come with a somewhat steep price tag for Oscar, prompting him to opt for a more budget-friendly alternative – pitching a tent on the premises for a reduced fee. The establishment, functioning dually as a hotel, offered an outdoor seating area adorned with plush mattresses atop the sofas. It was during this that I made a curious observation: one of the sofas was conspicuously devoid of its cushioning. Oscar admitted to having taken the mattress for a more comfortable night's sleep within the confines of his tent. How Funny!

On that particular day, I ventured to a river accompanied by a handful of new-found comrades, all eager for a dip. The water was nothing short of freezing, significantly chillier than the Blue Eye. A mere moment in this water left you with the sensation that you were being transformed into an ice sculpture. Our initial plan involved a two-night stay in Valbone, but Oscar and I decided to just stay one night and go the next day.

For this ambitious trek, I equipped myself with a trusty shoulder bag and an additional plastic shopping bag that carried all the provisions I required. Given the somewhat inflated prices at local shops, I'd opted to bring my own food. The hike was primarily in the company of Oscar, although the others from the hostel forged ahead at their own pace. We commenced with a valley traverse before beginning our ascent into the mountains. The temperature soared to 31 degrees Celsius, yet curiously, I didn't find it excessively hot. Perhaps I had acclimatized sufficiently due to my earlier hiking exploits during this journey.

I decided to forge ahead solo at a certain point, parting ways with Oscar. The hardest section of the hike loomed before me – an uphill snake-like path that led to the summit. The relentless incline necessitated frequent pauses in the scant shade for respite before tackling the next stretch. As one turned to gaze back at the panorama, the view was nothing short of breathtaking. The valley seemed to dwindle in size with every gain in elevation, revealing an ever-expanding view.

Curiously, my choice of hiking gear raised eyebrows among fellow trekkers, who couldn't help but comment on my reliance on a humble plastic bag. Remarks such as "You've packed quite a lot, haven't you?", "That can't be easy!" and "been shopping" and to be fair, they were not far from the truth. Carrying my possessions in this manner presented an unconventional, but amusing, challenge.

After a demanding climb of approximately three hours, I triumphantly reached the summit, encircled by a panorama of majestic mountains. The experience was simply spectacular. At this juncture, one could opt for a brief, perilous, additional hike to an even higher peak. I decided to leave my belongings below and embark on this precarious ascent. Navigating the rocky terrain, I exercised utmost caution, prepared to adopt a sitting position should my footing slip. The summit provided an unparalleled 360-degree view, encompassing the entire mountain range. The journey downwards was undertaken with equal diligence. As Oscar was trailing behind me, I relayed messages of encouragement received from fellow hikers to bolster his motivation.

Descending presented one particularly precarious section with a precipitous drop and the necessity to cling to rocks while inching along the precipice. Although the inherent risk was undeniable, the presence of numerous fellow trekkers offered reassurance.

Upon reaching the base, the sight of a bar, shop and restaurant was nothing short of welcoming. In the company of my small group once we met up again, we paused for a well-earned break, during which I indulged in a slice of pizza. However, my accommodation was still a two-hour walk away, a prospect I found disappointing. I eventually decided to hitchhike, an endeavour that proved astonishingly swift – a generous Italian family graciously extended a ride and we engaged in lively conversation throughout the brief journey. They deposited me right at the doorstep of my accommodation, a basic lodging, but its elevated location offered commanding views of Theth. Sharing my room was another random traveller and together, we had to wage an ongoing battle against the unwelcome incursions of wasps, an insect both of us had a mutual dislike. Our tactics predominantly revolved around hiding behind doors and using shoes.

The following day saw me embarking on a double waterfall excursion. The first of the two waterfalls remained blissfully untouched by the tourist hordes and boasted a splendid azure pond at its base, ideal for a refreshing swim. The tranquillity, however, was short-lived, as an influx of tourists soon descended, eager to document the scene with their cameras like the news. Subsequently, I ventured to the second waterfall.

Having temporarily divested myself of luggage at the subsequent hostel, I embarked on the journey to the larger waterfall. This waterfall complex was of grander proportions, featuring a substantial pool at its base. Here, I went in the cooling waters, amplified by the mist. As I settled on a nearby rock, I indulged in sunflower seeds, relishing the time-consuming task of shelling each one. The shifting temperature was palpable as I left the area.

The following day commenced with a sumptuous buffet breakfast, following which I attempted to hitch a ride before my scheduled bus departure. Sadly I couldn't get a ride so had to take the bus. As I strolled, the booming echoes of thunder resonated through the mountains, creating an atmosphere enhanced by the dramatic backdrop of clouds and peaks. Boarding the bus, I witnessed an unremitting deluge of rain, which evoked a profound sense of sympathy for those hikers braving the elements. The roads, inundated and treacherous, bore testimony to the tempestuous weather, a stark contrast to the serene waterfall I'd encountered the previous day.

My trip led me to Shkoder once more, briefly, as I merely passed through. I took up residence in another city hostel, this one nestled in the heart of the urban landscape. It afforded me ample opportunity to explore various places of the city over the course of the day, thereby cultivating a more comprehensive impression of Shkoder.

The following morning I embarked on a brief bus journey to Podgorica, the capital of Montenegro. Heeding the warnings of travellers, who'd cautioned me against expecting much from this city, I arrived with minimal expectations. In hindsight, even these modest anticipations proved true. Podgorica, I discovered, boasted scant attractions – a church, an ancient bridge and a tower constituted the main highlights. The urban sprawl seemed meticulously designed, with an unmistakable communist-era aesthetic permeating the streetscape. In terms of architectural character, it was arguably one of the most unremarkable cities I had ever encountered. My stay, therefore, amounted to just a solitary night and I could scarcely wait to continue my journey. My initial plan of mountain hiking was ultimately abandoned due to the inclement weather, leading me to revise my itinerary in favour of a detour through Kosovo before eventually circling back to the mountains.

Kosovo

My journey continued as I ventured into the little-known and less-explored territory of Kosovo, a destination that had long piqued my curiosity. While some parts of this country carried an air of danger, my intention was to steer clear of those areas and explore the safer regions.

During my bus ride, a young Kosovar girl aged around 6 years old kept waving and saying hi to me, she spoke with a slight American accent. Her proficiency in English was little and she tried to share how she had learned the language in Kosovo. The people I encountered so far seemed friendly. In fact, this young girl, excited by the novelty of meeting an English person, even requested to take a photo with me. Her mother trusting me completely, asked me to keep an eye on her child while she stepped away to the shop on a bus break. It felt like a brush with celebrity status, a testament to the rarity of encounters with English individuals in this region. From what I had gathered, Kosovars held a deep fondness for the English, owing to our support for their country's bid for independence and their desire to distance themselves from Serbia. The political situation was indeed tense, with Russia, Serbia and China all asserting Kosovo's status as part of Serbia. I was determined to avoid the Serbia-Kosovo border during my stay.

The bus journey lasted approximately six hours, during which I would need to navigate through four border crossings. My goal was to engage with locals in this relatively unexplored country, as I believed it had much to offer.

Navigating the political intricacies of the region, I was aware of the need to choose my entry and exit points in Kosovo with utmost care. For if I were to enter Kosovo via Serbia and then depart through Kosovo, Serbia might still consider that I had not truly left its territory, given their stance on Kosovo's sovereignty. The border crossings in this region held significant political implications and I aimed to avoid any complications during my journey.

Upon reaching Kosovo, due to the limited number of passengers heading there, we were taken off the bus and transported by taxi to our destination. As I disembarked, a friendly local approached me, helping with my belongings and even purchasing a cold bottle of water for me. It was one of the warmest welcomes to a country I had ever experienced. The city itself was enchanting, with a river meandering through its heart and a bustling street adorned with cafes and bars.

My early impressions of Kosovo were overwhelmingly positive and I was eager to delve deeper into its culture and history.

After the bus dropped us outside the city, I sought information from a fellow traveller about the current situation. I then shared a taxi with other passengers from the bus and made my way to the hostel. The accommodation was modern and vibrantly designed and I quickly extended my stay to two nights, drawn by the welcoming atmosphere and positive experiences I had encountered so far.

Occasionally, the hostel experienced power cuts, a reminder of the country's economic challenges and the need for infrastructure improvements. This could be frustrating, especially when trying to book my flight. However, the hostel owner came to my rescue by sharing his hotspot, enabling me to secure my flight booking. Finding affordable flights had become somewhat of a personal profession during this trip and I managed to book one for two weeks ahead. This flight also included a stopover in Copenhagen, allowing me to explore the Danish capital for a few hours before my onward journey to London. I was pleased with my skills for discovering travel deals.

In all honesty, this hostel was pretty much perfect in many respects but there was this one nagging issue that put a damper on the whole experience. The smell, I mean it was absolutely revolting. You see this place had a policy of no shoes worn inside which generally is a good thing for cleanliness. To make up for it, they handed out slippers to guests, but here's the issue – those slippers were downright disgusting. I mean, they were so vile that the very essence of sock smell seemed to have taken up permanent residence in every nook and cranny of the hostel.

Most visitors to Kosovo seemed older travellers and I didn't encounter many individuals my age. Perhaps this was due to the limited activities on offer or the fact that Kosovo didn't hold as much appeal for younger tourists. Nevertheless, I was eager to uncover the hidden gems this unique destination had to offer.

Prizren (my first stop), though pleasant, didn't offer an overwhelming array of activities. It had its attractions like a fortress and a charming old town where I sampled some local buurack, though it couldn't quite compete with the buurack I had in Macedonia (my apologies, Kosovo). What made my time here truly special were the people I met at the hostel. We engaged in deep, meaningful conversations that spanned a wide range of topics, enriching my experience.

One memorable evening, we set out to find a bar and stumbled upon a hidden gem, a secret bar tucked behind a curtain, masquerading as a discreet door. The place had a trendy, almost ruin-bar-like vibe, complete with trees and a unique atmosphere that added to its ambience. But the standout dining experience came from an unassuming restaurant that, on the outside, seemed ordinary. However, upon stepping in, I was greeted by a surprising sight—a pond with ducks! It created an open and natural ambiance that I never expected to find in a restaurant.

The bustling main square was alive with activity, boasting numerous cafes and restaurants. This communal love for coffee culture was a recurring theme in the Balkans, where people would spend hours at cafes, contributing to the lively atmosphere.

I then took a bus to the capital Pristina, I had the pleasure of reuniting with Yaprak, whom I had met at a Couchsurfing meetup in Skopje. She provided me with valuable suggestions and insights into her travels. Later, I met her friend Mat, who was also an avid traveller, with Japan next on his list. In a kind and generous gesture, he insisted on covering all our expenses for food and drinks during our gathering.

My visit took an educational turn with a free walking tour of the city, during which I explored various places, including the Kosovo National Library, often dubbed one of the world's ugliest buildings. Inside, it felt ancient and spacious, yet it was heartening to see young people working diligently there, preserving the place's history.

During the tour, I talked with some travellers who shared an intriguing story about a small town they visited which was divided by a river. One side housed a predominantly Serbian population who believed Kosovo should belong to Serbia, while on the other side of the bridge lived Albanians aspiring for independence. The stark division made this place a unique and intriguing destination. As part of Serbia's goal to join the EU, resolving tensions with Kosovo was imperative, making this small town a microcosm of a much larger, complex issue. I had to see this, although it had its risks, I decided to take a bus there, planning to spend a night exploring this remarkable divide. To my delight, both the girls from our small walking group were equally intrigued and joined me, taking an early bus to meet me there the following day.

Upon my arrival, the place exuded a sense of calm and life seemed to be flowing at its usual pace. Moreover, it happened to be the most budget-friendly place I'd stayed in while traversing Kosovo. My interactions with the locals were limited, always accompanied by their cheerful attitude. I found it challenging to engage in anything more than brief conversations here.

As I settled in, I enjoyed a simple pasta meal and took a leisurely stroll around. I encountered the bridge which separated both sides, which, to my surprise, was not entirely open. It was guarded by police cars and barricades, though pedestrians could still cross. Interestingly, on the other side of the bridge, they used Serbian currency instead of the Euros that were in circulation on the Kosovo side. It added an element of intrigue to my journey, especially considering the lack of Google Street View for this area, making it feel like I was truly venturing into uncharted territory.

For my overnight stay, I opted for a budget Airbnb, relishing a good night's sleep before the significant day ahead. My Airbnb host expressed his fondness for English visitors and reassured me of the safety in the North side, a comforting sentiment from a local. With all my luggage, a friendly shopkeeper kindly allowed me to store it at his shop free of charge the next day while I explored, in return I brought some snacks from his shop.

The situation at the bridge was a source of anxiety. Online sources painted a different picture from the one I was experiencing firsthand. Occasionally, there were reports of gunfire aimed at the police. Crossing without insurance coverage beyond the bridge was unsettling, but I felt compelled to see for myself. On the South side stood Kosovo's police, while the Serbian police manned the North side, preventing cars from passing but allowing pedestrians to cross. The atmosphere around the bridge was tense, with few people in sight. Upon reaching the other side, the streets were lined with Serbian flags and the paint on the ground bore messages like "NATO not welcome." It was evident that they were prepared for any potential conflict. Graffiti on the walls expressed strong sentiments, including support for Russia and claims of Kosovo belonging to Serbia. The experience was surreal, offering a glimpse into a perspective rarely encountered.

For our safety, we meticulously planned our route and refrained from speaking loudly or in English to avoid drawing unwanted attention. Our initial destination was a hilltop church and when we inquired about entry, the locals seemed taken aback, as if they rarely received visitors. From there, we proceeded to a miner's monument atop another hill, affording us a splendid view of the city. Aside from a father and son en route to the church, we encountered no other tourists. We then embarked on a half-hour uphill trek to reach the fortress, which we had entirely to ourselves. Approximately 20% of the vehicles passing us were emergency vehicles, but they paid us no attention. We were also accompanied by a friendly dog on our ascent. Crossing back over the bridge safely was a relief and we celebrated our unique journey at a renowned café nearby. Remarkably, I even spotted some British soldiers who were peacekeeping during my visit, a remarkable coincidence given that there were only about 84 stationed in Kosovo.

My next destination was Peja, a city in Kosovo nestled near the Macedonia border, known for its picturesque mountains that invite hikers like me. I chose a hostel that offered the option of pitching tents at an incredibly affordable rate, but for my first night, I opted for the comfort of a dorm room. After a long and eventful day, I needed a good night's sleep.

The following morning, fuelled by a complimentary breakfast, I laid out my plans for the day. My goal was to visit a resort that boasted a waterfall, a cave and a restaurant right by the water's edge. The only hiccup was the nearly three-hour walk to reach it on foot. So, I decided to try hitchhiking when I was on a more direct route and after just five cars, a friendly man picked me up. It turned out he worked at the resort, so I found myself conveniently dropped off right at the entrance. During the ride, we engaged in pleasant conversation about travel and Kosovo and his act of kindness saved me from an extensive hike.

My first stop at the resort was the waterfall, followed by a visit to the caves, for which I paid a nominal 2 euros for admission. A group guide accompanied me and thoughtfully translated everything into English, enhancing the experience. The cave, a testament to the passage of over 2 million years, was formed by water centuries ago and housed a colony of bats.

Finally, I concluded my excursion at the resort's restaurant, where I savoured a delightful cappuccino. By the water's edge, seating was scarce, but I found a spot higher up that offered captivating views. It was a modern and charming resort. When it came time to settle the bill, the gentleman who had given me a lift earlier insisted I needn't pay, despite my insistence. In the end, we took a photo together to commemorate the gesture.

Returning, I attempted to hitchhike once more but had no luck this time around. Few cars seemed to be headed in the direction I needed, so I embarked on an 11-kilometer walk down a road. Along the way, I was taken aback by the pollution, which made for an unpleasant experience.

On my final day in Peja, I embarked on a several-hour walk along a road to reach a canyon. Upon reaching a restaurant with a splendid view, I indulged in a healthy salad before retracing my steps. The people of Kosovo take great pride in their canyon, which stands as one of their most cherished natural treasures. I would have loved to explore more of it, but doing so would ideally require access to a car, as there were few, if any, established paths.

My next leg of the journey involved travelling from Peja to Ulcinj on the west coast of Montenegro. Unfortunately, the prices remained somewhat high due to the time of year, but I remained hopeful that they would taper as I ventured further up the coast. My flight was booked for the 6th and I aimed to explore some of the coastline and perhaps squeeze in some hiking before spending a night either in Sarajevo or at the airport before my departure.

The coach ride initially took us through a series of mountains, offering breathtaking views of Kosovo. At the border, the patrol seemed to conduct meticulous inspections of all luggage. When the border patrol officer boarded the bus and inquired about my destination, I responded with "Montenegro," to which he simply replied, "Okay." Sometimes, I wondered if these questions were merely meant to fluster travellers. With the prospect of sunny weather and a return to the coastline ahead, I couldn't help but look forward to the next leg of my adventure.

Upon arriving at my hostel in Ulcinj, named the Pirate Hostel, I was greeted by a pirate-themed atmosphere, which added a unique touch to the experience.

The warm welcome included an introduction to all the local activities on offer. That evening, the hostel organized a meal for around 30 of us, which surely left a memorable impression on the hosts. Following dinner, we headed to a bar for a few drinks and I relished the opportunity to spend time with this fantastic group of fellow travellers.

The following day, I embarked on a delightful walk commencing from the historic part of the city and tracing the coastline. The azure waters stretched as far as the eye could see, though the shore was a bit rocky. The leisurely stroll took about an hour and upon reaching the end, I found myself at one of the lengthiest coastlines in the Balkans. I marvelled at how far the sandy shore extended into the sea, prompting me to sunbathe for a while on the beach. My plan was to then return to the hostel by heading in a different direction.

In the evening, the hostel had organized a beach sunset event, drawing a substantial group of us. For a nominal fee of 5 euros, we were transported to the beach, where we swam and spent quality time together, chatting and enjoying the water until darkness descended. I cherished these moments. Later that evening, a group of us ventured to a local bar. While the party scene wasn't a dominant feature of the town, with enough fellow travellers from the hostel, it could turn into a memorable night out.

On what was planned to be my final day in Ulcinj, we embarked on the hostel's flagship event—a boat trip to explore the local beaches and the surrounding area. Our day began with an early rise at 9 am as we gathered at a waiting car that would transport us to the boat. It was a brief 15-minute drive and we made a pit stop at a shop to stock up on provisions for our journey. With a group of about eight participants, we were in for a fantastic day ahead. Our boat driver was exceptionally friendly and ensured that we didn't feel rushed throughout the trip.

Our first destination was a set of caves. I had no specific expectations, but the experience turned out to be incredibly enjoyable. The water was a stunning shade of blue and pleasantly warm for swimming. While the cave had sea urchins along its sides, once you passed them, it was safe inside and you could stand comfortably. Afterwards, we swam through a small opening that led to another area—a dark yet intriguing space where the play of light filtering through the water created a mesmerizing effect. Our guide then informed us that we needed to swim underwater below the rocks to reach the other side of some rocks. It added a thrilling dimension to our adventure and I absolutely loved it.

After everyone clambered back into the boat and had a chance to recover from all the swimming, we sailed to a beach that could only be reached by boat. The water here was too shallow for swimming, but it was an ideal spot to play some music and relax. I assumed this marked the conclusion of our excursion, but to our surprise, our captain took us to another part of the island, where there were opportunities for cliff jumping. Initially, I told myself I wouldn't partake in such risky activities, but when we reached the jumping spot, it was about 3 meters high. Although no one in the group seemed eager to take the plunge, I decided to push myself and give it a shot. It was a tad nerve-wracking, as timing the jump in sync with the steps was crucial, but it felt incredibly rewarding to be the first in our group to take the leap.

To our amazement, our captain then led us up to the top of the cliff where there was a house. We initially thought he was joking, as the structure seemed to merge a lighthouse with a conventional dwelling. However, much to our astonishment, he produced a key and unlocked the door, revealing his family's house. We were taken aback and amused by the unexpected turn of events. He proceeded to give us a tour of the house, sharing various treasures and fascinating artifacts he had acquired during his diving expeditions. It was one of the most unique tours I had experienced, all from the deck of a boat. Our day on the boat fostered a deeper connection among the group, making it all the more bittersweet to bid farewell, especially considering that most of them would be departing the following day.

As my time in the region dwindled, I made the decision to not head North, given the associated costs and unfavourable hiking conditions due to the weather. Fortunately, "Co Co," the hostel owner, had an opportunity for me to volunteer for a few days and I eagerly took on the role. Having become familiar with the area, I felt somewhat responsible for leading groups to the best cafes and eateries during their evening outings.

During this period, I found myself contemplating how I would adapt to normality after spending so much time with people and being constantly social. I knew it would be a challenge. Although I had taken a job in a bar upon my return to England, it just wouldn't be the same as the hostel experience and I couldn't shake the feeling that I would want for more adventures. I was already counting down the days until my next grand trip, which was slated for Asia.

My volunteer duties typically commenced around 10 AM. I'd begin by emptying all the bins in the hostel, including those in the rooms, which was quite a task and required multiple trips down the road to the main bins. Next, I'd move on to cleaning the kitchen, which involved wiping down surfaces and mopping the floor. This usually took 1 to 2 hours and after that, I'd assist the other volunteers in cleaning the rooms to complete our tasks. It was a relaxed atmosphere and once you finished your duties, you had the freedom to enjoy your afternoon and evening. I found satisfaction in this work, as it kept me occupied during my remaining days before my flight.

Living this lifestyle brought me immense happiness. Sometimes, it was refreshing to focus on relaxation rather than constantly moving from place to place, which could occasionally feel like a chore. Over the following days, I became more efficient in my work, often completing my tasks by noon. This left me with the afternoon to enjoy beach trips or anything else I fancied. The beaches were excellent for socializing, playing games in the water and occasionally lighting a beachside bonfire.

On one occasion, I recall returning from the beach with a Polish guy and other guests/volunteers. We were jamming to the local music played by the driver, even pretending our bottles were guitars. The driver then turned off the lights in the cab and I began flashing my light while the Polish guy mimicked playing the guitar. It was a hilarious moment and everyone was laughing.

I decided to go on the boat for a second time because it was quite affordable at £12 and I was in the company of an enjoyable group of people. During this outing, we encountered some jellyfish in the water, which made us cautious when entering and leaving the cave. There was a humorous Polish guy who seemed to have a childlike spirit; he paid little attention to the boat driver's instructions. However, he later surprised us all by successfully making a fire on land and with the driver's assistance, catching and preparing sea urchins. It was my first time trying them and I found their taste reminiscent of salty salmon, with a delightfully soft texture that allowed you to easily squish them. These sea urchins were exceptional due to the pristine clear water they came from. Opening them was an intriguing experience; if not killed properly, they would move in your hand, resembling something out of a sci-fi movie. Afterwards, we returned to the jumping spot where I took the plunge into the water. One of the guys in our group amazed everyone with a belly flip, seamlessly transforming it into a surprising dive.

My connection with my friends in the hostel grew stronger and it was becoming more and more like a second home. I had grown to know the bar staff, the restaurant workers and even some of the café workers in the area. The culture in Eastern Europe felt incredibly friendly and it seemed like everyone knew everyone else. It was a stark contrast to some Western countries where people often felt more detached.

When it was finally time to leave, it was difficult because I knew I wouldn't be returning anytime soon and the hostel had started to feel like a familiar and comfortable place. I said my goodbyes and left around 11 AM, catching a bus to Podgorica and then another bus to Sarajevo. Fortunately, the bus stop was only a half-hour walk from the airport, where I intended to spend the night before my flight.

During the bus ride, I struck up a conversation with an English guy who had just arrived and had no plans. We ended up going for some food and a beer together. This was particularly helpful for me because I didn't have any local currency, so I paid him some Euros and he bought food and drinks for both of us.

Upon arriving at the airport, I discovered that it closed at midnight. This meant I would have to walk to a nearby petrol station and spend some time there until the airport reopened. I met some local people who were living in Copenhagen and we chatted while we walked to the gas station together where we would spend the night. It was heartwarming to see two older gentlemen travelling with big maps and backpacks. Their passion for exploration was truly inspiring.

As I sat waiting for the airport to reopen, I couldn't help but reflect on the incredible experiences I had during my time in the Balkans. The friendships I had formed, the breathtaking landscapes I had witnessed and the adventurous spirit that had carried me through it all had left an indelible mark on me. While I knew the journey had come to an end for now, I couldn't help but eagerly anticipate my next adventure, counting down the days.

Denmark

After a smooth flight during which I managed to secure a window seat thanks to a fellow passenger's seat change, I slept for about two hours, just enough to keep me going. Arriving at Copenhagen Airport was a bit surreal after spending the past few months in the Balkans, where time sometimes seemed to stand still and modernity and cleanliness were rare sights. Passport control was swift and the friendly officer stamped my passport without any hassles.

With some energy left, I decided to head straight to the city. It was a stark contrast to the Balkans, as Copenhagen is known as one of the most expensive cities in the world to live. My day trip would be a whirlwind tour, perhaps a bit rushed, but I was eager to explore.

One of my most anticipated stops in Copenhagen was the community of Christiania. This self-governing area is one of the rarest places in Europe. In 1971, a group of hippies took over an abandoned army base and transformed it into a self-sustaining community. While the Danish government initially resisted, they have since come to an agreement for the most part to leave it alone.

One of the most striking differences in Christiania is its rules. Marijuana is legal within the community and running is prohibited, as it might cause panic, fearing a government raid. Occasionally, authorities do try to crack down on the illegal street dealers in an area known as "Pusher Street." Christiania's central location in Copenhagen makes it easy to find and there are multiple entrances.

The moment you enter Christiania, you're greeted by vibrant artwork that adorns the streets and buildings. The art often conveys meaningful messages about caring for the world, respecting community rules, living without regrets and more. It's clear that this place is home to open-minded individuals who want to live life on their own terms, outside the constraints of societal norms.

One particularly impactful piece of art was a statue holding a globe with the words "The world is in our hands." It was a poignant reminder of the responsibility we all share for the planet. I also witnessed a garbage truck adorned with artwork, making it a beautiful sight. The main area for dealing and buying marijuana is Pusher Street and signs abound, reminding visitors not to take photos/videos, a rule that must be respected to avoid trouble. Dealers in Christiania don't want to be tourist attractions and are simply trying to make a living.

Many people were conducting transactions, which appeared to be quick and discreet. The scent of marijuana hung in the air and tourists were taking it all in while respecting the no-photo rule. The locals in Christiania had a distinct look, often wearing bucket hats and exuding a hippie vibe. I saw groups of people laughing and relaxing, embodying the community's laid-back spirit.

In Christiania, nobody owns a home; you can only rent. If the community members don't like you, they can vote to have you leave, effectively forcing you out. I also ventured into a skatepark, both indoor and outdoor, though there weren't any skaters at that moment. I could only imagine the vibrant atmosphere when it's bustling with activity. Unfortunately, I was only able to take a few photos of the places where it was allowed, so I highly recommend visiting if this unique environment appeals to you.

For the remainder of my time in Copenhagen, I embarked on a stroll around the city. However, it was a bit challenging with all my luggage in tow and fatigue had set in. I would have loved to spend a few more days in Copenhagen to truly soak in its atmosphere, but my tight schedule didn't allow for this. The weather was beautiful, with warm sunshine and a refreshing breeze, reminiscent of my first trip to Budapest. The canals and people cycling around the city reminded me of Amsterdam.

To ensure I had enough time for my flight, I made my way back to the airport a few hours in advance, bidding farewell to Copenhagen and reflecting on the incredible experiences I had throughout my journey in the Balkans and this brief but memorable stop in Denmark.

England

Back in England, I found myself with some free time after catching up with work and friends. However, my travel bug was still very much alive and I knew I needed to find a way to continue my adventures. Given my limited budget, I explored opportunities to work either in the UK or abroad to fund my future travels.

I managed to secure a job at Vestry, an old club/bar that I used to visit frequently. This job would be a valuable opportunity for me to gain bar skills, which would open doors for working abroad. I even contemplated the possibility of working in Australia, where the pay is good and it could be a rewarding yet challenging experience. I recognised the advantages of the excellent working holiday visa arrangement between the UK and Australia.

Returning to England had its challenges, though. Many of my friends were at university and there was a prevailing societal expectation to settle down and follow the conventional path. This pressure to conform to societal norms was something I shared with fellow travellers who had similar experiences. However, I was determined to find ways to continue my nomadic lifestyle and avoid the traditional route for as long as possible.

I had some exciting ideas in my head, including the dream of opening my own hostel. The idea of creating a unique space, hosting events and ensuring that everyone has a great time appealed to me. While I knew it would be a lot of hard work, I believed it would be a fulfilling endeavour that would also provide a sustainable income. It was a concept I wanted to explore further in the future.

In the meantime, I dedicated time to learning Spanish, a valuable skill that would not only allow me to travel to South America but also enable me to communicate with more non-English speakers. I felt a sense of responsibility to make an effort to speak the local language rather than expecting others to speak English for my convenience.

I eagerly anticipated saving up enough money to embark on my next adventure in Asia. The world was full of opportunities and experiences waiting to be discovered and I was determined to continue my journey of exploration and discovery.

Morocco

I opted for Morocco as my next destination, primarily due to England's chilly weather and my desire to try my hand at some surfing. I had plans to explore Asia in the future, but I didn't want to miss Christmas this time around. My decision to visit Morocco had been brewing for some time and I had already conducted extensive research on the country, building up anticipation for the trip. My interests spanned the beautiful beaches, amazing cuisine and rich cultural experiences it had to offer.

My flight was scheduled to land in Agadir, which marked the southernmost point I intended to visit in Morocco. Agadir, a relatively small city, had undergone modernization efforts after being severely damaged by an earthquake and subsequently rebuilt.

While waiting at the airport, I struck up a conversation with a few fellow travellers. Among them was a woman flying out to meet someone she had previously encountered and a couple who were exploring various parts of Morocco. We engaged in a friendly chat and the couple eventually asked if I'd like to share a taxi once we landed, I gladly accepted, deeming it a stroke of luck.

On the plane, amusingly enough, I found myself seated next to the English woman with whom I had chatted earlier. It turned out we had both chosen seats randomly. After a three-hour flight, we touched down and I had to navigate the border patrol. The process was rather sluggish, with the officers posing a few queries, such as my occupation and the address of my stay. The officer appeared somewhat surprised when I mentioned that I didn't currently have a job, a response that seemed to raise a red flag for them.

Planning the initial stages of my trip presented some challenges. My flight arrived late, so I was glad I would be sharing a taxi which would be waiting for me when we landed. Also, I had the foresight to book an Airbnb in Agadir, where I could spend a night before embarking on a bus journey to a surfing hostel further up the coast.

Given that Agadir's residences lacked specific addresses and the local road names appeared incredibly confusing to me, I resorted to showing the officer the location of my Airbnb on my phone. His tone quickly turned aggressive, demanding the exact address even as I pointed to the road name. He stamped my passport with visible irritation and tossed it back at me in a rather confrontational manner.

Following the rather unpleasant encounter at the border, I met up with the couple with whom I'd agreed to share a taxi. I was pleasantly surprised by the driving in Morocco, which was notably better than my experiences in Egypt. Our driver, who also happened to be their Airbnb host, spoke excellent English and doubled as a surfing instructor. We engaged in a delightful conversation about Morocco and he assured me of the laid-back atmosphere in the country.

As we drove through the streets, I noticed palm trees lining the roadsides, occasionally adorned with locals selling fruits to passers-by. Our driver also shared an interesting story, mentioning that many Muslims in Morocco indulged in drinking and partying, despite their religious background. He dropped me off right outside my Airbnb, which I had previously booked—a private room with shared facilities, including a kitchen and toilet. Given the absence of hostels in Agadir, it was an economical choice that allowed me to explore the city at my own pace.

In the evening, I decided to take a stroll and explore the local neighbourhood. I noticed a few curious glances from the residents, but no one bothered me. The streets mostly consisted of gravel, contributing to a dusty atmosphere and there was a noticeable amount of litter along the roadside. I observed impoverished individuals scavenging through the rubbish, salvaging anything of value to sell for sustenance. Unfortunately, the Moroccan government did not provide adequate rubbish collection services in the area, leading to a build-up of waste.

I also ventured into a local food café, where I enjoyed a panini, fries and a beverage for a mere £1.50. The young man working there engaged me in conversation, expressing admiration for my travels. I took care not to give too much information, particularly after my past experiences in Egypt.

After my meal, I decided it was time to get a good night's rest before my journey to the surfing hostel the next day. With a few hours to spare in the morning, I left my luggage at the apartment and took a stroll to explore the Agadir market. To my surprise, the market was more relaxed than I had anticipated and I was hardly bothered by vendors. Most people spoke French to me, suggesting that this area didn't see many tourists passing through. I sipped on a smoothie and observed the market's bustling yet well-organized chaos. Vendors shouted their wares, the sound of tea being poured filled the air and metal poles clanged as stall owners set up their merchandise. At one point, I noticed a man on a rooftop working with hot sparks falling dangerously close to a shop below. The locals seemed unbothered, except for the shopkeeper who hurriedly protected his goods from potential damage.

Upon reaching the Taghazout hostel, I was greeted with my first taste of Moroccan tea. It was a delightful introduction to this unique tea culture, featuring a preparation method involving an abundance of herbs and precisely the right amount of sugar. The tea is poured and then returned to the teapot to be poured again, ensuring that all the flavours are extracted. A key aspect is gradually increasing the distance between the teapot and the glass to allow the bubbles to settle, resulting in a perfect Moroccan tea. Unlike traditional English tea, Moroccan tea is robust and served without milk, brimming with flavours and utterly delicious.

The hostel itself was nothing short of fantastic, having earned recognition as the second-best hostel in Africa a few years back. It boasted a rooftop area with foosball (table football) offering breathtaking sea views, especially during sunset and served a generous and complimentary breakfast and dinner for a small fee.

Eager to immerse myself in the surf scene, I wanted to get acquainted with fellow travellers during my stay in this surf-rich region of Morocco. On a Friday evening, the hostel provided a complimentary couscous dinner, which turned out to be a fantastic and incredibly tasty meal.

Considering my lack of experience in surfing, I wisely decided to sign up for a lesson offered by the hostel at a reasonable cost. I was not alone in this endeavour, as a few others were also trying their hand at surfing for the first time. The day was scorching hot, with temperatures reaching around 35 degrees Celsius, as indicated by the car's thermometer. To protect myself from the sun, I applied water-resistant sun cream to exposed parts of my body and borrowed some zinc from a fellow surfer to shield my face from the sun—a handy and effective solution. The lesson also included transportation to the beach, which was a convenient arrangement.

As we reached the beach, we were confronted with cold water, around 18 degrees Celsius, necessitating the use of wetsuits. In my eagerness, I initially put my wetsuit on backward, a rookie mistake quickly rectified. After a brief briefing and tutorial on how to stand on the board, which was quite challenging in the sweltering black wetsuit under the blazing sun, we eagerly ventured into the water.

Catching the waves proved to be relatively easy, but standing upright on the board presented its own set of challenges. The process of pulling oneself up and maintaining balance was trickier than it appeared, often resulting in me tumbling into the waves. Fortunately, my confidence in the water allayed any concerns about drowning, as the waves were small and there was minimal current to push us down the shoreline.

The surf instructor was quite helpful in assisting us to catch the waves by providing a boost, allowing us to body surf initially. However, standing up on the board proved to be a far more challenging task. Despite numerous attempts, I struggled to achieve a stable standing position. It was somewhat frustrating, but by the end of the day, I did manage to stand up once. We surfed until sunset and I was among the last surfers to come ashore.

As I sat on my board, awaiting the perfect wave with the sunset painting the horizon, I experienced a moment of sheer magic and tranquillity. I found myself immersed in a serene moment. It was a time of calmness and a wave of happiness washed over me. As I sat there, I couldn't help but reflect on the journey that had brought me to this remarkable point in my life.

While I hadn't completely mastered standing on the board, I felt content with my progress and was eager to give it another shot the following day. Exhausted from the day's efforts, I returned to the hostel that night and enjoyed a pizza while engaging in lively conversations with my fellow hostel mates around a campfire, all the while indulging in card games.

One notable difference in this hostel compared to others was the absence of alcohol in the town. Obtaining an alcohol license was notoriously challenging in the area, leading to very few people consuming alcohol at the hostel, a unique experience for me which was refreshing.

On the second day, I decided not to do another lesson, opting instead to practise what I had learned. Along with some new-found friends from the hostel, we rented boards from the hostel and set out early in the afternoon. It was during this outing that I had my first wipeout experience in the water. I caught a rather substantial wave, which sent me soaring high above the water before tumbling into the wave's depths. It felt like being inside a tumble dryer, a disorienting and somewhat frightening experience. Nonetheless, I remained remarkably composed in the water and within a few seconds, I resurfaced. Such experiences are par for the course in surfing and every surfer encounters them. Exhausted from the day's efforts, I took a much-needed shower and went straight to bed, hoping to recover for the next day's adventures.

On my last day of surfing, I decided to challenge myself by attempting to ride the green waves, the waves just before they break. To achieve this, I had to paddle past the white waves, which required both energy and technique, as it's easy to get pushed back to shore. To navigate past these waves, I often had to endure a few impacts to progress. This was when I decided to put into practice a new technique, I had watched online the day before, known as the 'turtle' technique. It involved lying on your board, flipping over underneath it and allowing the wave to crash onto your board, thus shielding you. Afterwards you could resurface and continue swimming. While it initially felt a bit scary, once I tried it, it was a fantastic feeling and allowed me to get beyond the white waves. It marked the first time I had ventured past these waves, creating a more relaxed atmosphere. Beyond the white waves, I could either lie on my board or use my arms to gently move around, providing a meditative experience. However, I had to be cautious as the current was quite strong and a competition was occupying most of the beach, leaving only a small area for surfing. The current threatened to push me towards the rocks, so I needed to stay within the safe zone.

I thoroughly enjoyed my time at the hostel and the surfing experience, but I noticed that the waves were deteriorating, which signalled that it was time to move on to my next destination. I decided on Marrakesh as my next stop. A friendly Italian couple, whom I had befriended, were headed in the same direction and kindly offered me a ride. The journey featured roads in good condition and it offered picturesque views of small villages and houses along the roadside, piquing my curiosity about exploring them.

The Italian couple's generosity was heartwarming, as they didn't expect anything from me upon our arrival. I found myself just a short walk away from the hostel in Marrakesh. The hostel was tucked away in an alleyway that, admittedly, seemed a bit sketchy at first, but all was well. It was a riad-style hostel, featuring a lounge area with no roof, but a cover to stop the sun and rooms spread across three floors in the middle section. Additionally, it boasted a rooftop that provided a captivating view of the surrounding buildings, igniting thoughts of the potential for parkour, given how closely spaced the buildings were.

Marrakesh was a city I had mentally prepared myself to explore, having received warnings about its bustling, at times chaotic streets and the likelihood of attracting a lot of attention. My initial impression was the overwhelming presence of mopeds on both the roads and pathways, which could be quite scary. It felt as though I might get run over at any moment and the noise and pollution they generated, spewing clouds of noxious smoke, made navigating the streets an adventure.

I soon discovered that sticking to the left side of the path was the safest approach, as mopeds tended to pass on the right. This rule held true even within the medina, the ancient city's historic centre, where the limited space was further constrained by shop stalls encroaching onto the paths. The medina also featured the occasional house and the odd donkey, creating an environment of organised chaos.

I was taken aback by the sheer size of the medina; it felt like I was wandering endlessly and had barely scratched the surface. The medina attempted some form of organisation, with certain areas designated for food vendors and carpenters kept slightly away from the main stalls. Perhaps I had honed my skills in avoiding hassle because I was pleasantly surprised by the relatively low level of people trying to sell me things. While vendors would call out as I passed, it was a far cry from my experiences in Egypt, where I'd often been followed or had people physically obstruct my path.

The following day, after breakfast, we embarked on a trip into the Imill Mountains. There were three of us since I met some guys who were keen to go in the morning. We decided that taking a taxi would be the best option. We knew the going rate was between 200-300 dirhams and we aimed for a fair price within that range. However, upon reaching the taxi stand, the driver initially demanded 500 dirhams, nearly double what we knew was reasonable. "Good price," he asserted, but we knew it wasn't. Fortunately, one of us spoke French and managed to haggle the price down to 300 dirhams, a much more acceptable rate when divided among the three of us and a near 50% reduction.

The journey commenced with several stops, including one at a random government building where the driver filled out some paperwork for himself and another at a shop for cigarettes, which he later smoked in the car, enveloping us in a cloud of smoke. In total, there were four stops, with one occasion where we thought he might leave us stranded in the desert, but it turned out he simply needed to use the restroom.

After a scenic drive through the mountains, we paid the driver and set out to find accommodation. Surprisingly, the street was quite commercialised, with shops, cafes and rental places for hiking supplies. Many locals frequented these establishments, which kept costs very reasonable. After a short walk, we approached a local who had rooms available and we managed to negotiate a rate of 150 dirhams, an excellent deal. We were provided with complimentary tea, which the generous owner brought over. We didn't have heating and slept on mattresses on the floor, but it was all part of the experience.

We found a charming café by the river, offering both indoor and outdoor seating, where we enjoyed a tasty panini. The service was a bit slow, but the overall experience more than made up for it. Along the way, we stopped at a shop to purchase supplies for our hike. The shopkeeper grew impatient with us as we declined to buy his sugared nuts and he became quite aggressive whilst handling our money. We also purchased some water which was in a conspicuously bright pink plastic bottle, which appeared somewhat dubious, but it turned out to be perfectly safe. Towards the end of our transaction, the rather irate shopkeeper scolded us to "stop 'zig-zagging,'" a memorable quote that provided us with a bit of humour to share amongst ourselves throughout the remainder of our journey. What great customer service - not!

We had a well-planned hike marked out on our map that would take us to a waterfall and a local village known as Aroumd. It turned out to be one of the most contrasting hikes I had ever experienced. One moment, we were trudging through a rocky desert with sand beneath our feet and the next, we found ourselves on a muddy path alongside a babbling stream. Locals were a common sight along the trails and while a few offered their services as guides, they generally left us alone.

However, a couple of guides managed to catch our attention with an intriguing story: they claimed that Richard Branson, the founder of Virgin Galactic, was staying nearby. We couldn't confirm this with absolute certainty, but we did some checking and discovered that he had recently invested in a hotel in the vicinity. So, perhaps they were telling the truth after all.

Our first stop on the hike was a waterfall, where a little café stand served local tangerine and orange juice. What I found particularly charming was the design of the café, which featured a fountain connected to the waterfall, keeping the oranges cool. We also indulged in some fresh water from the waterfall, which was perfectly safe to drink. Continuing our path, we reached the mountain village, composed of stone houses and donkeys laden with local supplies making their way up the steep slopes.

As we continued along the road, it suddenly opened up to one of the most breathtaking views I had ever encountered. In the distance, the imposing Toubkal mountain, the largest in North Africa, still bore a snowy crown. Below it, the landscape transitioned from sand and rocks to lush trees and greenery, accompanied by the distant sounds of a small waterfall. It was an awe-inspiring moment.

The village itself beckoned us to explore. I was captivated by its picturesque appearance from afar and was eager to witness firsthand how its inhabitants lived. We ventured onto some random roads, passing by a farm area and exchanging greetings with locals along the way. The pathways around the village featured numerous rocky trails and many steps, given the steep hillside. Local children greeted us warmly and even invited us to join in a game of football.

According to my maps, there should have been a café in the village. However, we noticed a sign that read 'cyber cafe.' Thinking it would be a nice opportunity to interact with the locals, we decided to seek out the café. We followed the signs, got a bit lost and eventually approached some locals to inquire about the café's location in French. Initially, they thought we were asking about internet access, but when we mentioned it was a café, they burst into laughter, saying there was no café to be found. So, perhaps the signs were either outdated or intended to amuse tourists while giving the locals a good laugh.

Afterwards, we attempted to venture a bit farther into the valley, but some shopkeepers insisted that we turn back and did not let us further without a guide. So, we embarked on the long walk back. We decided to grab some food, but most places were still closed due to the early evening hour. After a stroll around town, we settled on a place that had a gas heater to keep us warm. We endured a lengthy wait because they had to set up the kitchen for us. We positioned ourselves near the gas heater to keep warm, but people constantly left the door open letting the freezing air come in, which was quite frustrating and, oddly enough, amusing due to their unawareness. One individual walked in, left the door open, we closed it and then they promptly went out, leaving the door ajar once more, which made it quite funny. Finally, after about an hour and a half, our food arrived and it was delicious. I indulged in a satisfying pasta meal and we decided to stay for a hot drink afterward, mainly because it was nice and warm and we had no desire to return to our 4-degree room with no heating.

After, a kind German solo hiker joined us for a chat and we learnt something that sent shivers down our spines. In 2018, four years before our visit, two young hikers had been walking in Imill, likely taking a similar route to ours and going a bit further. They had decided to camp under the stars on the mountain, not suspecting that their lives were in imminent danger. Later that night, they were brutally attacked by a large group of men affiliated with ISIS and were beheaded on camera. The gruesome incident had made headlines worldwide and we couldn't believe we had been unaware of such a horrifying event that had occurred so close to where we were. That evening, we spent hours reflecting on how naive we had been. We thought a shopkeeper was merely angry when it was a police checkpoint meant to deter people from going further. We also considered the lack of tourists in the area and how persistent the guides had been. While it was possible that there was no current danger as the Moroccan government had tightened security in the region, we still felt like complete fools. Adding to the sorrow was the fact that I had met many travellers around that same age who were also into hiking and similar activities, making me realise that I could have been someone like them a few years ago and met that tragic fate.

It served as a stark reminder of the world we live in today, emphasizing the need to never let one's guard down. It was an emotional day, but we tried not to let the news spoil the amazing experiences we had earlier in the day.

The following day, we shared a large taxi back to Marrakesh, where I spent a night in a hostel. To save money, I opted for a 14-bed dormitory. The bunk beds were triple-deckers and I ended up on the top bunk, which was a bit unnerving due to the lack of a proper barrier. To put my mind at ease, I ingeniously fashioned a makeshift barrier using my towel, tying it securely at each end of the bed. It made me feel a bit safer during the night.

The next day was spent planning my next moves, including a 40-minute walk to an ATM that I thought wouldn't charge me any fees, only to be surprised with an unexpected charge. I also ventured into Marrakech at night with a few fellow hostel guests and it turned out to be a great time. Derek, one of the guys I quickly befriended, was particularly amusing. He had a knack for scoring free smoothie samples from food vendors and playing their own game with them, which was highly entertaining. As a group, we were frequently called "skinny" by the vendors, which we found amusing as they were just trying to entice us to buy their food.

Many travellers often opt for organised desert tours during their Morocco adventures, but due to my budget constraints and ample time, I decided to plan my desert excursion independently. The following morning, I shared a taxi to the bus station for my next destination, Ouarzazate. Situated to the east of Marrakesh, Ouarzazate is a famous city known for being the backdrop of numerous films and TV series, including classics like Ben Hur and Prison Break (one of my favourites).

Upon arriving, I walked to a hostel where I discovered that I was only the second guest there. The other person informed me that he initially had the entire hostel to himself for the past two days, indicating that it wasn't a particularly touristy spot. This was precisely what I was looking for—a less crowded destination where I could experience the authentic Morocco.

As I explored the city, I noticed that it had a much more relaxed vibe. There were hardly any aggressive sellers in my face and everywhere I looked, I saw locals rather than tourist traps. I dined at a restaurant where I had a tuna sandwich and I was the sole patron. The owner was incredibly kind and even brought out some complimentary tea and olives, striking up a friendly conversation. It genuinely felt like he cared about providing a good experience rather than just chasing money. In appreciation, I left him a generous tip.

During my stay in Ouarzazate, I took the opportunity to explore a few of the museums in the city. While I found them interesting, I couldn't help but wish that I had a deeper knowledge of the films that were featured in these museums.

After arriving at the bus station, I embarked on a 10-hour journey to reach Merzouga, the desert town where I would be staying. The journey was rather monotonous, as it mainly consisted of desert landscapes with occasional interesting views. What proved to be frustrating was the frequent stops along the way. I was eager to reach my destination and check in at my hostel.

Upon my arrival in Merzouga, I checked into my hostel and met Hassan the owner, where everyone was already having dinner. Thankfully, I was warmly welcomed and invited to join in. The hostel owner was incredibly friendly and immediately made me feel at home. I was relieved to find fellow travellers heading in the same direction and doing it solo, it seemed like everyone I spoke to had plans for the desert tour.

That evening, we gathered around a campfire and engaged in conversations, but I decided to turn in early as I was quite tired from the long bus journey. (Surprisingly, even sitting down doing nothing for an extended period can be mentally exhausting.)

The following morning, we were served a breakfast of pancakes, bread and tea, which was incredibly sweet due to the addition of six large sugar cubes – a Moroccan specialty. I learned that I could rent sandboards at a reasonable price and use them for the day, so I teamed up with Lucas, a fellow traveller I met at the hostel, to share one. It was about a 10-minute walk to reach the dunes and as I approached the desert, I was awestruck by the sight of the enormous sand dunes in the distance. I had never seen anything quite like it, even during my time in Egypt.

I was thrilled at the prospect of climbing to the top of one of the dunes for a panoramic view of the desert, a full 360-degree experience. The ascent was challenging, with the hot sand making the hike tough, especially while carrying the sandboard to some of the higher points. Once I reached a good height, I strapped my feet onto the board and prepared to descend. Sandboarding proved to be quite different from snowboarding, as the sand was much thinner. This meant that I could only go straight, as any attempt to turn caused the sand to get stuck on the board, leading to a fall. Perhaps if the sand were denser, it would have felt more like snowboarding.

While Lucas had his turn with the sandboard, I decided to hike to the summit of the dune. The climb was arduous because for every step I took, I would slip back down the sand, losing about 50% of my progress. I had to take several breaks along the way. However, when I finally reached the top, it was incredibly rewarding. On one side, I had a view of the small town where I was staying, with its unique architectural designs. On the other side, the vast desert stretched as far as the eye could see. I could even spot parts of Algeria, a neighbouring country with which Morocco had a closed border due to differing views on the Western Sahara issue.

In the desert, I could see camels, quad bikes and 4x4 vehicles, as people enjoyed various activities in the dunes. What surprised me the most was the silence – with no wind, I could hear for miles. The only sounds were those of motorbikes and distant conversations.

I had initially planned to take it easy for the day, but the lively atmosphere at the hostel and the prospect of missing out on an exciting desert adventure convinced me otherwise. Fellow travellers were gearing up for a desert hike, spending in a night spent under the dazzling desert stars. The opportunity was too enticing to pass up, so I decided to join the expedition.

With a few hours to prepare, I ensured I had enough supplies for the journey. I packed an ample supply of fresh fruits and two litres of water, essential provisions for our desert trek. A diverse group of approximately eight adventure enthusiasts, including myself, gathered in anticipation of an exploration deeper into the desert's heart. To shield myself from the desert sun, I ingeniously fashioned my towel into a headscarf, an impromptu and practical solution given the harsh desert conditions.

Our planned route covered roughly 4 kilometres, which seemed manageable on paper. However, the ever-shifting dunes and soft sands of the desert terrain posed challenges, ultimately extending the hike to around one and a half hours. To navigate, we relied on both maps and prominent landmarks, such as a colossal sand dune that served as a guide. The sprawling desert landscape provided ample opportunities for capturing breathtaking photographs. The seemingly endless expanse of sand stretched as far as the eye could see, offering an almost surreal backdrop for our journey.

Navigating the undulating dunes required careful route selection to avoid the inconvenience of scaling back up a sand dune if we made an errant turn. Despite the challenging terrain, the stark beauty of the desert and the camaraderie of our fellow hikers made the trek an unforgettable experience.

Our destination was a desert camp nestled behind a dune, strategically positioned to shield it from the intense desert sun. The camp boasted an oasis-like setting, adorned with verdant trees and cozy little structures for rest and dining. What truly set this camp apart was its complete isolation from the digital world; no Wi-Fi or phone signal was available. This lack of connectivity created a true escape from the bustling modern world, allowing us to immerse ourselves fully in the desert experience.

Following a brief respite, we ascended a dune to witness a mesmerizing sunset, a sight that left an indelible mark on our memories. Observing the shifting shadows of the dunes as the sun descended felt akin to witnessing a live version of an Apple screensaver. The tranquillity of the desert was occasionally punctuated by the laughter and chatter of fellow explorers nearby.

As darkness blanketed the desert landscape, we decided to descend the dunes with enthusiasm. During my descent, an attempt to secure my phone from slipping out my pocket led to a comical tumble into the sand, much to the amusement of the group. For the return journey, I joined arms with one of my companions and we careened down the dunes in exhilarating fashion.

One of our fellow travellers, a German girl, had thought ahead and purchased vegetables. This thoughtful provision allowed us to prepare a delectable vegetable tagine with rice, utilizing the gas stove available at the camp. Although the cooking process spanned about 2.5 hours, we whiled away the time with snacks and lively conversation. The resulting meal was a warm and comforting dinner, particularly welcome as the desert night grew increasingly cold.

During our meal, we engaged in conversation with the camp's owner, uncovering a sobering reality: much of Morocco disposed of plastic waste by burning it, a less-than-ideal approach to waste management. This information saddened us, highlighting the need for more sustainable waste disposal solutions.

Following dinner, the camp owners treated us to a captivating musical performance. Their voices and traditional instruments merged to create enchanting melodies. Inspired by their artistry, they extended the opportunity for us to participate, handing us three drums, each producing unique sounds and a metal instrument to clank together. Mastering these instruments proved a fun challenge, requiring practice to achieve the right techniques and maximize the range of sounds. The drums' timbre varied with the point of impact and it was crucial to ensure that their bases didn't fully touch the floor, as this would muffle their resonance. Our impromptu jam session was immensely enjoyable, evoking a sense of tribal unity and fulfilling a longstanding desire to partake in such musical expression.

However, the most awe-inspiring spectacle of the night was the star-studded sky. The absence of light pollution in the desert allowed the heavens to unveil their true majesty. Winter in Morocco, we discovered, is an ideal time for stargazing, as the celestial display was nothing short of spectacular. Under this canopy, we marvelled at the cosmos, a humbling reminder of the grandeur of our universe. I saw so many shooting stars!

I stood there for about 20 minutes, gazing up at the stars in awe before deciding it was time to retire for the night. Our sleeping arrangements consisted of sharing a tent with other friends from the group. The camp had provided us with approximately three blankets each, in addition to the warm clothes we had packed. Despite these efforts to keep warm, the desert nights were bitterly cold and I struggled to get a restful night's sleep.

The following morning, I made do with some snacks I had brought for breakfast. We embarked on our journey back to the hostel, where our paths gradually diverged as everyone went their own way. Arriving at the hostel first, I had the luxury of immediately taking a shower to wash away the desert sand and freshen up. Hassan, the hostel owner, surprised us with breakfast, even though it was already noon, demonstrating his genuine hospitality. I ended up with surprising Hassan with a tip at the end of my stay, he was a really great guy and cared for us all.

After my desert adventure, my next destination was Fez, a city located in northern Morocco, boasting the largest pedestrianized Medina in the world. I couldn't wait to explore this remarkable location. I took a bus and had already booked a hostel before my father planned to join me for a few days on this trip.

Fez quickly became one of my favourite places in Morocco. Unlike Marrakesh, it was pedestrianized, meaning there were no motorbikes within the Medina. My hostel had a lovely balcony where I enjoyed watching the sunset and it even featured traditional dance performances. I was fascinated by how the dancers used their voices to enhance the music.

Navigating the Medina in Fez presented a unique challenge, especially since GPS didn't work reliably in the winding alleys. However, I embraced this challenge and often tested my ability to navigate without relying on GPS. By the end of my trip, I was quite proud of my knowledge of the local area and I could find my way around with confidence. It's worth mentioning that shopkeepers and some locals occasionally tried to mislead tourists, leading them in the wrong direction to confuse them. They would take longer routes, hoping for a tip, which was a common tactic to trick travellers into believing they were genuinely helping.

Fez was also known for its beautiful parks, which added to the overall peaceful ambiance of the city. However, when I ventured a bit away from the tourist areas, I noticed a significant issue with litter. The city lacked a proper rubbish disposal system and it seemed like they were trying to hide it from public view. The architecture in the city was truly exceptional. The buildings were adorned with intricate details and vibrant colours, not only enhancing their aesthetic appeal but also serving a practical purpose by helping to keep the interior temperatures lower.

During my time in Fez, I participated in a captivating walking tour that unveiled many of the secrets hidden within the Medina. The tour even took us to a leather factory where they dyed and dried the leather in the sun, with hides hung all over the buildings. The smell was quite unpleasant, but they provided us with herbs to hold to our noses, making it more bearable. It was during this time that I struck up a friendship with a fellow traveller named Derek, who worked remotely and spent a month in each place he visited.

I was fortunate to be in Fez when the Moroccan national football team was performing exceptionally well in the World Cup. Football holds immense significance in Morocco and I was eager to immerse myself in the local passion for the sport. After the walking tour, Derek and I discovered a local café filled with enthusiastic locals and decided to join them. They welcomed us warmly and made space for us and we ordered some delicious drinks and food.

The atmosphere in the café was electric as everyone was glued to a small TV with an antenna that kept disconnecting, requiring constant adjustments to maintain the signal. The entire city of Fez seemed to be on lockdown as everyone tuned in to watch the game. Remarkably, Morocco won the match and the celebration was surreal. People were cheering and celebrating both inside the café and out on the streets. Drumbeats, chants and jubilant gatherings created an unforgettable atmosphere and I knew I couldn't miss another game in this vibrant football-loving nation.

The next day marked a significant event as my father was joining me on one of my adventures for the first time. This journey was his first time in Africa. It was a monumental step for him. I had my breakfast in the hostel and ended up meeting an English guy called Benedict it turned out he was a brother to a girl I use to go to school with!

My primary task for the day was to relocate from the hostel to an apartment I had booked, complete with a shared pool. However, finding the apartment proved to be a challenge as it was tucked away in a labyrinth of alleyways. I could only imagine the difficulty my dad would face since he didn't have a local SIM card to contact me for guidance. Despite my initial struggles, the apartment was a delightful discovery. It was a modern Moroccan building adorned with beautifully decorated traditional tiles, a perfect place for our first night's stay.

My father's arrival was scheduled for the evening, so I had prepared a set of instructions for him to navigate from the airport to the apartment. His main tasks included withdrawing money and using it to secure a taxi to reach my location. I was slightly apprehensive about throwing him into this challenging situation, but it was a necessary step for him to join me. A few hours later, he finally arrived. When he spotted me, I greeted him, saying, "My friend, this way for a taxi," fully aware of the exhausting journey he must have endured. He burst into laughter and enveloped me in a warm hug.

My dad recounted his airport experience, explaining that he had successfully withdrawn money. However, upon exiting the airport, he found no official taxis, only a dubious group of individuals lurking in a corner. They claimed to be taxi drivers and after some negotiation, they agreed on a price to take him to my location. Navigating through the Medina's labyrinthine streets proved to be a challenge, especially considering the language barrier, as the driver did not speak English. My dad found himself making numerous wrong turns before being dropped off about 10 minutes away from my location. Fortunately, I had insisted that he download offline maps since he had no access to mobile data. This proved to be a wise decision, allowing him to eventually find his way to me.

After settling in, I was eager to take my dad for a walk and show him some of the night time activity and local cuisine. I decided to take him to a place I had visited before, a spot where I had shared some laughs with one of the employees. As we strolled through the Medina, most of the shops were closed, but I told my dad to remember this moment because the next day, this street would be bustling and nearly unrecognizable. Despite getting a bit lost along the way, we managed to navigate without maps, which I was quite proud of when we finally arrived at our destination.

The friendly man at the restaurant remembered me and greeted us warmly. He led us to a balcony with a view overlooking the bustling street below. I ordered a vegetable tagine for my dad, as it's a traditional Moroccan dish and it turned out to be one of the best meals I had in Morocco. The vegetables were incredibly tender, requiring minimal chewing and the flavours were exquisite. We also had some bread to dip into the savoury sauce. It was a delightful experience, enjoying our meal while observing the chaotic traffic and life unfolding below.

The following morning, we enjoyed breakfast at the hostel, which was included in the accommodation cost. It was a spread of traditional Moroccan dishes, offering us a wide variety of flavours to savour. It was also the first time my dad tried traditional Moroccan tea, which features mint and sugar. He enjoyed it but noted how sweet it was. Fortunately, the hostel allowed us to leave our luggage behind while we explored Fez for the day, sparing us the inconvenience of carrying it with us.

Our day began with a walk around the Medina and I aimed to take my dad to some of the same points I had learned about during my previous visit. We had a few people follow us and attempt to guide us in different directions, but it wasn't too bothersome. We expected more of this since people could hear us speaking English, but it didn't make a significant difference.

A few hours later, we decided to stop at a café, a common occurrence when we spend time together. In the café, we met a friendly man from the UK who struck up a conversation with us. He was an interesting individual who shared stories about his travels and his belief in things happening for a reason. Despite our backgrounds in science, we found his perspective intriguing, offering us a different way of looking at life. However, after a few hours of conversation, we both developed headaches and had to part ways. It had been an engaging chat, nonetheless.

Our plan for the day was to head to a place called Ifrane, located south of Fez. We returned to the hostel to collect our belongings and then headed to the taxi stand. The first taxi stand we visited didn't operate the long-haul taxis to Ifrane, but at the time, I suspected they were trying to overcharge us. I managed to communicate in Spanish with someone who confirmed that we needed to go to another location for these taxis. After another taxi ride, we arrived at the proper taxi depot for the long-distance journey. While we could have taken a bus to Ifrane, the inconvenient schedules and higher ticket prices made the taxi a more attractive option. Riding in a cramped car with no seatbelts proved to be an interesting experience for my dad. The music the driver played was peculiar, with a man's voice singing seemingly without any accompanying music. I would have loved to translate and understand the lyrics.

Ifrane was often referred to as the 'Switzerland' of Morocco and upon reaching our destination, it became abundantly clear why. The houses in Ifrane were notably larger and the ambiance had a distinctly European feel, which was a stark contrast to the bustling streets of Fez. We also couldn't help but notice that the temperature was significantly colder since we were at a higher elevation. This part of the trip would be etched in our memories for its persistent chill and we found ourselves longing for warmer clothing.

Fortunately, we had booked an amazing apartment with two rooms, a kitchen and a living room. Despite having heating, the cold seeped in and the only time we felt truly warm was when we were both wrapped up in our beds, cocooned beneath the covers. Living in one of the rooms within these spacious, Swiss-style houses added a unique dimension to our Ifrane experience.

During our time in Ifrane, we decided to embark on a hike in the mountains. It proved to be an enjoyable adventure as we navigated and explored the forested terrain together. Along the way, we encountered a large group of kids who were using a plastic bottle as a makeshift football. Their enthusiasm for the game was amazing!

Hungry from our journey, we set out to explore the local dining scene. The food in Ifrane was surprisingly affordable and the restaurants exuded a level of luxury that exceeded typical Moroccan standards. We stumbled upon a place that seemed to blend American and Moroccan styles, resembling a fast-food joint but offering a wide array of high-quality menu items. It was a relief to savour our meal in the warmth of the restaurant, a stark contrast to the chilly weather outside.

After our mountain adventure, we made our way to Chefchaouen, also known as the Blue City. This picturesque village nestled in the mountains is famous for its buildings painted in various shades of blue. Upon our arrival, we found ourselves in the midst of another world cup football match and despite lugging all our luggage, we managed to locate a cafe where we could watch and support the game. As we cheered for Morocco, we ordered some much-needed food. The cafe's owner added to the fun with his lively and enthusiastic support and people on the streets were also glued to the match peering through the door.

Morocco emerged victorious once again and we were eager to join in the celebrations. After dropping off our luggage at the hostel, we hit the streets. It seemed like the entire town was in a jubilant mood as a parade took over the road, accompanied by cheering drums and even red smoke, creating a festive atmosphere that was impossible to resist.

Chefchaouen was undoubtedly one of my favourite places for taking photos and exploring the city. Its beauty lay in the countless hidden gems waiting to be discovered around every corner. One day, my dad and I hiked up to a local café that offered incredible views of the city in the distance. It was also close to the famed weed farms, for which Chefchaouen is known. This made for some amusing encounters, as many people assumed we were seeking weed and would often approach us, whispering offers or asking if we wanted some. Walking around the city sometimes felt like being surrounded by ghosts whispering "hash" into your ear. My dad's swift reactions and humorous escapes from these situations were quite entertaining to watch.

We also immersed ourselves in the hostel culture, spending one of our nights at the rooftop, engaging in conversations with fellow travellers. They were genuinely pleased to see my dad travelling with me and his presence added a unique dimension to their experiences. Many of them mentioned enjoying conversations with my dad, as it provided a change from always talking to younger travellers. Getting to sleep there proved difficult due to the large number of cats outside that were often meowing so loudly it sounded like screaming.

Our paths eventually diverged, as my dad had to catch a flight from a different city that was in the opposite direction from my next destination in the north. Though he felt a bit nervous, he was confident in taking a bus and then a flight from the city later that day.

I encountered a significant challenge when a power outage in Chefchaouen prevented me from printing my mandatory flight ticket and none of the local ATMs were functioning. I was against the clock to print my ticket and pay for my hostel, where the staff was beginning to get quite agitated. Fortunately, I devised a backup plan with the help of a kind individual from the hostel who covered my hostel expenses, with the understanding that I would reimburse him once the ATMs were functional again. The next hurdle was acquiring the flight ticket, which I managed to print at a hidden shop nearby with a working printer. I boarded a bus and finally arrived in Tangier, where I intended to catch my flight. The city was bustling with locals and the bus system proved complex and crowded, leading me to opt for a taxi and part with all my remaining money to cover the fare.

Spain

My journey continued with a brief 30-minute flight to Seville a picturesque city in southern Spain. I decided to stay at a social hostel that offered nightly events, including game nights and group chats. What made this hostel even better was the complimentary coffee and breakfast – a fantastic start to my days. Seville's charming streets were filled with shops and cafes and I was particularly eager to explore its rich tradition of tapas, which people enjoy throughout the day.

I also had the incredible opportunity to experience Flamenco dancing, a traditional dance in Spain that involves passionate footwork, intricate hand and body movements and intense emotional expressions. It was a unique and mesmerizing performance and the energy displayed by the dancers was truly amazing. Throughout the show, they danced with seemingly endless vitality and the rhythmic sounds of their footwork reverberated throughout the room, causing the tables and chairs to shake in response.

Spain exudes a vibrant and joyful atmosphere. The bustling cafes, lively street acts and abundant music create an infectious energy that permeates the entire city. Simply walking around, you couldn't help but feel the happiness in the air, with the local people contributing to the overall positive mood of the place. It's a country that effortlessly spreads happiness to all who visit.

One of the most peculiar and memorable days of my travels unfolded all in 24 hours. While strolling the streets of Seville with a small group from the hostel, I heard someone call out "Ollie." To my surprise, it was Benedict, an acquaintance from my travels who I met in Fez. What were the odds that we both independently chose Seville as our destination? That same night, while at a club, I was recognized by someone else. A quick check of Instagram confirmed that she knew me from my time volunteering in a hostel in Macedonia. The next morning, still baffled by the chain of events, I shared my experiences with some people at the hostel.

To my astonishment, Mica, another traveller, shared similar stories, including her time in Budapest. I was confident that we must have a common friend given our intersecting travel experiences. She initially had doubts, but after comparing Instagram, we discovered that Hann (a friend I had met in Egypt and Sofia) was among her close friends. To add to the intrigue, a couple who checked in later that morning were the same couple I had shared a taxi with at the very beginning of my journey in Morocco. These occurrences couldn't be mere coincidences.

Mica and I found ourselves in a dilemma as the weather in Spain had turned unfavourable. She suggested an escape to an island, Las Palmas, known for its pleasant weather and a short flight away. We checked the flight prices and were astounded to find only two seats left for a flight departing the next day, at an excellent price. It seemed almost too good to be true, but we seized the opportunity. At this point, I didn't even know Mica's name, yet we had booked a flight together for the following day.

We woke up early and before we knew it, we were in Las Palmas. It felt like an entirely different country, with lush greenery and tropical plants everywhere. The bus system on the island was efficient and we took a bus from the airport to reach our hostel. Las Palmas was attracting many visitors looking to escape the heat elsewhere.

While the island had a lot to offer, some areas were challenging to explore without a car. I was eager to rent one, but it came at a relatively high cost due to my age and experience. However, when split between friends from the hostel, it turned out to be quite affordable. Driving a car on the opposite side of the road, an automatic vehicle and in a different country was a new experience for me, which made me a bit nervous. The rental car was modern and filled with features. Our initial plan was to head north and explore that part of the island before covering the rest. The freedom to go anywhere was exhilarating and driving through the high mountains was both exciting and technically challenging – an absolute blast.

Las Palmas offered some of the most stunning night skies for stargazing, thanks to the minimal light pollution in the area. I had a plan to explore a remote part of the island, far from the hustle and bustle of the city and consequently limited transportation. Since I no longer had access to the rental car, my English friend from the hostel and I made it our mission to reach this distant stargazing spot. The journey involved taking two buses, with the hope of hitchhiking the final stretch, or else facing a 3-hour hike.

We successfully navigated both bus rides, but our stop left us in the middle of nowhere, high up in the mountains. The desolate roads raised concerns that we might indeed have to endure the full 3-hour walk. The few locals who drove past us must have found our situation rather amusing. Picture two British travellers with minimal provisions, hiking with plastic shopping bags in the middle of nowhere. Those who passed us in their cars must have been utterly shocked by how we ended up in such a predicament. As we watched car after car drive past us, we began jokingly considering desperate tactics like pretending to be injured or claiming we had an emergency to flag down help.

Then, our stroke of luck arrived in the form of a confused Dutch traveller who was headed to the beach at the end of the road, precisely where we wanted to go. He generously offered us a ride and took us straight to our destination.

The hostel was conveniently situated by the stargazing beach, a popular spot for enthusiasts to enjoy the night sky. The hostel even boasted features more commonly found in resorts, such as a pool and restaurant. That night I made it a priority to stargaze. I sat on the beach gazing up at the sky where I was treated to the sight of shooting stars and a multitude of stars that gradually became visible as my eyes adjusted to the darkness. It was a truly magical experience.

Following my wonderful time in Las Palmas, I decided to return to the UK to reunite with my family and spend Christmas with them. It was a much-needed break after extensive travels and a fantastic way to celebrate the holiday season.

London

Before heading home for Christmas, I decided to spend a few days in London. Although, I hadn't explored my capital city much before, I was open to the idea of possibly living there in the future. Despite the constant rain and my negative thoughts about the country, particularly the political chaos in Parliament, I was determined to make the most of my time in London and try to like it.

The public transport system proved to be efficient, with only a few minor delays, making it easy to reach the hostel. Initially, the hostel seemed promising based on its ratings. However, little did I know at the time that the ratings were fraudulent—my first encounter with such an event in all my travels. Arriving exhausted and desperate for some rest after an entire sleepless night, I hoped to check in early. The streets around the hostel were rough, littered with rubbish and most places were closed except for a few kebab shops. It wasn't the most pleasant area and my heart dropped as there was no one at the hostel to allow an early check-in. I had no idea how I was going to kill so much time.

Eventually, a man let me in after a considerable wait, during which I observed unsettling scenes of people smashing bottles and engaging in drug deals outside. Additionally, a woman confronted one of the girls waiting outside the hostel for having a flight sticker on her bag, claiming it revealed too much information about her. It was one of the most negative introductions to a city I had ever experienced and I really hoped the rest of my trip wouldn't follow the same pattern.

When I finally managed to drop off my bags, I encountered the owner of the hostel, who turned out to be one of the most unpleasant individuals I had ever met. The owner's behaviour was beyond rude; he insisted that I could only drop off my bags and then demanded I leave, using offensive language and displaying a serious anger problem. His drinking habits on the streets by night led to frequent police visits, creating an atmosphere akin to a prison with excessively strict rules. Despite my attempts to secure a refund, I decided to endure the unpleasant conditions because some of the fellow inmates—sorry, guests seemed much friendlier.

Most residents were individuals trying to settle in England, giving the hostel an unusual vibe with fewer travellers. The stringent rules, including hefty fines for not cleaning dishes promptly and a prohibition on using common areas before check-in, created an unwelcoming environment. I questioned the legality of such practices, especially when they forcibly ejected a paying guest for raising his voice too much. It seemed like they sought reasons to remove people, presumably to sell beds again at higher rates. The volunteers were equally problematic, often engaging in arguments with guests.

Every encounter with the hostile owner made me anxious and I kept my head down to avoid unnecessary confrontation. I felt compelled to inform anyone considering the hostel about its chaotic and rude atmosphere, dissuading some potential guests. Many hostels in London seemed more like places for homeless individuals and workers rather than welcoming spaces for travellers. Coupled with the constant rain and the negativity in the city, my experience became overwhelmingly depressing.

Amidst the raindrops in London, a glimmer of joy emerged—the enchanting Christmas theme. The city, adorned with sparkling lights and a festive spirit, cast a spell that even the gloomy weather couldn't fully dampen. Strolling through the cleaner streets, I enjoyed walking around.

Reflecting on my tumultuous experience, I realised that London, had its highs and lows. The hostility I encountered seemed to stem from specific elements rather than the city's essence. Perhaps, in the warmth of summer, the city might reveal a different side—one less overshadowed by rain and unpleasant encounters.

Malta

After Christmas I decided to go to Malta due to very cheap flights. My dad kindly dropped me off at the airport and I was amazed at how they managed to offer such low-cost flights. The journey to Malta took about 3 hours and upon arrival I hopped on a bus from the airport. However, I mistakenly got off at the wrong stop, which meant I had to walk across a part of the island to reach my hostel. I had chosen an excellent and reasonably priced hostel with a rooftop offering stunning views of the surrounding area. I had a return flight booked and intended to spend a week in Malta, a small country just off the coast of Italy. It was one of the few countries I had yet to visit.

My expectations for such a small island were modest, but Malta turned out to offer much more than I had anticipated. The architecture of the houses in Malta was a delightful surprise, reminiscent of Italian style architecture, with stone buildings featuring charming balconies. Some houses showed signs of their age with weathered exteriors revealing their history.

During one of my day trips I visited a location known as the Blue Grotto, which is an area just off Malta featuring a massive rock formation extending into the water. It happened to be a very windy day, I ventured down to the coastline and marvelled at the violent waves crashing against the shore. They were so tumultuous that attempting to go for a swim would have been a risky endeavour. Navigating around the island proved a bit challenging due to limited bus services and schedules that often did not align with their actual arrival times.

Malta is also famous for its stunning Blue Lagoon. However, I decided not to visit it during this trip due to unfavourable weather conditions. I wanted to save the experience for a future visit when I could see it in all its glory. A fellow traveller I met at the hostel had been to the Blue Lagoon a week before my arrival and even showed me a scar from a jellyfish encounter. The area is known for its abundance of jellyfish.

The nightlife in Malta was surprisingly vibrant, with plenty of restaurants and bustling areas on the island. I was amazed to find that some places in Malta were among the first I had been to in the world to offer free shots and drinks to entice visitors. This made for a budget-friendly night out. I even ended up swapping clothes with people from my group and pretending to enter venues as different people to score additional free drinks. This was a fun and cost-effective way to enjoy the night.

During this time, I was focused on growing my website development business. I dedicated a lot of effort to expanding my client list, my skills and working on my portfolio website to showcase my abilities to potential clients. I also noticed that the hostel I was staying at didn't have a website of its own. To my pleasant surprise, I plucked up the courage to speak directly to the hostel's owner about the idea of creating a website for them. They agreed and I was thrilled to have the opportunity to build their website. It was a fantastic addition to my portfolio, especially because they were the only hostel in Malta. I not only gained valuable experience but also got paid for my work, making the trip to Malta doubly worthwhile.

Malta turned out to be a very diverse place and I had the chance to meet people from all over the world. Many were there to learn English. I recall two Irish guys who became close friends during their stay. They were a constant source of entertainment, with their amusing stories and antics. For instance, one of them managed to break down the door to their room because they had misplaced the keys. Overall, my time in Malta, despite being a short break, was incredibly enjoyable and I look forward to returning to this charming island in the future.

UAE

I decided to spend a few days in the United Arab Emirates (UAE) since it was en route to Thailand and I was eager to explore this part of the world. My journey began with a landing in Abu Dhabi, where I had booked a reasonably priced private room for a two-night stay. The Abu Dhabi airport was an incredible sight, featuring impressive artwork and ceilings. I easily hopped on a bus to reach my hostel and navigating with google maps was no problem. The city had a different vibe compared to Dubai, feeling somewhat less traditional. Surprisingly, I found the food quite affordable due to the presence of smaller, budget-friendly eateries. I befriended a few people at a Moroccan restaurant, which further showcased the diverse culinary scene. UAE turned out to be more affordable than I had expected.

During my stay in Abu Dhabi, I had the opportunity to visit the iconic and stunning Sheikh Zayed Grand Mosque. It was one of the most breathtaking mosques I had ever encountered. The sheer size of the mosque was awe-inspiring and the way the colours reflected and illuminated as the sun set was a sight to behold. Each room within the mosque had unique features, including sundials on the walls used to mark prayer times. I also had a conversation with the owner of my accommodation, who explained how Abu Dhabi was more traditional and relaxed compared to the westernised and costly Dubai.

Travelling from Abu Dhabi to Dubai was straightforward, thanks to an easily accessible bus service. There weren't many hostels in Dubai, but I managed to secure a spot in a skyscraper about 20 floors up, offering panoramic views. It was like living inside an Apple screensaver when I was on the balcony. I often found myself gazing at the dazzling buildings and the famous river below. My initial impression of the hostel residents, most of whom were Russian, was that they were rather rude, but I soon realised this wasn't the case. Once we got to know each other, I discovered that they were a group of individuals who had escaped from conflict zones and they were actually really fun.

Dubai had many attractions, but some were too expensive for my budget. For instance, the Dubai Frame was a notable tourist spot, but I decided to admire it from the outside instead of paying a hefty entrance fee. This approach allowed me to save money while still taking in the city's sights. I also visited the Burj Khalifa, the world's tallest building, which offered spectacular light shows and water displays. I couldn't help but marvel at how they managed to install all those lights on the building. I even did an Instagram live stream here, which my friends and family back home thoroughly enjoyed.

However, amidst the glittering skyscrapers and luxurious lifestyle, I couldn't help but notice a sober aspect of Dubai – the sight of migrant workers leaving their workplaces. The roads were often filled with buses stuffed with these workers, leaving me to wonder where they were being sent. It shed light on the less glamorous side of Dubai, often overlooked by tourists and labelled by some as a form of modern-day slavery.

One peculiar feature of Dubai was the near absence of pedestrians. The city is known for its car culture and walking is not a common mode of transport. However, I decided to challenge this norm by relying on public transportation and walking to explore the city. The scorching heat made this a challenging endeavour, but I was determined to see as much as I could without relying on taxis or personal cars. While they did have E-scooters in some areas, Dubai was pedestrian-friendly and not as bad as the internet makes it.

My strong desire to experience Dubai's club scene led me to discover an age requirement of 21 for entry and I was just 20 years old at the time. My resourceful Russian friends devised a plan – we decided to stick together as a group. First, my Russian friend went through and the bouncer checked his ID. As I approached, I held my breath, but luckily, the bouncer waved us all through. Perhaps he recognized my friends from previous nights out.

Once inside the club, I quickly realised that the drinks were exorbitantly expensive, making it one of the priciest places I had ever been. However, the DJ's performance was exceptional and the overall atmosphere felt very mature.

To get to Thailand, I had to take a flight passing through India via Mumbai. I was particularly thrilled at the prospect of witnessing the landscape as we approached the airport, knowing full well that Mumbai stands amongst one of the most populated cities in the world. Peering out the window I saw a panorama dominated by houses and shacks, devoid of any greenery and what caught my eye was an astonishing amount of rubbish. The view from above made everything seem remarkably close, right up to the airport boundary.

Transitioning to the second flight wasn't a simple affair; I had to endure another round of security checks despite not entering India. This caught me off guard since I wasn't familiar with India's regulations. To expedite the process, I strategically positioned myself towards the back of the queue, hoping for a swift check without thorough scrutiny of my luggage. Amidst disappointed faces surrendering power banks and various items, I pondered the oddity of these seemingly harmless objects being confiscated. Planning to conceal my power bank beneath my laptop, I found it baffling why such items were targeted. Engaging in conversation with a friendly Egyptian man in line, I learned of his purchase—a bottle of vodka from Abu Dhabi Airport, intended for the flight. I feared they might confiscate it from him. When my turn arrived, the security check was quick and thankfully, my power bank went unnoticed. However, the real drama unfolded with the Egyptian

man. They adamantly prohibited him from taking the vodka, sparking a clash of cultures. He stood his ground, familiar with such tactics in his own country. For a tense 15 minutes, they argued, resorting to intimidation tactics and threats of flight denial. It was a standoff highlighting conflicting rules, with the Egyptian referencing the website's guidelines that allowed his possession. They even demanded the bottle be wrapped in plastic, contrary to Abu Dhabi staff who confirmed it wasn't necessary for passage through India. As the departure time loomed, they escorted him to the gates in a final attempt to pressure him into surrendering the bottle. The whole episode reeked of corruption, a blatant attempt to snatch the bottle for ulterior motives—whether resale or personal consumption. It was a disturbing reflection of corruption that seeped even into the airport's confines, preying on unsuspecting travellers. Discovering the sale of power banks post-security only added to the confusion, raising questions about the arbitrary confiscations. It was a troubling revelation, showcasing dubious practices within the airport's domain.

Thailand

I had landed in Thailand with no concrete plans, relying on the airport Wi-Fi to plan a route to my hostel. This involved taking a subway where a plastic coin served as my ticket, to be inserted into the coin gate to gain entry. I then hopped on a numbered bus, a colourful and elaborately decorated one, a common sight in Thailand. The excitement of being in this vibrant country was palpable. It was Valentine's Day when I arrived and the cultural significance of the occasion was evident all around. Many girls carried red roses and couples cozied up on the trains.

My hostel, though a bit far from the bustling city centre, suited me perfectly as I preferred to avoid the chaotic traffic of mopeds and cars in central areas. The hostel staff proficient in English were incredibly friendly and through late-night conversations with them, I delved into Thai culture.

During these discussions, I learned about certain challenges within Thai society. One particularly interesting conversation revolved around gender roles, with a focus on male children not being expected to contribute much to household chores, resulting in a lack of basic skills. One of the workers expressed her determination not to perpetuate this inequality with her own child, highlighting the need for change.

I also asked her about the one change she wished to see in her city and she spoke passionately about the need for more walkable paths and green spaces. Given the city's compact nature, where a moped often felt like the only practical mode of transport, her perspective made perfect sense. Additionally, I couldn't help but feel empathy for her as she discussed the challenges of pursuing travel due to visa restrictions and financial constraints. Despite these obstacles, her unwavering determination and resilience was truly admirable.

On my first night, I ventured out to explore the local area, which was bustling with life. It was a hot and humid night and I found myself sweating just from walking around. I decided to indulge in a Thai-style crepe with chocolate, a treat commonly found on the streets of Bangkok. As I continued walking, I unintentionally found myself on a unique street. The entire street was lined with girls, a phenomenon I had read about during my research and it was unlike anything I had seen before. I had previously visited the red-light district in Amsterdam, but that seemed like a drop in the ocean compared to this. The street was a bustling market, surrounded by bars and clubs. Some of the club doors were open, offering glimpses of girls dancing topless. I couldn't help but smile at the unexpected turn my first night had taken. I continued to explore the area, eventually turning down another street where hundreds of girls were waiting for someone to come along. However, that someone wasn't me and I decided to head back to the hostel after my interesting first evening out.

Over the next few days, I had a strong desire to explore more of the city. However, persistent rain severely limited my outdoor activities. What made it challenging was that Bangkok had so much to offer, but its sheer size meant that getting to the areas I wanted to explore took a considerable amount of time. Nevertheless, I managed to find indoor activities to keep me occupied.

One notable indoor attraction I visited was a market designed to resemble a water market with boats. While it was undoubtedly a tourist attraction, it was still fascinating to experience and sample some authentic Thai cuisine. I was accompanied by a friend and together, we tried a variety of Thai dishes, both sweet and savoury. One particularly intriguing treat called (ขนมบ้าบิ่น) was a cake that had a dark top and a flavourless taste. It was super interesting and I wasn't too sure what to make of the texture which was soft and sticky.

Fortunately, the rain eventually subsided and I seized the opportunity to visit Khao San Road, the city's renowned party district. A lively group of us from the hostel decided to hit the town. As soon as we arrived, we were bombarded by people attempting to sell us a wide range of items, from T-shirts to exotic bugs. It was a sensory overload. We grabbed some beers from street vendors and as we sipped our drinks, we were approached by individuals trying to sell bracelets with audacious statements that would undoubtedly be controversial in Western societies.

Khao San Road was a chaotic spectacle with bars facing each other, each competing to blast its music as loudly as possible. Conversations with friends became nearly impossible due to the deafening beats on both sides. While we were walking someone approached us offering scorpions for sale. We decided to give it a try and we found the taste to be interesting – like a salty crisp with a chewy texture. It wasn't bad and it got us thinking about the potential future of food.

Little did I know that this night would lead to one of the most profound experiences of my travels. Travelling has the power to be life-changing, especially when you meet individuals who leave an indelible mark on your life. I had the privilege of encountering such a person on this night, someone who profoundly impacted me for the better and whom I will forever remember. Our connection was so extraordinary and rare that I felt immensely grateful for this unforgettable experience.

As we strolled along the streets, resembling headless and slightly intoxicated chickens, we unexpectedly encountered another group of travellers and I struck up a conversation with them. That's when I met Erika, a solo traveller from Finland who had recently met the group at a local bar.

Right from the start, Erika and I hit it off instantly. We had a natural chemistry that led us to spend the entire evening together, dancing and talking without leaving each other's side. It was an exceptional experience to meet someone who could connect with me so quickly and we even joked about travelling together. We both loved the saying "Seek Discomfort" from a popular YouTube channel we followed and we shared a passion for exploring new and unfamiliar places.

Although I had not done much in Bangkok so far, meeting Erika made my trip worthwhile. She had a magnetic personality that drew me towards her and I knew that this was a moment I would never want to miss. However, we were both a little intoxicated and I did not want to get my hopes up in case nothing happened between us. Nonetheless, for me, this was an essential moment in my travels as it taught me the beauty of meeting new people and the value of keeping an open mind.

That morning, as soon as I woke up, I knew I had to act. I couldn't just let the opportunity slip away. So I messaged Erika and told her that if she was serious about travelling together, she should book my bus ticket. It was a bold move, but I didn't want to risk getting my hopes up only to be let down. To my surprise, a few minutes later, she replied that she had booked the tickets. My heart raced with excitement and nervousness. This was really happening - I was about to embark on an adventure with a beautiful and adventurous girl I had just met a few hours ago.

I had planned to take the bus to the station, but the traffic was unbearably slow. After a few minutes of waiting, I decided to take a bike taxi instead. It was a risky move, but I didn't want to miss the bus. The ride was stressful, to say the least. The driver had no idea how to get to the station, despite it being one of the main ones. He kept taking wrong turns and asking people for directions, even though he had Google Maps on his phone. It took over an hour to arrive and I was starting to worry that I might miss the bus. I tried to stay calm and remind myself that everything was going to be okay.

Thankfully, I had left with plenty of time and Erika had already checked us in for the bus. As soon as I arrived, she handed me my ticket and we boarded the bus together. I was both nervous and excited for what was to come. Would we get along? Would we have fun? I had no idea but I was ready to find out. This was the start of a journey that would change me forever.

When we reunited, I hoped that our connection from the previous night would still be strong and thankfully it was. The bus we boarded was unlike any I had experienced in Europe; it was decorated with cushions and blankets, making it a comfortable journey. I felt sorry for the other passengers as Erika and I chatted non-stop throughout the night and into the morning, discussing anything and everything. The bus staff even provided complimentary snacks and water and we were even treated to some delicious free Thai food during a stop at a gas station. The journey was amazing but the lack of sleep made us both exhausted upon arrival. Since the port was far away we decided to spend a night in the town. To avoid the expense of a taxi we wandered around to search for a local place to stay even though it was already 5am in the morning. We joked about being two random tourists with all our luggage searching for accommodation in the early hours. The first place we tried had a 24/7 reception, but the receptionist was lying on the floor and seemed unresponsive to our bell and just make some grunting noises. We sat outside sweating in the heat and trying to avoid the massive bugs on the floor while looking for other options. Eventually we found another place about a 15-minute walk from the first hotel, where we managed to book a room at a reasonable price. Both of us were in dire need of rest and I also took some time to reflect on the past 24 crazy hours.

The next day we checked out of our room and made our way to the ferry port. Luckily our ticket included both the bus and the ferry, making the journey easy and stress-free. We had some time to kill, so I grabbed us some coffee and we waited in the ticket area. While waiting the receptionist informed us about a discount we could get if we downloaded an app, which we promptly did and were thrilled to save some money. Boarding the bus was surreal as we were the only ones on it, almost like a scene from a movie. Despite only knowing each other for 24 hours I felt an inexplicable closeness to her as if we had known each other for a lifetime. The ferry ride was magical, we held each other close, gazing out the window as the ferry sailed along, sharing a kiss as we watched the scenery unfold. The entire experience felt surreal, like a dream and I was in disbelief that my life could feel so perfect.

I think we had an instant connection with each other that made us so comfortable with one another. We didn't hold back any part of ourselves and shared the same desires for our journey. I appreciated her adventurous spirit and she admired my calm demeanour, which complemented each other perfectly. Together, we felt complete, even though we knew it couldn't last forever. We made sure to cherish every moment of our time together and embrace each experience to the fullest.

Our first destination was Koh Samui, an island I had not researched beforehand, but I trusted Erika's recommendation. Upon arrival, we were both hungry and headed to a local restaurant to try some authentic Thai cuisine. I ordered pad Thai, but my appetite was not as hearty as I had hoped, possibly due to the overwhelming events of the past few days. Our accommodation was located far from the port, so we had to take a taxi. The fare was expensive, but I managed to haggle the price down a bit. Our driver was quite talkative, boasting about his wealth and how he helped tourists, though I knew it was all for show. I wanted a quiet ride, but I had to keep the conversation going since Erika was exhausted. We settled in our waterfront cabin, watched a movie and caught some sleep before waking up early for the sunrise.

The sunrise was breathtaking as we stood on the beach, watching the sky turn into a canvas of oranges, pinks and yellows. Two adorable local dogs followed us like our guard dogs, playing in the water as we swung on the nearby swing. As we walked back to our accommodation, the dogs trailed behind us, wagging their tails. When we got to our room, they tried to come inside, but we had to leave them outside because they were wet.

While Erika took some much-needed rest, I decided to go out and explore the area. I walked to a nearby 7/11 an American convenience store chain to get us some breakfast, but my journey wasn't without its challenges. A group of dogs had blocked the road, barking aggressively at me. I couldn't go around and coming back empty handed was not an option, so I decided to hitchhike just past the dogs. Within about a minute a tourist stopped with her bike and let me hop on the back all the way to 7/11 it was very kind. Once I reached the store, I picked up some breakfast and a piece of toast, which they had the odd habit of putting sugar on - not exactly what I had in mind. Going back, I spoke to a local woman and asked if she could walk with me past the dogs but then she gave me a lift all the way back, how kind was that! I offered her money for fuel, but she didn't want it. What a great little adventure!

As I got back Erika was very unhappy to see me and said jokingly "back already!" I think she wanted more sleep. However, the adventure only was getting started as we had to make our way across the whole island by walking and/or hitchhiking as we didn't want to waste money on a taxi. We thought alike. The first part of our journey was a peaceful walk along a quiet road, which eventually led us to a main road where we could hitchhike or take a bus. The heat was sweltering and I grabbed a cold coffee from 7/11 to cool down. However, I ended up spilling the coffee all over myself, making a complete mess of both me and the store. As we started walking again a lovely British local man asked if we wanted a lift, he let us hop in the back and drove us to the main road. I remember we looked at each other with the cool wind in out face and disbelief how that just happened so easily, we really were in a movie. As we got to the end of the road we walked for an hour which was a nice walk past all the local shops and I stopped at a local market to get some swimming shorts - which I left in Dubai annoyingly. We decided to try hitchhiking again when one of the local buses stopped. They were charging a huge amount of money and with our luck so far we decided to keep trying hitchhiking. This is when a friendly Thai family stopped after 10 minutes later and were able to take us to the port, this was a good distance to save us walking. The children in the back were very happy to see us and were sweet. They had big smiles and kept waving to us. We hopped into the back of the truck and they drove us to the port briefly stopping to drop off the children who waved to us as we left.

When we arrived at the port, we were surprised to see the same bus that had charged us a lot of money earlier now offering a very reasonable price. Despite our previous success with hitchhiking, we decided to take the bus as we had completed most of our journey for free already. The bus was actually a truck with two rows and a roof that could accommodate six people on each side, plus one adventurous person hanging off the end of the truck. We joked with some of the other passengers on the bus about how we were fitting in six on each side and next will be six on the roof. Just as we settled in for the ride, it started to pour down with rain, so we were grateful for our decision to take the bus.

When we reached our destination, we were only a few minutes' walk away from our next accommodation. As we walked, we were pleasantly surprised to find that the street seemed to be tailor-made for us, with a vegetarian café, a bar and shops. We couldn't wait to check in and relax, but unfortunately, we received terrible news at the reception desk: Fully Booked! Our booking had been a glitch in the system and the hotel was fully booked. We were both disappointed and frustrated, especially since most other places in the area were also expensive and fully booked.

Luckily, the receptionist had an alternative place nearby. It was much cheaper and had all the facilities we needed. We got there quickly as it was very wet and we had a warm welcome from the owner and her friends. They chatted and joked with us as well as sharing their KFC meal which was so kind. Despite hardly speaking any English we still felt welcome. This trip was full of lows, but everything always seemed to work out better. I remember we were sat there and just kept staring into each other's eyes in disbelief and amazement of the day, this trip was so magical and we were getting along so well. Once again we rested a little bit while watching a film waiting for the rain to stop. When it finally stopped we decided to walk down to the street and get some food from a local restaurant. That night we had some alcohol to relax and played a few card games together it was good fun.

The next day we wanted to rent a moped as it was the only way to get around the island cheaply. I had never been on one before so was a little nervous but didn't show it as I didn't want to worry Erika, however, she was aware I had not been on one before. We started by checking a local motorbike place before a magical walk along the beach which also involved going across the water which was a little scary, as for some reason I decided to take my laptop with me so didn't want to slip in. We did this so we could check a second dealership to see his prices, but we decided to go with the first one as we liked the dealer more. The man asked if I had been on one before and I said "yes!" in case he did not want to rent it to us, but I had no idea what I was doing. I was asking him some very basic questions and I must have looked so silly. I told Erika to walk back to the room while I went alone on the bike to build up some confidence. I went around some quiet streets where I practised turns, breaking and generally understanding how to ride it. The road sense was easy for me though as driving was on the same side as the UK.

We still had some time left in the afternoon, so we decided to take a short trip up to a nearby waterfall. The journey took us about 15 minutes on quiet roads, which allowed Erika to gain more trust in my driving skills. As we drove she mentioned feeling happy and safe, which was a great confidence boost for me. When we arrived, we parked the bike at the foot of a large hill and began walking up. At the top we stopped at a little café where I had my first cup of coffee for the day, while Erika opted for a refreshing coke. From the café we were treated to a stunning view of the surroundings, complete with birds chirping and people screaming from a nearby zip line.

We then took a short walk to a secluded waterfall but had to be careful as Erika had a bad arm from a previous injury in Finland. We didn't stay long as there was a massive spider with a web above the waterfall that gave us quite a scare. I had never seen such a large spider before! We then continued onwards to see the main waterfall which was quite impressive just requiring a little hike to reach.

There were a few hours left in the day so we went to a beach called 'W' beach. The beaches here were not private so despite being in a very expensive area we could still visit. It was very easy to get to as there were people who guided us from the hotel and so we found a nice spot to have a swim in the sea. It was very refreshing and the first time I had been in the water. It was a relaxing time for me to reflect on the whole trip so far and to be grateful for what I'd experienced on my adventure to date. It was very quiet and only seemed to have Thai people on the beach further up from the 'W' resort, so I think it was a good idea to visit here since it seemed a less well known beach in the area.

That evening, we decided to have a few drinks and play some card games and I thought it was a good idea to do some laundry. Little did I know that was the beginning of an epic battle against the forces of nature. As soon as I left my clothes to soak we discovered that the sink plug was stuck, that was only the beginning. Suddenly, we noticed a long line of ants marching towards the rubbish bin. I've seen fewer ants in an ant farm. It was like a scene from a horror movie. We knew we had to act fast, so moved all our clothes onto the bed and relocated the bin outside. Luckily most of the ants retreated. We were outnumbered, outgunned and out of our minds. Erika took some old pants she had and started squishing them, while I cheered her on like a sports fan. After a few minutes of hand-to-ant combat we eliminated most of the ants. Our room looked like a warzone. But then, we remembered the sink. With no plug-in sight, we had to resort to using our hands to pour the water on the floor and then wash it down the shower drain. It was like doing the dishes, but with our feet in the shower.

The following day we decided to do a tour around the whole island on the moped. The day started off well and we went to the vegetarian shop to have some food, we enjoyed it very much as was super filling. It was good to have some western food for a change. Following this we were going to go find another waterfall, sadly it started raining however we was able to buy some cheap plastic raincoats from a local shop nearby. The man was very friendly and helped put them on for us. The rain was horrendous but luckily it stopped once we reached the waterfall but we were a little wet. I then had a mutant chicken on a stick from a local store nearby and was the worst thing I had eaten it was disgusting and you could taste hard bits within it. They were like little surprises of flavourless despair.

Being the polite person I am, I went into the toilets to put it in the bin only on exiting kids demanded I pay the 10 baht for using the toilet. I tried to argue that I didn't even use the toilet, but they were not having any of it. What made it worse was then I had to pay double as they didn't even have change - having to pay to use a bin was very annoying. What a waste of money!

I had a great time hiking, although it proved to be quite challenging for my friend Erika, who felt a bit anxious due to her arm. I offered her encouragement and helped when needed. We both liked to push each other, when necessary, as deep down we both understand each other's strengths and weakness' showing how close we got on this trip. We reached our destination, a beautiful waterfall, where we took some time to relax before making our way back to our bike.

Our next stop on the road trip was visiting a temple and some statues, which were interesting to see but not particularly exciting. We then attempted to find a beach but were unsuccessful. However, on our journey, we did come across a snake that was approximately a meter long, which was quite an exciting and unexpected sighting.

The final stop of our trip was the one I had been eagerly anticipating: an abandoned holiday home. Initially, the road leading up to it appeared to be closed, but we noticed that the gate was open and assumed it was no longer in use. As we continued up the steep road, we saw that some of the other homes in the area were now inhabited by residents and tourists. However, the particular home we were seeking remained abandoned.

Despite the challenging ascent, we were determined to reach our destination and it proved to be well worth the effort. The abandoned holiday home had two floors, an infinity pool and a breath-taking bathroom with a view of the sunset. It was truly a remarkable sight and a highlight of my trip.

The next day we were checking out, luckily we had the bike so we somehow managed to fit all our items onto the bike squeezing my bag between my legs! We decided to check in at the next location so we didn't have to carry all our bags with us, this was situated right by the harbour which meant that we could catch the ferry easily to the next island the following day. WOW! This place was amazing they also let us use the room early and it was luxury. It had a WARM shower, a balcony, no ants, a kettle for NOODLES and best of all a view over the ocean where the sun set it was a dream. We wanted to see the local area and have some breakfast it seemed like a mix between tourist and local businesses but managed to find a very nice restaurant which I then later found out also had a record in the world for the largest buffet! I had an omelette, it was the best one I had ever had in my life. This was not just a normal one, it was slightly oily with bits of tomato, cheese and large enough to fit over the rice which was below it, the taste was incredible and the soy source topped it off. Erika was slightly jealous!

Erika expressed that she needed some alone time, which was perfectly fine with me. I had the moped, so I decided to venture out and explore some of the island's attractions. It was strange being alone again, but at the same time, it felt liberating to have some time to myself. My first stop was a beautiful garden that had a small entry fee, but it was well worth it. I enjoyed walking around, admiring the statues and taking some pictures. It felt like I was walking around a real-life movie set.

After the garden, I decided to stop by a 7/11 before returning the moped. I then caught a bus back to the hotel and I was the only passenger on board. I arrived just as the sun was setting and decided to rest in bed and enjoy the beautiful view. Erika chose to watch the sunset from the balcony while listening to music. We spent the evening relaxing and indulging in some noodles, making the most of the kettle in our room.

The plan for the following day was going to the next island where we would stay in a party hostel. I felt this might be difficult for me as I knew this could be a place where Erika would not be with me so much and we would meet other people. However, I knew this was best for us as we didn't want to get involved too emotionally. Funnily enough despite that we still spent a lot of time with each other. I think it just goes to show how strongly connected we were. While waiting for the ferry I did some work on my computer in the local café with a coffee, there I saw a rat in their kitchen ew! On the ferry we were making jokes and laughing most of the way to the end of the trip where we walked to the next hostel about 40 minutes away. The hostel was great and had a pool, gym and many sports activities.

That night, we decided to take it easy and unwind at the hostel bar, mingling with fellow travellers. Although being back in a hostel with Erika was a bit overwhelming, I tried not to let it affect me too much, especially with the added complication of catching feelings for Erika. Despite this we still did a lot together.

The next day, we rented a moped to explore the island and it was a blast. One of the highlights of our tour was a secluded beach to the north, where the water was so warm and clear that it felt like we were in a giant hot tub. It was pure bliss. Unfortunately, the second beach we visited was overcrowded and unremarkable, so we stopped for a quick drink. I ordered a Fanta, but it was tangier than the ones I had tasted in Asia and I didn't like it very much.

One day I needed a new towel, so I purchased one from a local shop before we both went to the beach together, I thought it was a plain grey towel. As I opened it up I found it said 'Happy Baby' with pictures of bears and baby symbols. Oh no, Erika and I found it hilarious.

A restaurant we found was excellent. The prices were affordable and the food was delicious so we enjoyed going there. With our time we spent days often with people from the hostel which was lovely to have the extra company and made the separation maybe a bit easier. We went for hikes and saw some viewpoints!

During our stay at the hostel there were times that was difficult for both of us. Despite spending lots of time with each other we decided it was best to separate before we caught too many feelings or could ruin the connection we had built. During our trip, we both wanted a tangible reminder of the time we spent together. I recall a particular moment when Erika decided to get a tattoo of a skateboard with a bird on it. She asked me what name the bird should have and since I knew she associated my name with positive memories and she liked my name, I suggested "Oliver." This small gesture served as a lovely reminder of our trip. In return, Erika choose me a bracelet, which I now keep close to me as a symbol of our bond. The memories we created together were precious and having these tokens to remind us of them was a beautiful way to hold onto them. Leaving was bittersweet. We had booked separate ferries, but somehow, they were leaving at the same time, which felt like the perfect end to our trip. As we walked up to the port together, we shared our last bowl of noodles from 7/11, knowing that this was our final moment together. It was difficult to say goodbye, after spending so much time together and sharing countless memories, but we both knew that it was time to go our separate ways.

As we checked onto our respective boats, the reality of parting hit us. We hugged tightly, our eyes brimming with tears. It was hard to let go of someone who had become so close, but I also felt grateful for the experiences we shared and the bond we had formed. Walking alone to our boats, I knew that this was not the end of our story and that our paths would hopefully cross again in the future however it was time for us both to seek new adventures.

Koh Tao, a small island near Koh Phangan, is renowned as one of the top destinations for backpackers to visit. The boat ride from Koh Phangan took about 1-2 hours and was packed to the brim with every seat taken, creating a rather crowded atmosphere. Even the hostels on the island were fully booked, but I managed to secure a last-minute bed at a reasonable price, extending my stay as I went along. The island itself offered a mix of beautiful beaches, lively parties and excellent diving opportunities. It's the second-cheapest place in the world to learn how to dive.

On my very first night I met up with a friend from Koh Phangan and together we joined a group to witness a drag show. I must admit I wasn't thrilled about this as I'm not a fan of being the centre of attention and I had been warned that the performers often interacted with the audience. When we arrived at the venue it turned out that every girl working there was a ladyboy and some of them were surprisingly convincing. To avoid getting chosen for the show my friends and I strategically sat to the side of the crowd. The performance itself was fantastic with some incredible acts and outfits. For the grand finale they selected a group of volunteers from the audience who had to dress up like girls and perform, looking more like a bunch of bewildered penguins in a bad dream. It was such a funny experience especially at 3 a.m. in the morning.

Another unforgettable experience on the island was the jungle party, held deep within an actual jungle. To reach this party we had to ride in the back of a pickup truck, holding on for dear life as the driver navigated the winding roads at speeds that would give Lewis Hamilton a run for his money. After this exhilarating journey our tickets were checked and we entered the jungle. The party featured three dance floors and various other attractions including a mechanical bull. The main dance floor was well designed with the DJ booth in the distance, people dancing in trees, tiny treehouses you could climb into and a sea of partygoers. I spent most of my time on the techno dance floor dancing until around 4 a.m., alongside the dedicated 10% who had survived from the start.

I also took part in an organised tour on Koh Tao which included a visit to a small island called Nang Yuan Island, where I had the opportunity to snorkel and enjoy a panoramic view from the top. The adventure began with a short hike to the viewpoint and I was looking forward to enjoying some solitude with nature and perhaps reading a book at the summit. However, as I neared the top I encountered a long queue of people, reminiscent of lines at Disney World. It seemed like everyone had chosen the same day to visit this viewpoint and was willing to wait in line for their turn. After tuning into different interesting British accents around me, I finally reached the end of the queue. While the view was undoubtedly stunning, I could hardly savour it as I had to make way for others taking their profile pictures. It seemed that all anyone wanted was Instagram-worthy photos. I'm pretty sure most people weren't even looking at the view; they would snap a quick photo and move on, like Instagram-addicted zombies. If I were in an episode of The Walking Dead, I would have been the survivor. I opted to enjoy the view further down the quieter section of the viewpoint.

After admiring the crowded profile picture location from a distance, I ventured into the crystal-clear water for some snorkelling. The tour company had provided the snorkelling equipment which I managed to wrestle onto my face after a bit of struggle. As I submerged into the stunning water, the underwater world unfolded before me. It was a mesmerising display of nature with fish of various shapes and colours just meters below. No Instagram fish filter could ever compete with this real-life spectacle and it truly felt like a magical scene. To add to the excitement, I even spotted some baby sharks!

Following our initial snorkelling session, we hopped back onto the boat to explore more areas around the island. It's always puzzled me why tour boats tend to follow each other like a pack of wolves. This results in hundreds of people splashing into the water simultaneously, potentially outnumbering the fish below. It also means you must constantly look up to avoid bumping into fellow snorkellers. On the bright side, the tour boat had a diving board and taking a plunge into the water from it was a lot of fun.

One of our last stops required us to follow a leader on a long swim towards the beach. After a while, when I didn't encounter many impressive fish, I decided to turn back. Little did I know that my adventure wasn't over yet. I swam back to what I thought was our tour boat, only to realise, to my dismay, that it was one of the other tour boats. So, I had to channel my inner Olympic swimmer and navigate the waters to reach my actual boat. Let's just say it turned out to be an unexpected and quite strenuous workout!

After exploring some of the islands, my next destination was Krabi, an area to the west of Thailand. Krabi was known for its touristy spots, but the city of Krabi itself had fewer visitors. I decided to stay there because of the hostel and the numerous attractions it had to offer.

One of the notable attractions was a steep hike to "Wat Tham Sua," a temple located atop a hill accessible via a staggering 1,237 steps. This temple offered more than just spiritual enrichment; it provided breathtaking panoramic views of the city and its surrounding natural beauty. I went with a group but one of the girls was late due to a brake failure on her bike. She was ok but bleeding and I was so surprised she managed to still do the hike. During my stay in Krabi, I crossed paths with many people I had already seen on my trip. We formed a close-knit group and spent a lot of time together, enjoying trips to beaches and markets. The sense of camaraderie and the shared adventures made it a fantastic experience.

The local markets in Krabi were some of the most affordable I had ever encountered. I visited them frequently to buy snacks and explore the variety of items they offered. These markets remained open late, providing a lively and bustling atmosphere. Our group often frequented a bar named the "OLE Bar," which was quite amusing due to my name being Ollie. The owners of the bar were exceptionally friendly and we received many complimentary shots. They always awaited our arrival and even stayed open later for us. We enjoyed our time there and on my last day we had a memorable photo session where they picked me up and held me in the air, in front of the "OLE bar" sign creating a fun and touching moment.

Among the friends I made in Krabi, one named Britt stood out. He was one of the most positively energetic people I had ever met, often making character noises such as Micky mouse and breaking into song at unexpected moments. His infectious enthusiasm added to the fun of our group. One moment I recall was when we were all on bikes and he was screaming "woo hoo", the locals around us burst into laughter and he would always make people laugh with his craziness.

Another friend, Paul from the Netherlands, had a passion for creating YouTube videos. One rainy day, we decided to rent a bike and explore an island just off the coast of Krabi. It was an adventure, involving moving my bike onto a wooden boat, with a local taking charge of manoeuvring it across narrow and precarious wooden panels. One mistake and it was straight into the water. Despite the potential challenges, we embarked on a thrilling journey, exploring the island. It was inhabited by a significant Muslim population and our presence caught the curiosity of the locals, especially schoolchildren, who would run to greet us from their schools. We documented this unique experience with Paul's GoPro, capturing the sights, sounds and interactions with the locals. This footage found its place in my YouTube video, showcasing the adventure.

A few days later, I embarked on a day trip with fellow hostel residents to visit one of the nearby beaches. During a small hike, a mischievous monkey seized an opportunity to snatch my chocolate bar when I briefly opened my bag and it saw the package. The swift theft left both locals and tourists in disbelief at the monkey's agility and speed.

One of the highlights of my trip was a hike I undertook with some friends. This excursion led us up a mountain and reaching the summit was no small feat. The journey, in 37-degree heat, took about two hours. Despite the challenging conditions, our positive attitude and camaraderie helped us persevere. Once we reached the mountain's peak, we were rewarded with breathtaking views that offered a complete panorama of Krabi and the surrounding area.

Following my thrilling time with the fantastic group of people in Krabi, my journey continued to Ko Lanta, which is a nearby island. Fortunately, many of my fellow friends from Krabi also decided to visit this island, allowing us to extend our adventures together. Our days on Ko Lanta were filled with exploration on our trusty motorbikes, shared meals to catch up on daily experiences and visits to some uniquely designed bars. One of the standout bars had fluorescent walls, inviting patrons to paint their names and artwork, creating a captivating ambiance filled with the creativity of previous visitors. We also discovered some fun and laid-back beachfront bars with fantastic chill DJs.

Ko Lanta had a close-knit and welcoming community, which allowed us to get to know many of the local residents. The island was teeming with monkeys, cheeky and agile, frequently swiping food, or drinks, especially when tourists momentarily left their belongings unattended. I vividly recall one incident where a poor man had his entire omelette snatched by a mischievous monkey within a minute of purchasing it, while the monkey mockingly feasted above him, mocking him.

During my stay on Ko Lanta, I couldn't resist trying the famed local tea, Lampang Tea, even though it wasn't my personal favourite (although afterwards a monkey seemed to like it). It was a must-try because of its reputation. Ko Lanta boasts some of the most stunning beaches I had ever seen, with truly phenomenal sunsets. One evening, I remember swimming as the sun dipped below the horizon. The sea was calm and the sunset was breathtaking. The tranquillity of that moment, the serene water and the mesmerising sunset created a unique and relaxing experience, unlike anything I had ever encountered.

For my stay in Ko Lanta, I had a cosy cabin to myself and a moped for exploring the island it was a perfect set up. I would frequently visit a nearby hostel to socialise and enjoy the camaraderie of other travellers. The availability of a pool was a welcome respite from the heat, providing an opportunity to cool down after adventurous explorations.

During my time on the island, some friends mentioned an abandoned holiday resort nearby. Curiosity arose and we decided to explore it. What we discovered was nothing short of extraordinary. The resort was immense, completely abandoned and we had access to countless rooms to explore. Some of these rooms were equipped with hot tubs, double beds, functioning air conditioning, water and electricity. There was even a fully operational gym and a library where I found a book to read. The state of preservation and the sense of having stumbled upon a hidden world was awe-inspiring.

After an incredible time spent with the best group of people, I made the decision to move on. I was the last to leave the group and I continued my journey to a lesser-visited city called Trang. This city, off the beaten tourist path, was characterized by its vibrant food culture, boasting an abundance of restaurants on every corner, a sight I had never witnessed before. It was a city primarily inhabited by locals and while the language barrier posed some challenges, my arrival in Trang coincided with encountering a fellow traveller I had met earlier in my journey. I only stayed for a few days before moving on to Hat Yai.

I then boarded a night train to Hat Yai since I needed to do a visa run to Malaysia to obtain another visa stamp and extend my stay in Thailand. Hat Yai was near the border making it a perfect place for a stop over and a destination for which I initially held low expectations but turned out to be a surprise. As always, I knew that the local people would play a significant role in shaping my experience. It became apparent that it was a hotspot for Malaysian tourists due to its proximity to the border, making it a popular holiday destination for them.

My Canadian friend and I had initially planned a straightforward night out at a bar. Little did we know that this night would transform into an unforgettable adventure. We began our night at a rock bar which from the outside appeared a bit sketchy with its dark doors. However, our perception changed drastically once we stepped inside. The interior was surprisingly modern and had a Western feel to it, adorned with plenty of lights and a spotless ambiance. However, we were in for a shock when we glanced at the drink prices, which we later attributed to the large number of Malaysian tourists in the area. Despite the upscale vibe, the bar was nearly empty, prompting us to seek out another venue after I managed to get the number from one of the most stunning waitresses I had ever encountered.

Our second stop led us to another bar. The girls there were locals who were studying, not the kind where you're uncertain about their gender. What followed was a fantastic opportunity to meet people our age, engage in conversations and learn about their lives as locals. They had excellent English and the drink prices were reasonable, so we ended up spending most of the night there. One of the girls gifted me a small metal device designed to clear your nose when you smelled it. I truly appreciated the gesture, even though I typically avoided accepting things for free. Her kindness touched me deeply and I promised to treasure it as a memento when back in the UK.

As the night progressed our new-found local friends invited us to join them for clubbing, an offer we gladly accepted believing that there could be no better company for a night out. We waited patiently until their bar closed and then hopped onto their mopeds to head to the club. Entry required being on a guest list and fortunately, we were on it now. I felt incredibly fortunate to be there that night, unaware of the incredible experience that awaited us.

The night kicked off with live Thai music and smoothly transitioned into a mix of English and Thai songs. The atmosphere was electrifying, with everyone dancing on tables and chairs, exuding an infectious energy. At one point, we even managed to climb onto the stage where a guy with a microphone was hyping up the crowd. He insisted that we weren't allowed up there, but I suspected he secretly wanted us to join because the locals went wild when they saw two white guys dancing on stage. It felt like we were the stars of the night, the main characters in an unforgettable story. As the night drew to a close, one of the girls entrusted me with the key to her bike. We somehow managed to fit three people onto it, with me taking the role of the driver and they dropped us back.

I felt a strong connection to this place and knew I was going to spend a lot of time here. The next day, I met up with Moosfi, the kind girl who had given me the gift. We went to a local café before her shift and it was great to chat with her. Originally from Malaysia, she was studying international studies in Hat Yai with the dream of becoming an airline pilot.

Moosfi was incredibly generous and allowed me to use her bike to explore the local area. She even trusted me with her motorbike overnight. As a token of appreciation, I always tried to fill up the fuel tank for her since she often let it run very low. One evening after her work shift, we ventured to the local market, which was open 24/7. It was around 2 am and we could find all sorts of delicious food. This city truly never slept.

One of the reasons I had come south was to reset my visa, as I was running out of days and needed to obtain a new visa stamp to extend my stay. This involved going to the Malaysia border and what should have been a straightforward process turned out to be much more challenging than I had anticipated. Firstly, there was a lack of clear information available online. However, I spoke to many people who assured me it could be done in a day and I was aware that many tour operators also offered one-day visa runs, so I knew it was possible.

The train system was very convenient, with a morning train to Malaysia and a later train back to Thailand, making it feasible to complete the process in a day. So, I woke up early and took the affordable train to reach the border.

Upon arrival, I left Thailand and was stamped into Malaysia, which was a straightforward process. However, when I went to exit Malaysia, the officer questioned whether I would be allowed back into Thailand on the same day. I replied that I believed I would, but the Thai passport control officer wasn't very pleased and informed me that I needed to spend one night in Malaysia. This was frustrating because I had only packed for a day trip and had no plans to stay overnight in Malaysia. As a result, I ended up with an exit stamp from Malaysia that was then stamped over again with a stamp saying "voided" since I had to go back into Malaysia. I hope that doesn't cause any more issues in the future. Thankfully, the Malaysia officials were understanding.

What added to the frustration was that the bridge over the train line was closed, so I had to walk along a confusing road and under the train tracks to reach the border town, which took quite some time. The other option was to take a taxi, but out of sheer stubbornness and because I had nothing else to do, I chose to walk.

I managed to book a very affordable cabin for the night, where I planned to stay and explore during the day. Unfortunately, it was during Ramadan and the town had a predominantly Muslim population, so everything seemed to come to a standstill. The whole town felt like it was frozen in time. Apart from one place where I managed to find some food, which turned out to be more expensive than what I was used to in Thailand, I spent my time eating and drinking in the town. For dinner, I asked a 7/11 worker what was open and he replied, "nothing." I eventually found another local spot in town; it was dimly lit and the lights above attracted a horde of insects that kept falling on me and my dinner. So, I decided to have my meal as a takeaway in my room. It was a very depressing experience and I couldn't wait to leave the next day. My room also seemed to be attracting various insects from outside, so I had to sit in the dark with only a small light on my phone. I watched as the insects would die from the light and then the ants on the floor would take them to their nests.

In the morning I retraced my steps back to the train station where I received some disheartening news. I struck up a conversation with other travellers who had tried to do the same visa run as me. They shared that when they attempted to return the following day they were told they had to wait an additional three days in the town. I knew I couldn't endure three more days in this place and I would have to buy new clothes and even a phone charger. So, I could only hope that I would get lucky and be allowed back into Thailand.

We had a lengthy discussion about the situation and ultimately concluded that it exposed corruption and a double standard where one rule applied to some and another to others. To avoid drawing attention to our group we decided to split up in the queue and I was incredibly nervous, to the point where I was shaking.

I had many questions racing through my mind as I approached the Thailand border. What would I do? Where would I stay? I hoped that I wouldn't have to go through this ordeal again and what I would do if they didn't let me in. That's when I saw some of the guys on the train through the window, which was reassuring. They pointed to the guard who had allowed them into the country. I approached the border guard confidently and she directed me to someone else. The next woman seemed like the boss, handling all the difficult inquiries. She felt like the final boss in a video game mission. I was the last person in the queue and people were passing through her into the country. When she reached me, she questioned me extensively about why I was doing a visa run, my purpose and where I was staying. It was quite a grilling, especially considering I was just a tourist who enjoyed the country. They should have welcomed me instead of trying to make me turn away.

Stamp!! She stamped my passport; I was so relieved that I didn't have to spend any more time in that depressing and sad little border town. As I boarded the train, my new-found travel friends all cheered and we were in great spirits that we had all made it through. I met a new guy on the train, an Englishman from a place near my hometown and we got chatting. To our surprise, we discovered that we had a common acquaintance – he was my auntie's cousin! In a train with very few tourists and in such a random place, it was unbelievable that we had a mutual connection. What a mix of emotions it was.

While I was in Hat Yai, there was a local party that happened once a month, where they closed one of the roads. It was a nice event with music, food and even a movie area with a very old traditional camera. While I was watching one of the acts, a man dropped a bottle next to me and I picked it up for him. I then realised he was a fellow tourist, as everyone around me seemed to blend in and I couldn't tell if they were Thai or Malaysian. I ended up chatting with him for some time and he turned out to be a teacher working at a Thai international school, teaching science.

Suddenly, one of the guys I had met at the border the previous day walked past and I pulled him in. The three of us travellers joined forces like magnets. We took a walk around and went to a bar in the main area of the market. It was a bit expensive but a nice place to be. While there, I was shown a hidden bar nearby, which turned out to be an amazing place. It was very dark and had incredible sculptures that incorporated nature and water. I only went in to look since I had already had a drink at the other bar.

Later, seemingly out of nowhere, an Indian man appeared who said 'hi' to me the other night and he was absolutely wasted. He offered to buy us all drinks and was being overly touchy, which made me feel uncomfortable. He kept calling us "brothers" and was trying to get us to go back to his apartment to continue partying. He also wanted to drive and I wasn't getting in his car when he was so drunk. I declined and decided to call it a night. Luckily, I did as he ended up crashing his car that night.

It was sad leaving Hat Yai and the friends I had made, but I couldn't stay forever and I was getting really bored during the daytime. My plan was to leave in the evening and head to Bangkok, from where I would then go to the North of the country. I had arranged to meet some family friends in Hua Hin, so I booked a train ticket that would take about 12 hours and also booked one night in a hostel in Hua Hin so I could get some rest before I would get picked up.

Dexter, an Australian family friend and his wife have a house in Thailand. They kindly invited me to stay and show me around Hua Hin. I had only met Dexter once when I was very young and didn't remember meeting him. Dexter rode a motorbike with a sidecar and I enjoyed my rides alongside him as a passenger. Despite his age, he was an excellent driver on the crazy roads. They lived in a bungalow with a grand garden in a nice complex. It was a little far from the main areas of Hua Hin, but it was lovely to stay with some "locals." We went for a drive and he showed me how the city had changed over the years. We then went to a local market and purchased some food for that evening.

As pleasant as it was staying with them, I wanted to experience more of the city, so I moved to a hostel after a few nights. The hostel was a short walk to the beach and near one of my favourite malls. This mall had a cheap ground floor full of food, like a big clean indoor market. What I loved about it was the large number of stalls everywhere and you could sit at any of the tables and chairs in the area. They served pizza, Pad Thai, noodles and even iced tea, which was my favourite. I came here often, sometimes three times a day to eat; it was the best. I love these big, air-conditioned malls with everything you needed under one roof; they were massive!

I then took a train back to Bangkok to meet Harry a friend flying in from the UK, havoc was going to be launched in Thailand that night. It was Harry's birthday and we were planning for a big night out. Harry was a good friend I had in the UK and he always talked about travelling. I inspired him so much that he wanted to join me. I was sceptical at first since he had never taken any flights in his life and wasn't the type of person to step out of his comfort zone. However, to my surprise, Harry made it happen and I was super happy for him.

When Harry arrived, he took a taxi from the airport and after some catching up, I hinted at a surprise I had in store for him on his birthday. I decided to keep the destination a secret and there was no better place to celebrate his special day than on one of the liveliest streets in the city. We headed out to Khaosan Road, with our accommodation conveniently located nearby. We met a fascinating mix of people and Harry had a memorable birthday celebration.

Over the next few days, we ventured out frequently and I developed a deep fondness for the Khaosan area. The constant change and the intricate alleyways made exploring the city a truly satisfying experience learning all the secret paths. I was even getting good at the Thai language and managed to order an omelette in Thai which I was very proud about. Within this bustling neighbourhood, I had discovered several hidden local restaurants that served outstanding food. One evening, while Harry was having a solo night out, he made a new friend named Dylan, another English guy. This friendship would add another layer of fun to our adventures in the coming two weeks.

Then, a surprise came our way. Tommy, the awesome friend I had met in Greece a year ago, who was currently teaching in Thailand was visiting Bangkok. We quickly arranged to meet at a café just outside the city. The café featured a captivating spinning globe in the centre, an excellent choice for our reunion. Harry joined me as we eagerly awaited Tommy's arrival.

The moment we saw Tommy, it was heartwarming. We spent hours catching up, exchanging stories and reminiscing about our past adventures. Harry listened with great interest and it was undoubtedly one of the trip's highlights to reconnect with Tommy in a different corner of the world. From there, Tommy had plans to meet another friend, a YouTuber and musician residing in Vietnam. We had the pleasure of briefly meeting this friend before bidding farewell to Tommy as he boarded his flight to his next destination.

Songkran was one of Thailand's most significant celebrations, marking the arrival of the Thai New Year. This incredible festival revolved around water guns, with everyone gleefully dousing each other in the scorching heat. It spanned five joyous days and we found ourselves right in the heart of the action on Khaosan Road.

We armed ourselves with water guns, readily available on every street corner and donned our swimwear, fully prepared for the aquatic battle that lay ahead. The streets in the vicinity had been sealed off, creating the perfect arena for the chaos to unfold. As we ventured down the road, we encountered people armed with water buckets, hoses and water guns, staying dry was impossible. The food stalls that usually lined the street were encased in plastic, attempting to ward off the water's invasion. Water stations, offering affordable refills, were conveniently scattered along the streets.

Upon stepping onto the street, an unexpected deluge greeted Harry in the form of a bucket of ice-cold water. His surprised reaction and jump, made me laugh, was a momentary foreshadowing from the inevitable soaking that awaited us.

During Songkran, the application of a white paste known as "talcum powder" or "talc" on faces and bodies could be added alongside vibrant water splashes. This practice was an integral part of the Songkran water festival, signifying blessings and protection. Referred to as "din sor pong" in Thai, this paste, when mixed with water, had a cooling effect on the skin. It symbolized purity and the cleansing of the spirit as people welcomed the New Year. If you happened to be without this paste, friendly individuals were quick to offer their assistance by applying it to your face.

In a twist of fate, our friend Tommy joined us in Bangkok for the Songkran celebrations. The festive spirit was so contagious that even Tommy, who typically refrained from alcohol, found himself sipping on a few beers. We managed to reunite on a nearby street to Khaosan, a wise move considering the massive crowds. It turned out to be an unforgettable experience, filled with water gun battles, impromptu dance parties in the streets and beer. This was a unique opportunity to truly let loose and I had never encountered anything quite like it before. Our favourite battles were often with patrons at the bars, leading to an epic one-on-one skirmishes around tables and hiding behind people. The bars also had the added benefit of offering free water refills from the bathroom. The ensuing chaos, resulting in a disgusting floor covered in water, paint and tissue, but that didn't deter anyone; instead, it added to the overall chaos. It was as if the wild and relentless chaos of the celebrations just carried on, day after day, with no end in sight.

The water war extended even to the roads and I hatched a plan to seize a bus for a mobile water gun assault. I teamed up with local Thai participants and we made use of the open bus windows as they were ideal firing positions. Meanwhile, mopeds zipped past with passengers wielding water guns and Tuk Tuks became mobile water gun platforms. Chaos reigned supreme as we targeted unsuspecting passersby, their laughter and screams filling the air. Despite the language barrier with my fellow passengers, we collaborated effectively to soak our mutual targets and sought cover when the return fire began.

Certain areas of the city were cordoned off and featured stages for music and revelry. Performers on stage, armed with water guns, would fire into the air whenever a musical drop occurred. These expansive areas allowed for a respite where one could enjoy food without getting drenched, a welcome breather. The festivities extended well into the evening and on one such night, amidst the burgeoning crowds, I serendipitously spotted Tommy's friend shooting a YouTube video. It was surreal to reconnect in the midst of the massive crowds and we all danced together with the locals.

After four days of perpetual wetness, fatigue began to set in and I developed an uncomfortable rash from the water. My familiarity with the city's alleyways proved invaluable in navigating without getting soaked, especially when running simple errands like buying food. It became akin to a real-life game of Pac-Man, dodging water-based ambushes. Most people were considerate and refrained from drenching you when you raised your hand in surrender, though a few mischievous individuals persisted in their sneak attacks. One evening, we sought refuge in a snazzy rooftop bar, offering stunning views of the city and had the luxury of staying dry while sipping fancy cocktails.

We also had a memorable visit to Chinatown, which turned out to be quite comical. We found ourselves in a 7/11 store, enjoying some noodles. Harry didn't have any chopsticks, so he resorted to trying to eat them with two pieces of plastic in the shop. The stark contrast between our previous experience in a luxury bar and this street-side noodle feast on the floor in Thailand was truly funny.

While we initially had plans to explore various parts of Thailand during our two-week stay, the vibrant life of Bangkok had a magnetic pull on us. We stumbled upon an exceptionally affordable hotel with a refreshing pool in an ideal location, which made us want to linger. We did manage to tear ourselves away for two days to visit the Rom Hub Market, a famous train market where the train tracks weave through the stalls, earning it the reputation of being one of the world's most perilous markets. To reach there, we embarked on a journey involving a train ride, a boat trip across a river and another train on the other side, which took us right through the bustling market.

The scorching heat with temperatures soaring between 40-43 degrees, made it quite an intense experience and we were in a constant state of perspiration. As we arrived at the markets the uniqueness of the setup became evident, waving to the market goers from the train as we passed by, we could reach out and touch the stalls through the train window.

Most visitors come for a day trip, but we opted for a two-night stay to soak in a more local experience. This turned out to be a fantastic decision because after the last train had departed, we found ourselves as the only tourists in the entire city. During our stay, there was a market on the streets and they had set up a small stage for the closing celebrations of the Songkran festival. With a sparse audience, we couldn't help but feel a bit sorry for the performers. On a particular night, as we stood out conspicuously, the host, spoke some Thai, causing laughter and looks from the few locals around us who were obviously talking about us. Two girls approached us who were dancing on the stage, took our hands and led us onto the dance floor. Suddenly, we were part of the performance, trying our best to follow their lead in traditional Thai dancing. The locals had smiles on their faces and for the next two days, we became local celebrities. Everywhere we went people recognised us and greeted us with dance moves or excited sounds. Word had apparently spread and we felt genuinely welcomed.

Our visit to the famous Rom Hub market by foot was equally fascinating. It was incredible to watch as the vendors swiftly packed away their stalls as the train passed, only to set them up again in a matter of seconds. However, we noticed a shift in the market scene, with a greater number of tourist-oriented stalls compared to local ones, suggesting that the locals might have shifted their shopping to another area. Each evening, the streets would transform with an array of stalls, creating a lovely atmosphere perfect for leisurely strolls. We would also enjoy a healthy lychee smoothie here as they grow the fruit in the area.

After taking a train back to Bangkok we wanted to cherish every remaining moment in this vibrant city. My adventures with Harry had undeniably ignited his own wanderlust and he was already contemplating leaving his job to embark on more travels. The prospect of our future paths crossing once more was exciting and I held out hope that we'd reunite sooner rather than later.

My plan was to spend a few days in the Kanchanaburi area of Thailand, known for the historical significance of the Death Railway. This railway was constructed during World War II using forced labour, primarily prisoners of war, with the intent of connecting Thailand and Myanmar. I walked along a portion of this railway known as the Hellfire Pass and listened to an informative audio guide as I strolled. It was a sad experience to learn about the hardships faced by those who were forced to work on this project, many of whom were Australian and British. The particular museum I visited was funded by the Australian government and was incredibly modern and informative, shedding light on a lesser-known aspect of the war.

One of my favourite activities in Thailand was biking around the city, exploring its streets and culture. I also took a walk along the famous bridge constructed by the prisoners of war. Seeing the bridge from a distance was a profound experience, particularly noticing the damage to one of its supports, a result of bombing attempts to disrupt and slow down the railway construction. Many prisoners of war engaged in sabotage to resist the project, but it was challenging as they were forced to work even harder to repair the damage. Later, I took a train ride along a portion of the track they built, known for being one of the most picturesque train routes in Thailand. The journey took me close to the edge of the track, offering breathtaking views of hills and cliffs.

I had a rather unsettling encounter while on a bus when I noticed a cockroach on the floor. In an attempt to prevent it from coming near my shoes, I quickly placed my heel on the floor and put my other foot on top of it. The bus journey was relatively short, so I wasn't too concerned. However, once I disembarked from the bus, I had a truly nerve-wracking moment. I glanced down to retrieve some money from my pocket and to my shock, I saw the cockroach had somehow made its way into my pocket.

In a state of alarm, I swiftly tucked my shirt into my trousers to contain the unwelcome visitor. Then, I turned to Google translate to ask a local for assistance in removing it. Thankfully, a kind local helped by pushing my pocket upwards, coaxing the cockroach to jump out. It was an extremely unsettling and unpleasant experience. What made it even worse was that this incident occurred during the onset of the rainy season, with torrential rain pouring down.

Despite this unnerving episode, my visit to Ayutthaya was truly remarkable. Exploring the ancient buildings and ruins allowed me to envisage how this old city must have thrived in its prime. Ayutthaya was one of Thailand's main trading hubs and the local museums offered fascinating insights into its history. I initially intended to explore Ayutthaya on a pedal bike, as the government encouraged biking in the area. However, I quickly realized that the roads in the vicinity were not cycle friendly and I found it to be a rather stressful experience. As a result, I promptly returned to the hostel and requested a refund for the bike rental, deeming it too risky to ride in those conditions.

After spending a few more days in Bangkok, I embarked on a 12-hour train journey to Chiang Mai. Coincidentally, Erika was also in Chiang Mai at the same time, so it was a pleasant surprise to reunite with her. We caught up as friends, sharing stories of our respective travels and experiences. Chiang Mai, situated in the northern region of Thailand, is renowned for its picturesque scenery and a thriving cafe culture, which I was eager to explore. It boasts the largest market in Thailand and the city itself is designed in a square shape.

Reconnecting with Erika was wonderful and she guided me through some of the city's highlights. Chiang Mai is famous for its numerous vegetarian restaurants, offering an array of unique and affordable vegetarian dishes. I enjoyed spending time in the city's diverse cafes, where each one had its own distinctive charm. Chiang Mai is also known for its many "weed bars." While I don't smoke weed, these establishments offer a relaxed atmosphere with board games and table tennis, making them a popular choice among remote workers and travellers. I attended a few meetups at these venues, which allowed me to connect with other like-minded individuals who were working remotely and trying to make Chiang Mai their temporary home.

During my stay, I rented another bike and ventured into remote areas around Chiang Mai. One of my memorable explorations led me to a mountain village, providing a fascinating glimpse into local life. It was an incredibly hot day, with temperatures reaching around 45 degrees. While riding through the mountains, I also encountered small forest fires on the roadside, but they posed no major threat. One of the highlights of Chiang Mai was its massive market, taking over the entire city. It required about 20 minutes of continuous walking to traverse from one end to the other. The market featured a plethora of items and I indulged in various foods. I also extended my visa to prolong my stay, as I was keen to explore further, including Pai.

During my time in Chiang Mai, I experienced a unique event where music played across the city through speakers mounted on electric poles. Although I wasn't entirely sure of the reason, it created a sense of unity and was an incredible experience. On another day, I visited a temple and ended up spending the day with a random Thai family. They allowed me to join them in their tuk-tuk as we explored various places. They only charged a nominal fee and I was deeply grateful for their generosity.

One day at my hostel in Chiang Mai, I had a rather unusual encounter. While working on my laptop, I noticed a Thai man who stood behind me for some time. He eventually headed to the restroom, but soon after, I observed two more men approaching me before rushing into the bathroom. Concerned, I turned my attention to the reception desk and the staff quickly beckoned me over. It turned out that the initial guy had stolen money from a temple and was being pursued by the police. This incident generated quite a buzz in the hostel that day.

Chiang Mai also delighted my taste buds with a diverse range of food and beverages, including longan juice made from dried fruits. This added to the richness of my experience in this incredible city.

Interestingly, as I was exploring one of the party areas of Chiang Mai, I spotted a guy sitting outside a bar. To my astonishment, I instantly recognized him as a fellow traveller who had stayed at my hostel in London many months ago. We had not been in touch since and I couldn't believe the chance encounter on the other side of the world. It was an unexpected and heartwarming reunion.

My friend from Bangkok called Song, who was a Thai girl living in Bangkok also joined me in Chiang Mai for a few days. On one of the days, we rented a bike to visit an airplane that had been converted into a cafe. Unfortunately, this day turned into a bit of a disaster, as it was about an hour away and heavy rain began. The road was soon flooded and we had to make multiple stops to seek shelter. Everything got soaked and even my Face ID was broken due to the wet phone. Despite the challenging weather, I felt confident on the bike, embracing the feeling of being a local. After enduring the long and wet journey, we finally reached the airplane cafe, had a drink and decided to take the longer route back. Although our hiking plans were thwarted, the relief of returning to warmth and dryness was rewarding.

I also attended an open mic event in Chiang Mai, which was an amazing gathering of local people who had migrated to or were currently living in Chiang Mai. The event had a strong sense of community and it was heartwarming to witness everyone actively participating and enjoying themselves. The following day, while exploring the mountains, I received a bike fine for not having an international driving license. Fortunately, Song, who is quite the negotiator, managed to reduce the fine to a more manageable amount, around £10. During that day, we ventured into the mountains, explored waterfalls and stopped at charming mountain cafes.

My time in Chiang Mai also included a cooking school experience, during which I learned to prepare Pad Thai and green curry. It was a fascinating process, from selecting fresh herbs from the garden to cooking the dishes. This experience gave me a newfound appreciation for the effort that goes into creating these delicious Thai dishes. Another unique Thai tradition is the love for pool (billiards), where they would often have a free table in the bars and all you needed to do was put your name on the whiteboard to play against the winner. It would often get competitive and it was such a good feeling when you made a great shot or won, as lots of people would watch and give you a clap. I went out many times on my own to join in with the pool games.

Before returning to Bangkok from Chiang Mai, I ventured to Pai, a stunning place nestled in the mountains. The journey there, via a winding minibus, was quite challenging, with countless twists and turns that made it hard to avoid feeling queasy. Despite the speed at which the driver navigated the route. Pai welcomed me with its breathtaking beauty and a vibrant community of fellow travellers.

During my stay in Pai, accompanied by a close friend, we embarked on a thrilling adventure to a view point. Online sources had warned us about the demanding motorbike journey, but I found joy in embracing the challenge. The hour-long ride involved conquering an extremely steep mountain, manoeuvring through gravelly terrain, cautious navigation around potholes, steep inclines and keeping a keen eye out for oncoming traffic on narrow bends. The ride demanded a considerable amount of skill but luckily my prior experience riding a moped in Thailand helped. Despite taking on the journey with a modest 150 CC bike the trip went well although most travellers attempted this route with more powerful engines.

During my final days in the country, I found myself staying with Song, who graciously opened her doors to me. Witnessing the day-to-day life of a local in the city was a valuable experience. Song's place was a bit on the outskirts, but conveniently close to the BTS, the sky train. She met me at the train station and guided me through a series of shortcuts, weaving through fences, creating a labyrinthine feel in the closely packed surroundings. It was a clean and safe area. Song was renting a modest room on the lower floor of the complex; it was a single room with an outdoor area equipped with a tap. Having a kitchen wasn't a necessity in the city, as most people preferred dining out. However, Song did have an electric stove that she occasionally used when she felt like cooking, which was a hobby she enjoyed.

The most challenging aspect of staying at her place was the absence of air conditioning. In the scorching heat, fans were positioned everywhere, but they still struggled to provide much relief in temperatures exceeding 40 degrees. Nearby, there was a small local shop and a plethora of food stalls. This neighbourhood was not frequented by many foreigners, so I often received warm smiles from the locals. On one occasion, a friendly woman commented in Thai, "Very handsome man," which brought a smile to my face. After a few days seeing how a local lived I had to move on. I then took a flight to Australia from Bangkok, as it was a place where I could work and save up some money for my trip while remaining near Asia. It was a good option for me.

Upon my arrival in Australia, I made the deliberate choice to establish a temporary home, aiming to balance my budget and find some much-needed relaxation. As I contemplate the uncertain path that lies ahead in my life, I'm filled with boundless enthusiasm. The world, in my eyes, is a realm of limitless opportunities. I'm confident that I'll soon venture back into the world of travel, armed with fresh adventures and a treasure trove of captivating stories to pen in another chapter of my life's book.

After months of incredible adventures, I had time to reflect in the many places I had visited, the people I had met and the experiences that had enriched my life. Travel had become my greatest teacher, a journey of self-discovery and a source of endless inspiration. The memories of bustling markets in Bangkok, the serenity of temples in Chiang Mai, the vibrant streets of Marrakech and the breathtaking beauty of the Greek Islands..

And so, with a passport filled with stamps and a heart filled with memories, I set my sights on new horizons, knowing that the world would continue to be my playground and my greatest source of joy.

The end of one adventure was only the beginning of the next and my journey was far from over.

Thank you immensely for taking the time to read my book - a project that has been two years in the making. I hope you found it enjoyable! For further updates and to follow my next ventures, visit www.BeyondTheBorders.me

Follow my journey:

www.BeyondTheBorders.me

Printed in Great Britain
by Amazon